STALKY'S REMINISCENCES

by

MAJOR-GENERAL L. C. DUNSTERVILLE

LONDON

JONATHAN CAPE 30 BEDFORD SQUARE

FIRST PUBLISHED 1928

FIRST ISSUED IN THE TRAVELLERS' LIBRARY 1930

JONATHAN CAPE, 30 BEDFORD SQUARE, LONDON
AND 91 WELLINGTON STREET WEST, TORONTO
JONATHAN CAPE AND HARRISON SMITH
139 EAST 46TH STREET, NEW YORK

PRINTED IN GREAT BRITAIN

Contents

Introduction

In the following pages I have attempted to give some account of my life experiences – episodes strung rather sketchily together, accompanied by occasional reflections and comments.

I am sorry that I have so little to say regarding the many famous or interesting people I have met, in fact there is little in this book about anyone but myself. Where others do come into the story, I have tried, as far as possible, to avoid giving names. I do not want to run the risk of a libel action, and one can libel people so much more freely by saying " I would not for one moment divulge his name. He is a tall, dark man, with a squint, well known to you all, but it would be unfair to disclose his identity."

I have endeavoured to confine myself to the lighter side of life, avoiding serious accounts of military episodes, and accentuating, as far as possible, the more cheerful events of a soldier's life in peace-time.

It may well be that the trivialities I record have no interest for the general reader, but to me the minor incidents of life are vastly more interesting than heroic achievements – if this is a personal failing, I cannot escape from it.

It is possible also that I have dwelt too much on the subject of manœuvres – but that portion of my book was written chiefly with a view of interesting soldiers in India to whom these memoirs were originally addressed – men who surely must be growing weary, after twelve years of novels, autobiographies and films, of the subject of the Great War.

In the accounts of my travels I have offered a few comments on the racial characteristics and conditions of life in various countries, but I do not forget the danger of such superficial generalities. It is also obvious that most of my experience was gained long before the Great War, which is assumed to have altered everything.

" Nevertheless it cannot be concealed from the enlightened judgment of the holy and good, to whom these discourses are specially addressed, that the pearls of salutary admonition are threaded on the cord of an elegance of language, and the bitter potion of instruction sweetened with the honey of facetiousness, that the taste of the reader may not take disgust, and himself be debarred from the pleasure of approving them."

SHEIKH SAADI. *The Gulistan*

STALKY'S REMINISCENCES

CHILDHOOD

ALTHOUGH this book is not intended to be a serious attempt at autobiography, still it may be well to begin on orthodox lines, and I may therefore record the fact that I was born at Lausanne in Switzerland on November 9, 1865.

My family name speaks for its Norman origin, being included in the Roll of Battle Abbey, and the somewhat unusual fact exists that it has never been shared by others than ourselves.

Up till 1300 we held large estates in Wiltshire, that of Castle Combe, near Chippenham, being the 'caput Baronæ'.

In later years the family found themselves in Devonshire, my great-great-great-grandfather having settled in Plymouth.

My grandfather, who was the last to reside in Plymouth, started his military career, in which he attained high rank, in the service of the East India Company in those palmy days when the pagoda-tree stood so invitingly on India's coral strand, awaiting just the gentlest shake to pour its golden fruit into the lap of fortune-hunters. The fact that he died possessed of very moderate means seems remarkable.

Few surnames are capable of being converted into anagrams, but ours is one of the few, and it makes

'NEVER SIT DULL.'

13

I do not remember when I first had this pointed out to me, certainly I knew nothing of it in childhood or early manhood. It is peculiar, therefore, that my outlook on life has been in exact keeping with the excellent advice of the anagram.

At the time of my birth my father had returned to India, leaving my mother and five sisters at Lausanne, where we remained for a year or two. As he continued to serve in India till after I had entered the army, I saw little of him, and my mother died when I was ten years old, so that I missed in childhood the advantages of a settled home.

My Swiss birthplace has often been a source of trouble to me. Families like ours spread their birthplaces all over the world. My father was born in India, my mother at the Cape, my wife in England, myself in Switzerland, and my eldest son in China.

The Swiss authorities were puzzled as to the correct manner of registering my birth, and eventually put me down as a Swiss subject, son of an African and an Indian; but the English authorities have never got over it, and seem to be in a perpetual state of perplexity.

In filling up certain forms for one of the Government Offices three years ago on behalf of my eldest son, I had to make the usual statements relating to age, parentage, etc. The fact that I was a Major-General in the Indian Army and that my father and grandfather had also attained the same rank in that service did not at all convince them that I was quite the genuine article — English for 857 years.

They wanted to know if I had been 'naturalized'! I had some difficulty in convincing them that it was quite all right and that I spoke English with no foreign accent.

I did not remain long in the land of my birth, as the family migrated from Switzerland to Jersey when I was about two years old, and from there we moved, a few years later, to the Isle of Wight.

I remember little of my early years and few of my childish recollections and small adventures are worth recording; but I have one very happy memory in connection with rum-and-eggs that my mind likes to dwell on. I absorbed this delicious drink for quite a long time — it was a special diet for an invalid sister who hated it, and I, on the contrary, liked it very much.

Fate has been good to me in this way. In schoolboy days I had an anæmic friend whose parents paid extra for him to have a small bottle of stout at night. Of course he didn't like it, and of course I did, so I helped him out of his difficulty. This pleasant state of affairs lasted for several terms. He got thinner and thinner, while I got fatter and fatter — in fact, I might attribute my later robust health chiefly to the consumption of this nourishing beverage.

Another unfading memory is that of the luscious smell of a frowsty hotel. That must have been when we left Jersey, when I was about seven, and we stayed at an hotel in Southampton. A warm smell of bacon, coffee, and cigar-smoke. I frequently encounter this well-

known mingled perfume nowadays, and I would naturally hate it, but childhood's memories make it sweeter
to me than the fragrance of flowers in spring.

It is well that I should not dwell too much on the
years of my early childhood, as I have no doubt in my
own mind that I was an exceptionally unpleasant infant. Like most men, I have had bad periods in my
life, and I believe that my first seven years were probably the worst.

I did not bother to think why I thought and behaved
as I did, but looking back on it now I dare say it was
partly the longing for assertion of a very small male,
surrounded at all times by seven females, all of whom
were, in greater or less degree, in a position of authority
towards this helpless little creature.

My mother being to a great extent an invalid, my
early training was chiefly in the hands of my five sisters,
and whatever I am to-day must be regarded as the
result of their methods. I express my gratitude to them.
I needed a strong hand, and I got five pair of strong
hands. Bless them.

But they went wrong on one point. That was not
their fault, they were not old enough to know. Fifteen
years ago after a scene of trouble with one of my sons
aged six, it occurred to me to explain to him that there
are, and must be, two separate sets of laws (though
based on unchanging principles) for grown-ups and
children.

This was never explained to me, with the result that
I hated all grown-ups with a hatred that no words can

express. They were just so many unreflecting tyrants, and the world was full of them.

Whatever I did or wanted to do, I was promptly told to 'don't'.

As a parent myself I know how unfortunately necessary this is, because, in keeping with the theory I have expounded above, whatever children want to do is what they should not: but a wise parent withholds some of the 'dont's' for fear of driving the child into the state of mutiny in which I found myself.

I cannot at all account for the vileness of my temper in childhood's days. It disappeared entirely with manhood and at my present age I find it very hard to get angry with anyone about anything. My fierce outbursts of rage were succeeded by long periods of sulks which made them worse.

In these days some kind-hearted faddist would prove that all the evil of my nature proceeded from the fact of something pressing on my brain, and a timely operation might suddenly endow me with the temper of an angel.

But in the Dark Ages when I was a boy, they thought it was just my wickedness (so did I), and they treated me on that assumption with no more serious operation than the frequent wielding of a slipper or a cane.

At Ventnor, when I was about eight years old, I decided to commit suicide. I was very miserable, and I attributed none of this misery to my own abominable temperament, but laid it all to the blame of the grown-ups, and suicide seemed to fill two necessary conditions — escape from my own misery, and inflicting misery on grown-ups in their turn.

I did not stop to reflect that possibly the disappearance of such a horrid child might not cause widespread misery — I simply had the one thought in my mind, 'They'll be sorry when I'm gone, and they'll repent them of their sins. But — ha, ha — it will be too late.'

I left the house in a raging temper one evening, probably about eight o'clock, and I walked down to the sea to throw myself in. It was bright moonlight, and the fresh night air both cooled my temper and weakened my resolve. What I did I cannot exactly recollect, but I got very wet, and then I must somehow have made up my mind to defer the business to some future occasion, because by about 10 p.m. I found myself back in the town finding life well worth living again.

The reason of this change of outlook on life was due to the fact that, with some other boys, I had found a loose flap in the big circus tent through which we could gaze on the prancing horses and buxom ladies in tights — a glimpse of Paradise.

While engaged in this pastime I felt a heavy hand descend on my shoulder, and, turning, gazed into the stern features of one of the town police — the authorities had been informed of my dramatic disappearance, and the incident terminated with my recapture.

When I was about nine years old my mother went out to India with my elder sisters, while my younger sisters and myself were sent to Woolwich to be under the care of a guardian, an officer's widow.

We remained under her care for about five years. Here I found my hatred for grown-ups diminishing. My guardian was a charming lady who let us do exactly as we pleased. It was like a fairy-story – I could not have believed there were such people in the world. She had three sons and two daughters, so that I was able to enjoy the society of other boys, another step in emancipation.

I should have rewarded this dear lady guardian for the unrestrained freedom she allowed me to enjoy by saying to myself, 'Here at last is a good, kind, grown-up who never says "Don't". I must be careful never to cause her any pain or worry,' but instead of this I simply thought 'Hurrah! Now I can do as I jolly well please.' And I did so to such effect that on more than one occasion the unfortunate widow was embarrassed by visits from the police.

My younger sisters were as bad as I was, and between us and the guardian's own children, it is a marvel to me how that dear lady ever survived. I remember one tutor and several governesses who all left in rapid succession declaring that they could do nothing with such depraved children.

In the winter term of 1875, when I was just ten years old, I was sent to school at the United Services College, Westward Ho, in North Devon.

This college was started about the year 1872 on a sort of co-operative principle by a lot of old Admirals and Generals who found themselves like most retired service-men unable, even in those days, to pay the high costs of Public-School education.

With their very limited funds they could not afford a large outlay on school buildings, and they were consequently delighted to find a real bargain waiting for them on the coast of North Devon.

Westward Ho had always been famous as a golf centre, and a company had been formed to turn it into a fashionable seaside resort with the additional attraction of the splendid links. A fine pier was built, swimming baths, hotels, and terraces of houses: but visitors failed to come and the property came into the market.

The founders of the college bought a long terrace of houses at the foot of the high ground facing the sea. These were adapted to form dormitóries, class-rooms, and quarters for the masters.

A long corridor was built to enable masters and boys to pass from one class-room to another in bad weather, and it also served under such conditions as a sort of makeshift playground for the boys. A gymnasium and chapel was built on the north side of the terrace, and a fives-court on the south. In this way at a very small expenditure of time and money, the college came into being.

We had a very poor lot of buildings compared with any of the well-known public schools, but as most of us had never seen any of these, no feeling of envy rankled in our bosoms. The locality was perfect, with wild scenery and glorious air, at a distance from any large town and out of the reach of parents.

Bideford was the nearest town, and was of course 'out of bounds', which added to its attractions.

My father being one of the founders, I was destined for the school as soon as I reached the age of ten.

As regards the staff and the boys, the former were, I should say, a particularly talented set of men and the latter were a rather unusual collection of rough specimens, all, with very few exceptions, being sons of officers in the navy or army. Kipling was one of the exceptions, his parents having wisely selected the school for him on account of the peculiar merits of the Headmaster – Cormell Price. Cormell Price was a very remarkable and gifted man, and the extraordinary success of the college in its earlier years was entirely due to his personality.

Boys are apt to look on schoolmasters as a sort of brotherhood all pulling together in a more or less successful endeavour to instil some learning – or better still, a love of learning – into youthful minds. It is only later in life that we realize that this team is seldom a team that 'pulls together', and I know now that this was the case at Westward Ho. The Headmaster could run the school, but its eventual failure was due to the fact that his 'team' were unmanageable.

And when I look back on those days with the proper perspective of old age, I can see what an impossible task he had.

The control of 200 wild lads was an easy matter for a man of his charming personality and intuition. But the control of the widely divergent characters of Crofts, Willes, Campbell, Pugh, Haslam, Green, Stevens, Evans, Bode, and others, not forgetting Messieurs Jacquot and Marner, the French masters who succeeded one another, was beyond the power of mortal man.

Of all the masters Crofts must have been the most impatient of control – he was not the sort of man who would care to accept any other person's opinion on any subject. He certainly had the great and uncommon gift of imparting instruction as distinct from mere teaching, but he was of a very irritable temperament and gave us the impression that he heartily disliked boys – quite rightly, I dare say, but when one feels like that it is better not to let the boys know it. A keen athlete and a fine swimmer, he was drowned at sea some years after the college had been transferred from North Devon to Harpenden.

Willes, the padré, was a genial, robust type, popular with both masters and boys and possessed of uncommon common sense that enabled him to settle many feuds by friendly arbitration or by kindly hints. Campbell, who preceded him as chaplain, was a very peppery individual, who endeavoured to rule by fear, which does not pay in the long run with boys. I can never recall his face without an expression of ferocity on it, nor his hand without a cane in it.

Pugh was a great, strong, 'hefty' fellow with very

large feet and a very kind heart. He would have been a very good house-master if he had not made the mistake of prowling and prying, which all boys resent and which made it extremely easy for us to entrap him. Kipling, Beresford, and myself enjoyed the privilege of being in his house and under his care, but I am not sure that he enjoyed the privilege of guiding our infant footsteps.

Of Haslam I remember little except that he was the only married master, and his good wife prevented him from getting into trouble.

Green was a house-master who wore a thick black beard which helped him to keep order. He was rather inclined to bark at us, which accounted for his nickname of 'Barky'.

Stevens, a parson, was a good, sensible fellow, popular with the boys and I should think equally so with the masters.

Evans, nicknamed 'Punch' because of a rather large and curved nose, I best remember as the founder and organizer of the 'Bug-and-tick' or 'Natural History Society'. His enthusiasm for this Society led him sometimes a little astray, but he understood us and I do not think any of us could have anything but pleasant recollections of his dealings with us – even though the 'dealings' sometimes involved the use of the cane. He had the additional attraction of being a good actor and won our affections by his performance in many comic pieces.

Bode, who later took Orders, is the only survivor of

the group – still in harness at Beechmont, Haywards
Heath. I am indebted to him for early training in
singing, which, as far as I remember, was a hobby of
his. He had nothing to do with the teaching of singing, but in some capacity or another I can recall him
waving a bâton and persuading me to sing glees.

I have given, with some diffidence, a few notes on the
characters of the various masters who composed the
staff of the old college in the days of my youth, chiefly
with a view of appreciating Cormell Price's difficulties,
but I think the greatest difficulty he had to contend
with was our lack of tradition, which is the main
stand-by for control. In our case there was no tradition,
and as each master brought with him fragments of
traditions of other schools, the Head was confronted
with an almost hopeless task: and as regards the 200
boys we were equally heterogeneous and lacking school
tradition.

Another difficulty was probably caused by the
absence of selection. At the start of a new school
financial considerations are of primary importance, and
the chief thing to do is to get the school filled up to its
fullest complement. Under such circumstances, and
with no 'waiting list', selection is almost impossible.
So among us were many rather tough characters.

The Headmaster had come to us from Haileybury
and brought a small nucleus of boys with him. The
great majority of the rest were little innocents like
myself, sons of hard-up officers. But there must have
been quite a large proportion of boys that no one else

wanted, possibly even quite a fair number who had been already tried elsewhere, and had been, to use an euphemistic term, 'rejected'.

I mention all this because so many people have taken a deep interest in Rudyard Kipling's inimitable *Stalky & Co.*, and have often expressed their inability to understand how 'things should have been so'.

Soon after the issue of that book I read frequent letters in the papers from old boys of various famous public schools, informing the world that their schools were not in the least like that. Of course they weren't. The above may help to explain why they were not.

Stalky & Co. is a work of fiction, and not a historical record. Stalky himself was never quite so clever as portrayed in the book, and the book makes no mention of the many times when he was let down. But he represents, not an individual – though his character may be based on that of an individual – but the medium of one of the prevailing spirits of this most untypical school.

I joined the school about 1875 and my number was 10. I owed that early number not to the date of my joining but to the date of registration at the time of the foundation of the college.

Kipling did not join till several years later – I cannot tell when, but one can form some estimate of the period from the fact that his number was 264. During those troublous years I had to develop my character, without his shrewd guidance, from artless simplicity to artful guile, and by the time that he and Beresford united with me in the occupancy of a study I was in the passive condition of a bundle of Chinese firecrackers to which his fertile brain eagerly applied the torch.

Beresford added to the combination an extraordinarily mature judgment combined with a malicious ingenuity. It is difficult really to score off masters in the long run, and in most cases when we were triumphant, it was due to his placid subtlety.

Our paths in life have proved the wide divergence of our characters, but this divergence made the youthful combination all the more dangerous. What one lacked the other had, and we really must have been a very difficult trio to tackle.

Beresford and I had our fair share of brains, but Kipling had a great deal more than his fair share, and added to it the enormous asset of knowledge – intuitive and acquired.

Our earlier escapades were on the lines of simple buffoonery, but we soon evolved on to a higher plane of astute plotting on more intellectual lines, the essence of each plot being that it should leave our adversaries nothing to hit back at.

The culmination of the plot was the appearance of the elusive criminals in the pleasing pose of injured innocence.

In spite of our many drawbacks there was a splendid spirit in the school, and a very strong sense of loyalty pervaded both masters and boys when confronting the outside world.

And I may say, finally, that Westward Ho was a notably 'clean' school, in every sense of that word.

CHAPTER II

SCHOOLDAYS

I MUST now deal with the first year of my school career, a rather trying period of life for any boy, but especially so for me under peculiar circumstances.

To begin with, I was much the youngest boy in the school. There were a few not much older than I was, but the majority began at the usual public-school age of fourteen. As the college had no preparatory school at this period and my father was anxious to send me as soon as possible to any school where I would get well smacked and kept in order, I was launched to begin the battle of life – in a rather literal way – at the early age of ten.

We numbered about 200, and, as I have mentioned, among the elder boys there were several who had started elsewhere, but had come to us because their previous institutions had not regarded them as particularly desirable.

I had no previous knowledge of the little points of etiquette common to all schoolboys. I was not altogether a 'little innocent', but I was extraordinarily ignorant of boys' ways – coming as I did straight from the mild tutelage of sisters and governesses.

I dare say Christian names are no longer 'taboo'. I seem to hear them used sometimes among modern schoolboys. But at Westward Ho we guarded ours with jealous secrecy.

My ignorance of this, and my fat cheeks, were the chief causes of my early sorrows.

I was a 'fat little beast' or a 'bloated mass of blubber' to scornful elders, and these epithets caused me great agony of mind.

My first recollection of events on the day of my arrival begins with my appearance in the corridor on a wet, cold, dark afternoon. Details of my journey from London up to that point have faded from my mind. I seemed to have dropped from the skies into a howling pandemonium.

A new boy always excites some little interest and I soon found myself surrounded by a group of boys clamouring to know my name. To their appeal I responded 'Lionel'.

This was received with delighted applause and yells of derision. I could not see why. And being again appealed to I once more responded 'Lionel', which seemed as unaccountably humorous as my previous reply.

After a little of this I began to realize that I was not the object of spontaneous popularity but that I was having my leg pulled, and my brain suggested to me that perhaps my surname would be a more correct answer.

So in reply to a new-comer in the rapidly increasing crowd, who asked me 'What's your name?' I replied 'Dunsterville'. But this only earned me a cuff on the head and the repetition of the question 'What's your name, you fat little beast?' And cuffs were administered in increasing intensity until at last I gave once more the ridiculous reply 'Lionel', whereupon my interlocutor left me with a parting kick, to give place to another of the same kindly nature.

This went on for several days, at the end of which I had begun to loathe the sound of 'Lionel'.

During the first two or three years of my school life I naturally formed lasting friendships which helped to balance the very rough side of life. I think none of these earlier companions are now alive.

Life was certainly very rough, and bullying was rampant. It was bound to be so in a school such as I have described, and although the Head was aware of it, and did all in his power to put it down, it was a good many years before it was reduced to reasonable limits.

As the smallest boy in the school I was an easy prey, and the life of perpetual suspense that I led during those harrowing years, probably taught me a great deal of cunning.

In addition to the blows and kicks that inevitably accompanied the bullying, I suffered a good deal from the canes of the masters, or the ground-ash sticks of the prefects. I must have been perpetually black and blue.

That always sounds so dreadful. Witnesses in court say that the victim had black and blue bruises, and tears fill the eyes of listeners.

But the truth of the matter is, any slight blow produces a bruise. A cane, however lightly applied, must always leave a blue-black mark. It in no way indicates the severity of the blows. And, with one or two savage exceptions, I am sure that the blows I received as a result of bullying or legitimate punishment were harmless enough. They certainly did me no injury, and may have done me good.

Kicks and blows I minded little, but the moral effect was depressing. Like a hunted animal I had to keep all my senses perpetually on the alert to escape from the toils of the hunter – good training in a way, but likely to injure permanently a not very robust temperament. I was robust enough, I am glad to say, and possibly benefited by the treatment.

It would serve no useful purpose to dwell at length on the various forms of bullying, but it may be interesting to give one or two examples.

One amusement for elder boys was to hold the little ones out of the top-storey windows by their ankles. As the buildings were five stories high this was rather a terrifying performance.

Another cheerful game was 'hanging', which was carried out from the top landing of the staircase which wound round a sort of square well so that over the top banisters one could look straight down to the bottom floor.

The condemned criminal – myself or another – was taken to the top floor and the sentence of death was read out as he stood by the banisters. His eyes were then blindfolded, and a rope with a slip-knot placed under his arms. A certain amount of slack was allowed for the first 'drop', to give an uncomfortable jerk. With this preparation he was launched into space, and after the first check at the end of the slack he was lowered slowly down till he got near to the bottom floor. Here an assistant hangman was placed, whose duty it was to inform the Chief Executioner above when to let go the rope.

He calculated by eye how much 'drop' you would be likely to stand and then gave the signal, when you fell to the floor with a resounding thud. He over-calculated on one occasion, when a boy broke his leg, and that led to the discovery of this innocent pastime, which ceased to exist from that time. It was not a pleasant performance for the victim, but at the same time not painful, though perhaps a little unnerving to a beginner.

Criminal lunatics must have been boys once and consequently one may assume that among any large group of boys there must be some embryo criminal lunatics. On no other assumption could one account for forms of bullying that are just sheer infliction of pain.

There were not many who revelled in these forms of torture; their expedients were simple enough and I need only give one example of a particularly refined form of cruelty. The assistant held your ear up against the thin wooden panel of a form-room door, and informed his master, the bully, when you were in position. The latter had a hammer in his hand and with this he struck a violent blow on his side of the panel.

The result to the victim was a sort of sensation of a bomb exploding in his head; this was followed by a headache which soon passed off.

How wonderfully we human beings are made! It is

hard to imagine anything more delicate than the tympanum of the ear, and my ear was frequently subjected to this horrible treatment. Yet, at the present day, my hearing is extraordinarily acute.

Learning to swim was not quite the same as being bullied, because one realized that it was well meant. But it was just as terrifying.

There were two methods. The first and the only orthodox one was as follows. The school sergeant had a sort of fishing-rod with a canvas belt at the end of the line. You were fixed up in the belt and pushed into six feet of water, while he was supposed to half-support you by taking some of your weight on the rod, and to encourage you with kindly words of advice.

This usually started quite well, but presently old Cory the bath-man would come along and get into conversation with the sergeant, and while they discussed the chances of the next Derby, or some such eternally engrossing topic, I was left to sink to the bottom. Then the sergeant, feeling an unusual drag on the pole, would look round, grasp the situation, haul me out half-drowned and leave me to empty myself of the gallon or two of salt water that I had imbibed.

But when the sergeant was not there, some of the elder boys kindly took his place, applying unorthodox methods.

I hear, even now, people putting forward the theory that as the action of swimming is a natural one, if you throw a child into deep water he will quickly learn to swim by inherited instinct.

B

This was the theory they put into practice.

I was thrown into the deep end and allowed to sink once or twice — in the belief that a person always rises three times to the surface before he sinks for the last time — and then they had an amusing competition, to save the drowning man. So I was eventually 'saved', and as before allowed to empty myself of the salt water I had swallowed.

I learned to swim all right somehow, but I do not think that either of these methods helped me very much.

We were very well fed on good wholesome food, but being boys we were insatiable and I was always hungry, and devising expedients (honest or otherwise) for filling up the blank spaces.

A favourite subject of correspondence in the papers to-day is the question of diet for boys at public schools.

Parents fret more about their children now than they used to do.

When the average size of a family varied from six to twelve, parental supervision was wholesomely diluted and the children were all the better for it. I don't think my father knew anything about 'vitamins', or wanted to. A diet of meat, vegetables and bread and butter, was good enough for his son, and I suppose that these, with various additions, contained all that was necessary for a growing boy even including the then undiscovered 'vitamins'.

Our supper would be considered a quaint one in these days. Hunks of bread and chunks of cheese, washed down with plenty of flat but wholesome beer. We had this just before going to bed and I slept very well on it.

Some boys had parents who sent them frequent tips which enabled them to fill themselves out at 'Keytes', the school tuck-shop. I had very little in this way and my weekly pocket-money of sixpence was a sum of considerable importance to me.

Pocket-money was given out by one of the masters at the dinner table. He was supposed to be provided with the requisite number of sixpences, but sometimes he ran short and he would then hand over a two-shilling piece to the biggest boy of four, with instructions to change it and pass on their shares to the other three.

It was the stupidest way of doing things that you can well imagine, and was putting a very strong temptation in the way of the elder boy. And the elder boy with whom I was generally bracketed was the sort of boy who needed little tempting. So I often got no six-pence at all, or was glad to compound for twopence and a ball of twine, or a penknife with both blades broken.

So I learnt two valuable lessons. First, to earn money honestly, to be spent in the tuck-shop. Second, to procure eatables from the world at large without expenditure, and honestly – if possible.

I earned money in various ways, little odd jobs rewarded by richer boys with a penny or two. I got half a crown out of a rich youth one Sunday for diving into the swimming-bath in my Sunday clothes with my top-hat on. And I made and sold a great many sets of miniature golf-clubs and balls for use in a popular game of miniature golf played on the floor of the form-room. The clubs were about eight inches long and were accurate models.

I made a little money almost honestly by collecting copper nails, and bits of copper sheeting from pools on the beach, and selling them in Bideford where I got quite a good price for them.

Wrecks were not uncommon in Bideford Bay, and my copper came from sailing ships that had gone to pieces on the bar. I suppose these things belonged in law to 'the Crown', but you had to be pretty clever to find them, and I am sure the Crown would never have done it.

The eatables I procured for myself were such things as blackbirds, potatoes, turnips, hens' eggs, apples, with good fortune a rabbit, and on rare occasions a whole loaf of fresh bread.

With the exception of the bread these were just things that bountiful Nature provided or that farmers and hens had left lying about and that seemed to come my way. The bread, I am afraid, was real theft, but it did not seem to be so to me. It was our own college bread and part of the supply intended for our con-sumption — but they only gave us slices and I wanted a whole loaf after I had eaten all my slices. And it took some getting, I can assure you.

One had to descend into forbidden regions, and dart

from passage to passage with domestics passing backwards and forwards all the time. And there was no escape in flight, because you were known, and to be seen was equivalent to being captured.

I am sure that no parent who reads the above will want to write again to the Headmaster to inquire whether Cuthbert gets enough to eat. Once for all, it is quite certain that he does not. As far as my experience goes, no healthy boy has ever had enough to eat. I have sometimes as a boy had too much, but never once enough.

I know that I am not, and never was, abnormally greedy, and my fat cheeks were purely natural and not in the least due to my large appetite. In my recollection it was always the thinnest boys who ate most, and the fatness of my cheeks brought tears to my eyes when I noticed a sort of living skeleton always eating two to my one.

This food problem not only exercises the minds of parents with regard to boys at school, but a fond mother often betrays the same anxiety for a full-grown man.

During the Great War all sorts of 'mothers' darlings' found themselves unexpectedly in the ranks of the army. A mother of one such lad wrote to me when I was commanding a brigade, asking me if I would assure myself 'personally' that her boy had enough to eat.

I hadn't really time to do that, so I told the Brigade-Major to write to her and advise her to have a good look at the next batch of British soldiers she met, and judge from their prime condition whether army food was ample or not.

I managed to get through a good deal of reading in the intervals of work, games, and being hunted. Like most boys my fancy ran to rather lurid works of fiction. I owe a deep debt of gratitude for many happy dreams of love and adventure to the authors of two splendid books. My first favourite was *Ned Kelly*, The Ironclad Bushranger, with a thrill in every chapter. The second favourite was *Jack Harkaway*. I also read most of Fenimore Cooper's splendid stories of Red Indians, and Captain Marryat's books of adventures at sea. Another author was 'Gustave Aimard', who wrote of Spanish adventures and vendettas. From his books I learnt a whole set of Spanish oaths and imprecations, which still linger in my memory.

Spain is one of the few countries I have not yet been able to visit. I hope to get there some day and try my vocabulary on the inhabitants.

It was about this time that I took to signing in my blood the letters I wrote to my sisters.

I don't believe that they were much impressed by it, and it was an unpleasant job getting the blood from my arm, and blood is most trying stuff to write with, it congeals very quickly and won't run off the nib – I doubt if it was worth while.

About my second or third year at school I ran away to sea, during the summer term.

In taking this action I was impelled by many considerations. I had a great love for the sea which has never left me. I never had the least desire to be a soldier, I wanted to be a sailor, but I was never consulted.

I wanted freedom and adventure – something on the lines of being wrecked on a desert island where one found conveniently to hand all the things one needed, not forgetting a parrot and a Man Friday.

I wanted to get away from the tyranny of masters and boys, to get out into the wide world, to make my own way in life, to find possibly a gold mine, and return in a few years and say 'Ha, ha!'

My effort ended in complete failure. I sought employment with the small coasting brigs and schooners, but they laughed at me and told me to go back to school. It worried me that they should spot so easily that I was a schoolboy when I had taken, as I thought, great pains to disguise myself.

I must have been away about three days and two nights, getting a crust of bread here and there at farms, a turnip or two from the fields, and sleeping concealed in the thick Devon hedges at night. At last hunger compelled me to surrender and I made my way back to school to give myself up. As I crossed the football field I was spotted by various people, who 'captured' me, and rather boasted of their capture. This annoyed me more than anything. To be regarded as a 'capture' when one was really a 'surrender' – quite a different thing.

I was taken before the Head, who showed considerable tact in his treatment of me.

Although I had failed in my endeavour to go to sea, I had had an interesting time, and the excitement caused by my recapture helped me to feel somewhat of a hero. I was, on the whole, rather pleased with myself. The fact that I should have to undergo a severe licking and perhaps be expelled, did not worry me in the least. I was very, very hungry and the thought uppermost in my mind was that whatever they did, they would have to give me food!

So I was full of assurance as I was marched by Sergeant Schofield into the awful presence of the Head. I expected him to leap from his desk and do or say something dramatic, but to my pained surprise, he continued writing and seemed barely aware of our presence.

The silence was very unnerving. Nothing beyond the sound of my own breathing, and the ticking of the clock.

At last the sergeant ventured to attract attention by clearing his throat, on which the Head asked him what he wanted, without even turning round.

My assurance was trickling out of me fast.

It trickled out to the last drop when I heard the Head say 'Dunsterville? Dunsterville. Oh yes, now I remember. The boy that ran away.'

Then turning suddenly round and facing me he asked, 'And what do you want?'

'What did I want?' This was quite a new proposition. I had thought that it was they who wanted me, but the Head assured me that that was not so at all. Having run away, my name had just been erased from the rolls and that settled it. I no longer belonged to the college and so 'What did I want?'

Visions of cups of hot tea, and plates of nice meat and bread, faded from my mind, as I burst into tears. No amount of beating or reproaches could have made me weep like that, or made me feel such a crushed worm.

To cut a long story short, the Head saw that, like a condemned criminal, I was given plenty of good things to eat. Then there was a public licking before the whole school in solemn assembly, which somewhat restored my assurance. And there the matter ended.

The net result of this escapade was distinctly advantageous – it gave me a sort of status in the school and enabled me to shake off finally my sense of inferiority.

My life still remained sufficiently exciting, and I had my little adventures frequently enough to save me from a feeling of stagnation.

One of these was perhaps serious enough to merit being placed on record. Among my many rambles in forbidden places my favourite haunt was the quarries where men were at work blasting the rocks.

I soon found out where they stored their blasting powder (black) and also found how to get at the store and help myself to the precious substance unobserved. With this I used to carry out very interesting experiments in small blasting operations on my own.

Somehow or another — I cannot remember how — I became possessed of some fine grain black sporting powder. This I proceeded to use in the same way as my blasting powder, but of course it burnt much more rapidly; in fact, with the short trail I laid, the explosion was almost instantaneous. I hadn't time to jump out of the way before the charge went off practically in my face.

It is an extraordinary thing how quickly one's nerves move by instinct. In the fiftieth part of a second, I suppose, I must have shut my eyes and so saved my sight. But my eyebrows and eyelashes were burnt off, and my face was as black as a nigger's. It hurt a good deal, but it hurt much more having to wash the black off my scorched skin in salt water on the beach. But it had to be done. To have returned to school with that face would have been to confess my sins.

I had to be treated in hospital, but was soon all right again. In explaining the extraordinary condition of my face I invented some plausible tale in connection with the burning of a newspaper while drawing up the fire in one of the class-rooms. It went down all right. At any rate they kindly accepted that version of the affair and said no more about it.

I had some conscience even at that early age and I tried to persuade that censorious part of my make-up that I had not really told a proper lie because the damage had been caused by fire — in a sort of way — and my skin was really burnt — in a manner of speaking.

CHAPTER III

'STALKY & CO.'

I cannot remember exactly when Kipling or Beresford came to the school, but I suppose it was in my third year, which would be about 1878.

We eventually shared a study together, but must have formed our first alliance long before that time. The greater part of our 'study' period was passed together, but not all. There were changes in the combination at one time or another, the details of which I cannot recall.

From the details I have given of my life up to this point, it will be realized that I had gained some considerable experience, and had probably a good deal of skill in manœuvre, coupled with other traits that might give promising results when combined with the precociously mature mentality of Kipling and the subtle ingenuity of Beresford.

I am sure we were not posing, and we were not setting out merely to defy authority, but almost unconsciously I am afraid that was our attitude. We must have been heartily disliked by both masters and senior boys — and with entire justification.

The first effect the combination had on me was to improve my tasté in literature. The period of Ned Kelly and Jack Harkaway was succeeded by Ruskin, Carlyle, and Walt Whitman.

We did a good deal of reading, hidden away in our hut in the middle of the densest patch of furze-bushes, or in a tiny room we hired from one of the cottagers. Our various huts were mostly 'out of bounds', but the secret entrance to them was sometimes in bounds, in which case one ran no risk of capture on entering or leaving. And capture in the hut itself was practically impossible. The furze-thicket was on a steep slope, the tunnel of approach between the prickly stems of the bushes was only just wide enough to admit a boy. A grown-up endeavouring to approach from above could only do so (as we did) by pushing through the furze-bushes and moving down backwards. Progress in this way was slow, and grunts and exclamations when contact was obtained with healthy furze-prickles gave notice long before the danger could be at all acute.

Approached from below, things were easier, but for that reason we never made our main road in that direction; the little track there was only an emergency exit and quite impossible for a full-sized man to negotiate.

The joy of a hut was manifold. It was out of bounds; it was one spot in the world out of reach of grown-ups. Then there was the joy of construction. Finally, there was the joy of smoking, often ending in the misery of being sick. Reading to ourselves or out loud was our only recreation, and the hatching of plots against people who had 'incurred our odium'. *The Confessions of a Thug* was one of the books we read aloud, and Walt Whitman we thoroughly enjoyed in the same way. You can't get the real effect out of W. W. in any other way. *Fors Clavigera* and *Sartor Resartus* and other works we absorbed in silence, broken only by occasional comments.

I can't remember why on earth we hired that little room from 'Rabbit's-eggs', but I suppose it was in the winter and our outdoor haunts were damp and uncomfortable. I call it a room, but I fancy it must really have been something more in the nature of a pigsty. But whatever it was, we cleaned it up and had the same joy in its occupancy as we had in our hut — the feeling of security and escape from tyranny. We did some cooking over a methylated spirit-lamp — the usual brews of cocoa and tea, and occasional odds and ends that a kindly fate had put in our way on our travels.

Old Gregory, from whom we hired this room, was a rather dull-witted peasant who was frequently under the influence of drink. His nickname of 'Rabbit's-eggs' was due to his having offered for sale six partridge eggs which he stoutly maintained were 'rabbut's aigs'. He genuinely believed them to be so. He was passing a clump of bushes when a rabbit ran out of them, and for some reason or another he peered into the bushes, and there, sure enough, were the six eggs, obviously the produce of the rabbit!

He was inclined to be quarrelsome in his cups and possessed a dreadful vocabulary of the very worst expletives, which gave rise to his secondary nickname of 'Scoffer'. These were traits that could obviously be used to advantage if handled judiciously.

We were given the privilege of a study about 1880. It was conceded to us rather reluctantly, though, as a matter of fact, we were just the sort of people who could get the greatest advantage out of such a privilege.

We took great pains over the æsthetic adornment of our study, the scheme being based on olive-green, and some grey-blue paint with which we did some remarkable stencilling. Curio shops at Bideford furnished us with quaint fragments of old oak-carving, ancient prints, and some good, but damaged, pieces of old china.

Finance was difficult. We were none of us very plentifully supplied with funds, and after the first month of term bankruptcy generally stared us in the face. On emergency the sale of a suit of clothes filled the gap, and we devised many similar expedients to tide us over a bad time.

At our most severe crisis, when the larder was quite empty, I made a useful discovery. In playing about with the fire I found by chance that used tea-leaves placed on a hot shovel crinkle back into their original shapes and look as if they had never been used. It was easy to turn this discovery to our immediate advantage. I did up about half a pound of tea-leaves in this way and put them back into their original package. Then I visited the study below and exchanged them for about half the proper tea-value of cocoa.

They returned the tea with threats on the following day, but in the meantime we had swallowed the cocoa. Peace was restored by our confession and an offer to regard the cocoa as a loan to be repaid when funds were available.

We did not spend much of our money on tobacco, because our smoking was really more bravado than pleasure. A clay pipe and an ounce of shag last a very long time. During one term we revelled in big cigars, or they revelled in us. We made constant efforts to smoke one to the end, but the attempt was either abandoned or ended in disaster.

I became possessed of these expensive luxuries in the following way: –

Having spent my holidays with friends in Germany, I was returning to school when I met an Englishman on the train who seemed a very pleasant fellow. He told me that he had a large number of cigars that he wanted to smuggle into England, and asked me if I would help him. I said I would gladly do so, whereupon he proceeded to fill the double lining of my top-hat box with his cigars, explaining that as I was obviously a schoolboy the Custom officials would not trouble much about examining my things, and I could restore the goods to him when we reached London.

I passed through the customs quite successfully, but I never saw the man again, and as a result I arrived back at school with sufficient material to make a hundred boy bravado-smokers sick for a year.

Nearly all our successes in our various schemes were based on simplicity. Things just seemed to come our way, like the cigars. I never asked for those beastly things or wanted them, and I wanted them less than ever after a few trials. For instance, an examination-paper found its way to us on one occasion in a most guileless way. The papers used to be printed off in copying-ink on a tray of gelatine. A short time after putting the negative on to the gelatine, the ink sank to the bottom and no further impression could be taken.

Beresford, wandering round a form-room one rainy afternoon, found a gelatine tray that had recently been used for the above purpose. The master who set the paper had carelessly left the tray on his table under the impression that the ink had sunk to the bottom. But it had not.

Just for something to do, Beresford applied himself to the task of endeavouring to recover the manuscript before it had entirely disappeared, and by an incredible amount of misplaced patience and assiduity succeeded in securing what proved to be a gem of the first water — a very feeble, but still legible, copy of the English Literature Examination paper.

Only one of us was up for this particular exam., and on his own merits he would have done well, but the opportunity of getting some amusement out of the affair was too good to lose.

The paper consisted of quoting ten or twenty consecutive lines of Milton's 'Comus', commenting on the derivation of words, references touched on, and various matters in the notes appended to the school edition.

The master concerned had a special pet pupil who always got top marks, and the joke was to see whether, when one of us was able to answer every question in full, the pet pupil would still emerge top — and he did.

It was certainly a form of cribbing – but a venial one. Our code of honour held that cribbing in a competitive exam. was a vile form of meanness, but in an ordinary exam. we could take what help the gods gave us.

The Natural History Society, founded by Mr. Evans in 1880, soon attracted our attention, and I think we all three became members. It was not so much the pursuit of butterflies, or the study of birds and plants, that drew us to the Society as the valuable privileges conferred on members, the chief of which was a relaxation of bounds. Places that we could only visit hitherto by stealth we could now walk boldly through, carrying in our hands some hastily-gathered botanical specimens or matchboxes containing beetles or caterpillars. With these we could smilingly confront the sergeant or any prowling master who had 'stalked' us with a view to punishment for breaking bounds.

But one's nature cannot be wholly evil, and a small spark of something good in mine was fired by Evans' enthusiasm for botany. I interested myself in flowers merely in order to carry out nefarious schemes with greater impunity, but I ended in loving flowers for their own sakes. My slight knowledge of botany has been a source of pleasure to me all my life.

The Literary and Debating Society attracted us in a more genuine way and we extracted quite a lot of amusement out of it. Kipling was made Editor of the School Chronicle, and some of his earliest efforts appeared in that paper. I remember 'Ave Imperatrix', written in the style of a poet-laureate congratulating a monarch on escape from peril. This was with reference to an attempt on the life of Queen Victoria about 1881. Poets would not be poets if they could know when the divine frenzy was going to inspire them, and when a poet happens to be also a schoolboy the inspiration is pretty certain to come at an unsuitable moment. So it happened that 'Ave Imperatrix' was written in French class at the end of a French textbook.

Looking back on my own school-days, I am filled with an intense sympathy for schoolmasters. What a wearisome and thankless task is theirs! I regarded them as a tyrannical lot of old men (some probably not more than twenty-six years old) who hated boys and wanted to make them miserable. So I, in my turn, tried to make them miserable. I know better now, and I hope that boys of these days are not so stupid as I was, and have a fairer estimate of the relative positions of master and boy than I had.

Kipling must have been a difficult youth. The ordinary boy, however truculent, generally quails before the malevolent glance of a notably fierce master. But I remember Kipling on such occasions merely removing his glasses, polishing them carefully, replacing them on his nose and gazing in placid bewilderment at the thundering tyrant, with a look that suggested 'There, there. Don't give way to your little foolish tantrums. Go out and get a little fresh air, and you'll come back feeling quite another man.'

Kipling's sight was a great handicap to him in the knockabout life of boyhood. Without his glasses he was practically blind. We fought occasionally, as the best of friends always do. He was quite muscular, but shorter than me, and this gave me some advantage. But as you cannot fight with specs. on, my victory was always an easy affair – taking a mean advantage of an opponent who could not see what he was hitting at.

Like all schools, we had compulsory cricket or football three times a week, but it was foolish to expect a boy with a large pair of specs. on his nose to take much interest in the 'scrum' of Rugby football.

Kipling's only nickname at school was 'Giglamps'– sometimes shortened to 'Gigger'– derived from the very strong glasses he was compelled to wear.

When I was about twelve years old my father came home on leave from India, and came down to visit the school and to have a look at his son and heir. I was a little awed by this large gentleman, whom I at once put in the same category as the masters. He was then about forty-nine years of age, and all I can remember of his visit is his rage when I offered to help him over a stile. He was a very active man and a noted shikari, but I thought a person of his age was probably infirm. As he had to return to India before our holidays began, we had no opportunity of learning more about each other.

During my seven years at school I spent my holidays with various people in various places. Sometimes a kind

Victorian aunt took me in, sometimes I returned to my guardian at Woolwich, and sometimes I had a good time in London or in the country, with friends.

At Greenway, Luppit, near Honiton in Devon, I spent my most exciting holidays, shooting rabbits with an old converted flint-lock lent me by a farmer – Gaffer Coles. The conversion of this ancient weapon from flint-lock to muzzle-loader with percussion cap had been very imperfectly carried out, and every time I fired a little spurt of flame came out of some leakage very close to my eye – rather a dangerous sort of weapon.

With my guardian at Woolwich I had a very good time. As I mentioned before, she was a kind, tender-hearted soul who never dreamt of exercising any control over us, and we were a gang that ought to have had the strictest control. There were eight of us: myself and my two younger sisters, the guardian's three sons and two daughters; and the girls were as bad as the boys – they always are when they're not worse.

We lived at 43, The Common, and our various pranks (which I certainly will not describe) attracted some undesired attention to the house. On more than one occasion the police had to visit the widow and threaten legal action unless she would guarantee our future good behaviour. This rather put a check on our youthful exuberance until I found a way out of the difficulty.

No. 43 was a storey higher than the terrace of houses on its left. I found we could get out of our attic windows, crawl up to the top of our roof and get down, with the aid of a bit of rope, on to the roof of the next house. From there we could make our way along till we were three or four houses down the row, and directing our operations from that point, we had the extreme pleasure of noticing indignant passers-by knocking at No. 39 or 40 to complain to the harmless residents of assault and battery.

Leading such a turbulent life, both at school and during the holidays, and with less check on one's evil tendencies than the ordinary bad boy gets under normal circumstances, it is hardly to be believed that religion played any part in my life. But it certainly did so in a quite unconscious way. 'Fear God and Honour the King' was the school motto, and our pride in this showed that we were not entirely heathen. The second commandment was also firmly rooted in our minds. Not in its true affirmative form of 'Thou shalt love thy neighbour as thyself', but in the diluted negative form of 'Don't do anything mean. Don't let anyone down'. And I think that in all our villainies we did try as far as possible to amuse ourselves without injuring others. That's not much, but it is something.

Owing to my wandering life, my religious education was extremely varied, which was an enormous advantage. Most religious people are shut up in little boxes, and they shut their children up in the same boxes, and they would never dare to peep into other people's boxes or allow their children to do so.

I received snatches of instruction from many varied

Nonconformist sects and from most of the bewildering sects within the Church of England. They each tried to instil their own particular teaching into me, and their efforts produced a contrary result. The one important thing about salvation to each of them was that they were right and all the rest were wrong. And from this I learnt the opposite, and that was that nobody is ever entirely right, and one's opponents are often very far from wrong.

Later in life I have made a practice of entering every open door and, in this way, have taken part in the services of all the great divisions of the Church in Europe, and I find they all teach the same thing: 'We are right. The rest are heretics.' What a lot of hatred is taught in the name of a religion of love!

My kindly guardian's religious ideas were of the simplest kind. 'I do not speculate on the number of stars I shall have in my crown, but I do try to love God and to love my neighbour.' And I am afraid that, in including us under the category of 'neighbours', she allowed her love to go to the extent of never saying 'no' to anything. If we had been good children we should not have taken advantage of her kindness. But where are these good children? I never meet them.

In touching thus lightly on the only side of life that really matters, I am aware that it is a subject that most well-bred people shy at — till they come to die, and then they make more fuss about it than any of us, as I know from experience. Also, I shall be accused of inconsistency. To be a robber of hen-roosts and 'the good young man' at one and the same time is verging on hypocrisy. Well, I plead guilty to the inconsistency, but not to the hypocrisy.

The point is that I am sorry to say I never was 'the good young man', but that is not to say that I was not trying, or at any rate wishing to be. Every one who has ideals fails, because as soon as he reaches what he thought was his ideal he finds he has only reached a point from which he can see something better, and he starts again, to fail again. But he is going forward all the time and in the right direction. Experience of life has convinced me that bad people are not so very bad, and good people are not so very good. We expect too much of each other and are disappointed.

From 43, The Common, my guardian moved to London, where I spent instructive holidays in the neighbourhood of Chalk Farm. Tottenham Court Road was not far away, and with complete freedom of action and no restriction as to time of coming home at night, I learnt a good deal more of London life than the ordinary country boy knows as a rule.

Other holidays I spent in Plymouth, the home of my forefathers, where I enjoyed the advantage of learning to handle a sailing-boat. Certainly I cannot complain that my life was lacking in variety.

Living all my childhood and boyhood by the sea has left me with the love for the sea that increases as the years go on. I remember our first house at Sandown. It had no garden on the side facing the sea because the brine made plant life almost impossible. There was just a tiled courtyard and a few tamarisk bushes, and when there was a big south-easterly gale the wind seemed always on the verge of lifting the roof off, while the spray from the big roaring breakers dashed against my bedroom windows. I never want to be farther from the sea than that.

That is probably the result of thwarted desire. I wished to be a sailor, and they made me a soldier. Doubtless, if I had been a sailor, I should have settled in retirement as far from the sea as possible. I not only failed to realize my wish for a seafaring life, but spent most of my life on or near the Indian frontier, a thousand miles from the sea.

Mingled with my childish memories of the wild sea-waves is always an unfading romantic affection for the rugged old red sandstone cliffs of North Devon, with the jackdaws and seagulls nesting in the crevices and the Atlantic rollers roaring at the foot.

The first break-up of our little band was in 1882, when Kipling left for India to take up an appointment with the *Civil and Military Gazette* at Lahore. Beresford left a short time later to join Cooper's Hill Engineering College, whence he also eventually found his way to India, in the Public Works Department; and I left at the end of the summer term, 1883, to enter the Royal Military College, Sandhurst.

My success at my first try at the Army Entrance examination startled every one, myself no less than the others. I had fairly good brains, but I was an unwilling worker and entirely lacked application. I went up as a sort of forlorn hope and passed, with rather intense competition, half-way up the list. This success was entirely due to the methods of the Headmaster, Cormell Price. You could not fail. I think I can say that without exaggeration, because, although I did not actually go as far as wishing to fail, I certainly had no desire at all to pass.

I had a sort of romantic idea of enlisting as a private soldier and working my way up to Field Marshal. I have to thank Price for saving me from that. I am not suggesting that going through the ranks is a bad way of beginning soldiering. I have several friends who have won their commissions in that way, and, on the whole, they seem to have enjoyed their experiences in the ranks; but it is a big handicap in later life when age and commissioned service are balanced against each other. Then you regret the four years' seniority you lost by going through the ranks.

At the time I am speaking of, competition for Sandhurst was very severe, and the normal procedure was for a boy to finish his time at a public school and then go for six months, or a year, to a crammer, and then take the exam. Price passed us all into Woolwich or Sandhurst direct from the school and without the delay and expense of cramming.

My year at Sandhurst passed uneventfully. Five or six of us had passed in together from Westward Ho and it was nice to be able to start a new life with a nucleus of old schoolfellows. I am afraid I had not even begun to 'settle down' at the age of eighteen, and there were times when it looked as if the authorities might ask me to select some other career than the army. But all's well that ends well, and I emerged triumphantly in August 1884 with my commission and appointment to the second battalion of the Royal Sussex Regiment, stationed at Malta.

CHAPTER IV

A START IN LIFE

I SAILED from Woolwich for Malta on board a hired transport on November 1, 1884. As my sisters had already gone to join my father in India, I was the last of the family to set out on my adventures, and there was consequently no one to wave a kindly farewell on the quay and no one appeared to care twopence where I was going or what was to become of me.

I was very far from feeling depressed on this account – in fact, I never noticed the omission. It has only occurred to me now, as I set down these reminiscences. Later life has convinced me how much pleasanter it is not to be seen off, or met on arrival. On both occasions one has plenty to do and to think of, and affectionate farewells and welcomes generally mean the loss of a trunk or two.

After an uneventful voyage I reported myself for duty at regimental head-quarters in Ricasoli Barracks, and soon found myself drilling with recruits on the barrack-square, which constituted my chief employment during the first six months of my service.

During these six months I was severely snubbed, and learnt, by committing each fault in turn, the intricacies of army etiquette.

On a regimental guest-night which I found rather boring I retired to rest about 1 a.m. while there were still guests in the Mess. At about 2 a.m. I learnt that

one must not do this. There is no need to give full
details of events, but fate was not unkindly to me.
My tub was at the foot of my bed, filled with cold
water ready for the morning. One subaltern proposed that I had better have my bath at once and proceeded to put me into it. We struggled across the
bath for some time and I evaded the ducking. Next
morning I found at the bottom of my tub this officer's
gold watch, which had fallen out of his pocket in the
struggle.

My quarters had whitewashed walls and the blood-
stains on these must have startled my soldier servant.
But it really was not a very serious affair. Noses bleed
easily, and the blood was not all mine.

On returning to the ante-room after parade one day, a
friend remarked with surprise that he had noticed that
I had broken the point off my sword. I at once drew
it to show him he was wrong, and so learnt that you
must not draw your sword in the ante-room (a wise
precaution from the old duelling days). The large
amount of Port-wine I had to pay for as a punishment
made this lesson easily remembered.

Three more occasions on which I had to stand the
whole Mess Port-wine were when I spoke of some
religious matter, when I opened a political discussion,
and when I mentioned a lady's name – three good
rules well learnt, though at considerable expense to my
father. A mention of Wellington's campaign in the
Peninsular cost me some more Port, and I was now
more than half educated, having learnt the excellent

rules that in a Mess you must not discuss religion or politics, or mention a lady's name, or talk shop.

Carrying the Colours for the first time was a costly honour, also involving expensive refreshment for my brother officers.

My pay was five shillings and threepence a day, and my father gave me the small allowance of £100 a year, which just doubled my pay; but this fell far short of my Mess-bill, and further parental assistance was necessary at frequent intervals.

Malta, being at that time the head-quarters of the Mediterranean squadron, was a pretty lively place, and there was plenty to amuse one outside barracks. Dances were frequent, as well as all the usual forms of social gaiety.

I went to a ball at Government House, looking, as I thought, very smart in my brand-new scarlet Mess-jacket with a good deal of gold lace on it. But the room seemed full of midshipmen, and I found to my sorrow that no girl will look at a scarlet coat when there is a bluejacket around.

I am grateful to the Royal Navy for many cheerful suppers on board ship very late at night — or perhaps early in the morning. A favourite menu on these occasions was a simple one: 'sardines, raw onions, and gin'.

Both officers and men had splendid boating facilities. I had a small sailing-canoe, out of which I got much enjoyment. A sudden puff of wind upset me when I was about a mile outside the harbour, and as I could not right the canoe, I proceeded to swim homewards, pushing it before me. Progress was slow and very hard work, so I was delighted to see a Maltese boatman coming to my assistance. With his aid I was soon ashore, when I gave him the liberal reward of ten shillings.

This, however, threw him into a perfect frenzy, and he shrieked 'What, do you value your life at only ten shillings?' I tried to explain to him that he had saved me trouble but not my life, and if when one had one's life saved one had to pay the value of one's life, it would be better not to be saved at all. I was none the worse for my ducking, beyond losing a rather valuable stone out of a ring — I shudder to think that I used to wear rings, but this was a family one.

In January 1885 we were ordered to Cairo, and hoped we might be sent up the river to join the Nile Expedition, but as our 1st Battalion was already there we were kept at the Base.

If Malta had been fairly lively, Cairo put it altogether in the shade. It was before the days when Cairo became a fashionable resort and, being war-time, there were no ladies there. So without their refining influence we were rather wild.

Our favourite amusements in the evening were roulette and baccarat, played in the numerous gambling-dens. Senior officers showed us the way and we were not slow to follow their example. I won at times a mass of golden coins, at other times I lost still more without pausing to consider that I had very little to lose.

The crash very soon came, before I could even wire

to my father for help. I awoke one morning to find my tent surrounded by Egyptian Police, and an evil-looking document was thrust into my unwilling hand. But before handcuffs could be actually applied, my brother officers arrived on the scene, and steps were taken that brought the matter to a satisfactory end.

I am now eternally grateful to them for what they did for me, but at the time I did not regard the possibility of having to leave the army as anything very dreadful. I was happy enough in my regiment, but disappointed, as we all were, at being kept at the Base, and the dullness of barrack-square routine in peace-time had already in one short year considerably damped my military ardour. I had wild ideas of starting life afresh in Patagonia, or Timbuctoo, or anywhere where one could feel 'on one's own' – which simply meant, I suppose, that I had not yet got accustomed to discipline. My father eventually adjusted matters and set me on my legs again, but with a warning that the next time I should have to extricate myself without his assistance.

Soon after this episode my company was sent to Suez, a dull place after the gay life of Cairo. We had detachments both in this town and at Port Said, and neither of these towns was at all the sort of place a mother would choose for her boy of twenty – in fact, they probably held in those days about the world's record for iniquity.

At Suez there were one or two gambling-dens which helped us to get rid of our pay, and roulette formed

our only recreation at night. But by day we were fortunate in being able to get a little shooting on the
marshes formed by the overflow from the sweet-water
canal.

There was just enough water, with a few clumps of
reeds and tall grasses, to tempt an occasional bird to
alight and risk the fusillade of the Suez pot-hunters.
Curlew, coot, and now and then a duck or snipe, was
all that our shooting-ground yielded us, but it gave us
outdoor amusement, and even the coots were a welcome change from our rations of bully-beef.

If we could have had it as our private preserve it
would have served all our wants, but being just outside
the town, it attracted every scallywag who owned a fire-
arm of any sort. It was amusing to watch the procedure. A single curlew would alight somewhere about
the middle of the marsh. Then from behind each
clump of reeds would gradually become visible the
various head-dresses of the seventeen nationalities
who had determined to make their evening meal off
that unfortunate bird. Bowler hats, a fez or two, a
tweed cap, a solah topee – and I think there was
once a Levantine Greek in a top-hat. If the bird was
killed there was always a dispute as to the ownership, because probably five or six had fired at the same
time. But more often the bird flew away unharmed,
leaving little to quarrel about except the accusation of
premature firing.

I shot a brother officer here. We were coming home
after sunset when a duck suddenly alighted on the

water. The bird was quite visible above the sky-line, but was lost in the darkness when he got below the line. But we knew about where he was, so we determined to stalk him by going round opposite sides of a big clump of tall grass and so getting him between us. It was a dangerous expedient and the duck got up exactly as we were facing each other. I shot Gilbert and he shot the duck.

The pellets were only just underneath the skin and were easily removed by the doctor, and I was compelled to stand a glass of Port for each pellet. There seemed to be an enormous amount of them, and it was an expensive affair. Gilbert and I still meet occasionally, and I think he still hopes to find a few more pellets.

In the summer our detachment was ordered to Suakim, half-way down the Red Sea on the East Coast of Africa – a nice place for a summer resort. If I were to state what the thermometer actually was I should not be believed, but it was certainly a long way over 120 degrees in the shade. We lived in tents with an extra matting roof to lessen the effect of the direct rays of the sun, but even with that we lost a great many men with heat-stroke.

I invented an excellent device for procuring a cool sleep in the long hot afternoons. I spread a date-palm mat on my bed and poured water on it, and then lay down on it without any clothes. The hotter the desert wind blew, the greater the evaporation, and I kept delightfully cool. But as a result I laid the seeds of

c

rheumatic fever, which developed some months later and nearly put an end to my career.

In the winter of 1885 we were ordered to rejoin regimental head-quarters at Cairo, which soon afterwards left for India. This was rather a disappointment to us, as we were not on the Indian roster and were hoping to go to one of the colonial stations; but the war in Egypt had upset all rosters, so our new destination was Rawal Pindi, in the Punjab, where we arrived in January 1886. Rheumatic fever bowled me out *en route* and I had to be left behind, sick, in Deolali, where, with good doctors and kind nursing, I was soon pronounced out of danger, and rejoined my regiment in a month's time.

Travelling up country, I was lucky enough to have a day to spend in Lahore and so met Kipling, and we enjoyed a talk over each other's adventures.

Kipling was then living with his parents, while employed on the staff of the *Civil and Military Gazette*, and had already risen to fame as the author of many witty satires on Indian life. We were both twenty years of age and looking forward eagerly to what life might have to show us. I was fortunate enough to be able to spend two days with him before continuing my journey to Rawal Pindi, where I rejoined my regiment in the middle of the training season.

Life in Rawal Pindi was a very fair mixture of hard work and social gaieties. The climate in winter is excellent, and a little shooting can be got in the neighbourhood,

From Pindi we were sent in April to a summer camp in the Himalayas — Upper Topa, where we had a damp and unpleasant time in our tents during the heavy and continuous rains of an extra liberal monsoon.

I soon began to interest myself in the people of the country and their languages, passing the Higher Standard Urdu within a year. This was a great advantage to me, as I soon found it impossible to continue the financial struggle in a British regiment with an allowance of only £100 a year, and being much attracted by the smartness and general appearance of the Indian units, Cavalry and Infantry, that formed part of the garrison, I decided to apply for the Indian Army.

This was no easy matter. I was told bluntly that my application would not be forwarded, and I received a good telling-off from the Captain of my company, who said, 'Do you think I've been training you for three years, and teaching you to be a decent representative of the regiment, in order that you may chuck the whole thing just when you are beginning to be of some use to us?' and more to the same effect, with various expletives.

I persevered, however, and in the end my application was forwarded and I had the good fortune to be posted to the 24th Punjabis, stationed at Mian Mir.

Here I soon found that the most important part of my education lay before me, as, in addition to purely military training, I had now to learn something of the history of India, and the languages, religions and customs of the men with whom I was now to serve.

The learning of languages is easy to some, but terribly difficult to others. I had the advantage of having passed in Urdu before I decided to enter the Indian Army, and within two years I passed in Punjabi, Pushtu, and Persian. From a complete ignorance of the religions of India, I was soon able to understand sufficient of Hinduism, Mahomedanism, and the Sikh religion to avoid hurting the prejudices of those races; but I naturally made mistakes at first, which occasioned a certain amount of trouble. Coming from a country where we are all of one religion, and where there is no 'caste', it was extremely difficult at first to realize the great importance that Indians attach to all matters concerning food and drink, and how each religion, and each caste in each religion, has its own different rules regarding these matters.

I took a great liking, however, to the Pathans Sikhs, and Dogras of whom the regiment was composed, and by availing myself of every opportunity of conversing with them when off duty soon got to know all that was necessary concerning their customs and modes of life, and in a very short space of time began to feel quite at home in my new surroundings.

CHAPTER V

THE INDIAN ARMY

THE change from a British regiment to an Indian one is, of course, considerable in every detail. In those days there were fewer officers in a battalion, and I found myself, very soon after joining, a mounted officer on parade, and Officiating Quartermaster.

I had to buy a horse in a hurry from a friend. The horse was guaranteed sound in all respects, and soon proved to be lame in all four legs, which necessitated my disposing of him for a trifle and making a more careful purchase. This was another step in my education.

The duties of a mounted officer on parade were not easy to learn. A favourite and quite useless manœuvre was that of 'a line changing front' in various directions. This necessitated two mounted officers galloping out to mark the points where the flanks would rest when the change of front was completed. The difficulty was to know who was to go where and, having got somewhere, to guess the approximate point for the flank.

I was not bad at guessing the point, but I rode a rather wild horse, and when he started to gallop he disliked having to pull up, so that instead of marking the point, I spent some time careering round in circles. Our chargers were not well trained. I remember one officer whose horse frequently ran away with him, leaving the parade ground and refusing to stop till he had reached his stables. As this officer was not remarkable for his keenness in the performance of his military duties, it was suspected that he allowed his horse to run away with him so as to escape from the parade.

He was of a type well known in the army, a specimen of which is responsible for the wicked but clever dictum, 'It is better to incur a slight reprimand than to perform an arduous duty.'

Taking over the job of Quartermaster also presented difficulties, and as there was no proper system of keeping accounts and I was not by nature designed for office work, I had many troubles, and was obliged to spend many weary hours adding up columns of figures which never produced the same total twice.

With the exception of actual parade work, most of our tasks were carried out in mufti, one of the most diverting of performances being the frequent inspection of lines by the Commanding Officer. It was an imposing affair. The C.O., shaded from the sun by a huge white umbrella with green lining, and wearing a large solah topee and blue spectacles, headed the procession, followed immediately by the Quartermaster, the Subadar-Major, the Chowdry, the Mutsuddi, the Regimental Police Havildar, the Jemadar-Sweeper and other people of importance. For about an hour and a half we wandered up and down the lines and the bazar, a halt being made every few yards to call the Quartermaster's attention to some small repairs to buildings, or to cross-examine the Jemadar-Sweeper on the subject of sanitary shortcomings.

A person of almost more importance than the C.O.,

except on the field of battle, was the Chowdry – Janki
Pershad – a refined and educated Brahmin, who had been
in the regiment nearly since the day of its being raised
and so constituted a living record of events. His chief
duties were normally connected with the regimental
bazar, and as Quartermaster I met him frequently in
this capacity. On one occasion when inspecting the
bazar I wanted to get rid of a lot of rupees that I was
carrying about. So I proposed to leave them, without
counting, with one of the shopkeepers. Before doing
so, I asked J. P., 'Is he an honest man?' and J. P.
replied, 'Yes, sir, he is honest.' On receiving this
guarantee I proceeded to dump the rupees down on
the man's table, but J. P. interposed and told me not
to do so. I said, 'But you told me he was honest.' To
which he replied, 'Yes, sir, he is honest, but not *so*
honest.' I had always been inclined to think that
'honesty' was a comparative term, but it was not till
Janki put me right about it that I felt quite sure of
the matter.

I can recall one other example of his quaint and
clever use of English. In an Officers' Mess expenses
for regimental guests are charged for under the heading of 'Mess guests', each officer paying a share calculated in proportion to his rate of pay – other expenses
are paid for by an equal division. There is sometimes
some doubt as to whether certain charges are to be
calculated on the proportionate rate or by simple division. A doubtful question arising concerning a tomb-
stone erected to the memory of one of the officers,

Janki Pershad, who kept the Mess accounts, asked for orders as follows:

'Please, sir, is tombstones Mess guests?'

Orderly-room was 'Durbar', and was held in the open air under a shady tree: a very informal affair at which many onlookers were present. Punishments were awarded to fit the crime, not strictly in accordance with Military Law, but very much more efficacious.

A sepoy's pay was Rs. 7 a month (about ten shillings), with some compensation for dearness of provisions, and Good Conduct Pay, and out of this he found his food. Regimental lines were invariably built and kept in repair by the regiments themselves. Things are very different now; rates of pay are much higher and rations are provided by Government; but the sepoy of those days was a very fine fellow, and I think there was more happiness in a regiment than there is now. Education was hardly thought of, and the lack of it probably accounted for the increased happiness. Many Indian Officers, perhaps the majority, could not read or write, but they managed to perform their duties with complete efficiency in spite of this. But some of them, while knowing all about movements relating to actual fighting, were lamentably deficient in ordinary or ceremonial drill on the parade ground.

At one inspection, when I was Adjutant of the 20th Punjabis, I trembled when the General said, 'I would like to see that tall Indian Officer over there drill his company.' Knowing the weakness at drill of this particular man, I purposely misunderstood the General's order and directed another Jemadar to carry out the performance, hoping that the General's attention might be distracted elsewhere for a moment. But the ruse failed and the General insisted on seeing the performance of the man he had chosen.

Thereupon Jemadar Falana started off with the simple manœuvre 'Change direction to the right', which was neatly executed by the company, who were then once more ordered to 'Change direction to the right', which continued until the General complained that he was feeling giddy and insisted on some change. On this the Jemadar started a series of 'Change direction to the left', until the General angrily told me to stop him. I got into trouble over this, efficiency in drill being in those days almost entirely the responsibility of the Adjutant.

Up to the outbreak of War I knew at least one Indian Officer who could not really read or write, although he had been forced through the tests necessary to secure his promotion, but the changed conditions of war and military training make the position of an uneducated officer quite impossible in these days.

I soon settled down in my new unit, but it was some time before I could accustom myself to the change — especially in Mess life. In most Punjab regiments a large proportion of the officers were married, leaving only three or four to dine in Mess. Mess furniture and plate were scanty and dilapidated.

Cocoa-nut matting did noble duty beneath our feet, and the furniture was mostly 'local'. A few prints on the walls, faded groups of old officers, some neglected trophies of war and the chase, and a dull collection of old books and albums, comprised the bulk of Mess property.

An electro-plated centre-piece was then much in vogue in Punjab regiments. I saw it so often in those early years that I came to the conclusion that it must be a sealed pattern issued from the arsenal. It was a simple design of a camel beneath a palm-tree and it had generally seen trouble. The camel's legs were screwed on to the base and the nuts worked loose or got lost, and this enabled the camel to strike most unusual attitudes; and the fronds of the palm-tree were bent and distorted.

Crested crockery was unusual. In one regiment I encountered much opposition when I proposed to abolish the heterogeneous collection of plates off which we ate and substitute a simple design with regimental crest, and I was very proud when I had accomplished my task.

But our old harlequin set would be a constant joy to me if I could get hold of it now. My favourite plate was one with a large fat canary on it; there were some with neat borders of ivy-leaves, and others with well-known flowers of the field. And to abolish this in favour of a monotonous old crest showed a distinct lack of perspective.

I remained at regimental head-quarters at Mian

Mir long enough to enable me to pick up the threads
of a new routine, and I was then sent off to Amritsar
to command a small detachment there. It was a great
pleasure to find myself in the position of a commanding
officer, even though my army was a very small one,
and I took the opportunity of being in the centre of
Sikhism to learn Gurmukhi and to get to know the
Sikhs well.

Amritsar is an important city from a religious, commercial and historic point of view, but negligible as a
military garrison. In fact, our little army rather sav-
oured of comic opera. There were a few gunners in the
fort – about twenty, I think. There was a detachment
of the Border Regiment, about 100 men, and my lot of
about the same strength.

But however microscopic a detached garrison may
be, it has to be controlled in the same way as an army
corps. That, of course, is sound enough; but it must
not be taken too seriously. The military situation
was quite Gilbertian because some of the more senior
officers failed to see how funny it all was.

And it was not only the army that was funny, but
there was lots on the civil side to make one smile.
Army officers numbered about six all told, and the
senior of these was ex-officio Officer Commanding the
Station, but he was equally, of course, O.C. his own
detachment. One was Station Staff Officer, and one
performed the duties of Cantonment Magistrate.
During an epidemic of malaria it was quite possible
for one officer to hold all four appointments at once,

and run round from one office to another carrying on a heated correspondence with himself in different capacities, even going so far as to demand from himself his 'reasons in writing' for some breach of regulations.

It is said that one officer eventually put himself under arrest for his behaviour towards himself in another capacity, and that he could not get out of arrest again because his being in that position prevented him from exercising his other official functions. '*Se non è vero, è ben trovato.*'

Among the civilians there were the Deputy-Commissioner and the Civil Surgeon, two people of real importance, and therefore not forming part of the comic element, a Police Officer, an Assistant-Commissioner, a Secretary to the Municipality, an Educational man, and two Commercial men.

I took up my abode in the Amritsar Hotel, run by an Indian gentleman, and persuaded others to join me there until we occupied the whole premises and turned it into a sort of Mess. Among its members were the Police Officer, a cunning old blade, the Assistant-Commissioner – a good fellow but a veritable 'Verdant Green', having just arrived from England – and an Irrigation Officer. We enjoyed the greatest comfort in our little hotel, but it was embarrassing for bona-fide travellers who turned up wanting a room for the night to find they had disturbed the privacy of a 'Chummery'.

I noticed our proprietor's advertisement in the papers, 'under European management', so I sent for him and asked where his European 'manager' was.

He replied, 'Your honour order everything, see kitchen, keep clean. I say European management.'

The policeman was an interesting character. He had
to do a lot of travelling in the district, which necessitated his maintaining a pony and trap. 'Verdant
Green' wanted a pony on arrival and the policeman was
glad to let him have his at a moderate price. Then he
suggested that V. G. really ought to buy a trap – a man
in his position, etc. – so that was provided. Then, as a
pony and trap without harness are not much use, the
harness was sold to him at a sacrifice. Then, you may
ask, 'How did the policeman manage to do his travelling?' Well, the answer is that he borrowed the pony
and trap from the good-natured owner six days in
the week, while the latter wore out the soles of his boots
in his enforced pedestrianism.

One of our number was a self-educated man – rather
a fine character, but often affording us amusement by
his misuse of quotations. He knew no French or
Latin, but he thought an expression now and then
from these languages added polish to his speech. On
one occasion we were speaking of something that had
been done on the sly, and he remarked, 'Oh yes. He
did that, but of course it was all *"couleur de rose"*.'

Amritsar was not a very lively station, but we had
facilities for most of the usual forms of sport – shooting
was poor, but we were able to get up a station game
of polo, and we even had our small race-course.

I personally enjoyed the polo very much, but I was
not a source of enjoyment to the other players. I had

several ponies, but only one of them fast enough for the game – and he was altogether too fast. He had a mouth of iron and his only pace was a mad gallop. I could never pull him up till we were well outside the ground, when I would wheel him round and aim him straight at the little knot of players with my return gallop. The small throng scattered in terror to let us through, on which I repeated the operation from the other side of the ground. It is extraordinary that I was never responsible for a fatal accident.

My cheerful existence in Amritsar came to an end early in 1887 when the regiment was ordered to march to Sialkot and my detachment was recalled to head-quarters. I only remember one event of importance on that march, and that was our entertainment at Gujran-wala by an old retired Sikh officer of the regiment – Subadar-Major Hira Singh. The occasion is impressed on my mind by the fact that I was introduced to quite a new beverage – an improved form of brandy-and-soda, with the brandy doubled and the soda replaced by champagne.

The garrison at Sialkot consisted of one regiment of British Cavalry, one regiment of Indian Cavalry, one battery Royal Horse Artillery, one British Infantry and two Punjab Infantry battalions – large enough and not too large and, being far from the main line in the days before motor-cars were invented, well out of reach of Inspecting Generals.

Pig-sticking in the neighbouring State of Jummoo was the favourite sport here and, as usual, I was well to the front in displaying my sporting proclivities. Riding a pony that was a confirmed bolter, I did unwillingly the most desperate things that called forth the applause of my brother officers.

But pig-sticking ground is invariably bad going, and with a pulling pony I often had to bring my right hand, with the spear in it, down on to my reins. The man in front of me, just about to negotiate a rather stiff jump, glanced over his shoulder and, catching sight of my spear-point a few feet away, wheeled round and exploded in unrestrained wrath. It was obvious that, whatever the risks were to myself, I was a source of danger to others and my friends would feel happier if I stayed away.

On the whole we had sufficient facility for sport and the usual outdoor amusements in Sialkot, but from a soldiering point of view things were not very bright. We were therefore all delighted when the regiment received orders to proceed on active service, to join the force that was to operate against the Hazaras in the Black Mountain country. The news was doubly welcome to me as I had already suffered one disappointment in the Nile expedition, where we had all the dull work of duty at the Base and never heard a shot fired.

Imagine my horror, then, when the C.O. sent for me and said, 'The regiment is ordered on active service and I have selected you for the command of the depot – a very responsible position and one that could not usually be entrusted to so young an officer; but as you already know the men so well and speak Pushtu and

Punjabi, I am sure you are just the man for the job.'
Even after this lapse of time I could hardly trust myself
to say what I thought of the situation. At the actual
moment I contented myself with saying 'Thank you' —
the rules of discipline would not have permitted me the
necessary scope to express myself more fully.

So the regiment departed, leaving me to groan over
my grievance and regret the day I ever came into the
army; but I made a gallant effort to make the best of a
bad job and I soon found plenty to interest me in the
command of the depot. In fact, I might have been
quite happy if I could have got over my sulks. But at
that age I had not properly developed the philosophic
side of my character, and my disappointment rankled.

However, there was always the pleasure of being
one's own master, and as O.C. Depot I had first-rate
opportunities of learning the customs of the men
and improving my knowledge of the language.

I collected a quaint old Hindu beggar — a Sadhu —
and in his companionship passed many pleasant hours.
He was a weird fellow to look at. Beyond one or two
little pieces of string here and there, he wore no clothes,
but as his chocolate-coloured body was neatly smeared
with ashes, he didn't appear so very undressed.

His hair was matted into a sort of felt, which looked
rather disgusting, but one does not inquire too closely
into the secrets of a Sadhu's toilet, and being a Hindu,
some form of daily ablution was necessitated by his
religion.

With a view to improving my Hindustani I paid frequent visits to the native theatre in the city. The plays were interminable, the players very poor and the whole performance very tedious, but I used generally to stay for three or four hours.

Meeting my Sadhu at the entrance to the theatre one evening, I invited him to come in and see the play. I paid for two seats in one of the front rows and introduced my friend to his place in the stalls. He was fond of tobacco, so I offered him one of my Trichinopoli cigars, at which he pulled with great gusto. Cigars coupled with nudity seem incongruous.

After a time I became aware that trouble was brewing. People seemed to be objecting to my nude companion occupying one of the best seats, and I must admit he did look a little out of place. As all Easterns have a superstitious regard for beggars of all religions, I thought they would be pleased at the civility shown by me to a Sadhu; but they had a sort of idea I was making fun of him and of them, so he had to go out.

My only other friend at this time was a Judge. He was a member of the uncovenanted Civil Service, and though he was old enough to be my father, his youthful spirits made him a charming companion. Our chief amusement after dinner in the Mess was cock-fighting, and at this sport he was a great performer.

Cock-fighting in its various forms is a rough performance, and it is difficult to keep one's hair tidy during a series of combats. Confronting him on one occasion as we sat trussed up waiting for the signal to begin the fight, I noticed the extreme neatness of his luxuriant growth of hair.

A few minutes later, when I had gained the victory and he turned over on his side, his entire coiffure became disarranged, and I then found that he was quite bald, but concealed this defect by growing hair about a foot long on one side of his head and neatly arranging this over the top. When it was dislodged it came off like a cup, hanging by a hinge to the side of his head. He was much annoyed at the exposure of his toilet secrets and never offered to cock-fight again, but we remained very good friends.

Nothing of interest occurred during the absence of the regiment except that my famous pony put his foot in a hole when we were galloping across country and I broke my collar-bone. The regiment returned from the Black Mountain before the end of the year and I tried my best to forget my disappointment, but it was a hard job to control myself when my brother officers started the usual talk of reminiscences.

Under these circumstances, I did not hesitate when I was offered the appointment of Adjutant in the 20th Punjabis, to which regiment I was accordingly transferred early in 1889.

CHAPTER VI

THE DIE-HARDS

HAVING now entered on my third year of service, I began at last to feel fairly settled into my profession, though as a matter of fact during the next ensuing six years there were many occasions when it looked as if I might have to make a fresh start in life in some other capacity.

It is forty-three years now since the day when I joined my first regiment in Malta. Forty-three years sounds a long time in the ears of young men looking forward with eagerness to the adventures of life, but in reality it is not a very long period, and to those of us who have the pleasure of looking back after the completion of our few adventures, it seems short enough. There are still officers serving on the active list in India and elsewhere who can remember those days.

But in one sense it has been a long period, because in those years the army has gone through greater changes than previous armies saw in at least two centuries.

Practically no great change had taken place in two centuries beyond the invention of breech-loading rifles and guns, increasing range and rapidity of fire. I began my service with the Snider rifle, a very good large-bore weapon though very clumsy compared with the rifle of to-day. With this humble beginning I ended my career in an atmosphere of aeroplanes and gas. The aeroplane has done more than anything to alter modern warfare. Tactics are entirely altered when secrecy becomes impossible. In the old days a clever commander could outwit his enemy by pretending to mass troops at one point when he was really assembling at another, and victory was often due to the skill of a commander in this respect.

But this has become impossible now that aeroplanes fly over the heads of troops and report all movements while they are still in progress.

And as for gas, what shall I say? It is an invention of the Devil, which puts the real fighting merit of a man into the background. One measly and undersized opponent armed with a gas-dispersing machine can overwhelm a thousand heroes.

When I joined the army in 1884 the general spirit of military training was much as it had been in the days of Napoleon. Officers and men were trained to a certain standard of elementary tactics, and a very high standard of efficiency in the use of their weapons — beyond that their principal duty was to look smart and wear very gorgeous uniforms. Higher forms of military education were advocated by the authorities, but were not received with much enthusiasm by regimental officers. In fact, in those days a young officer who displayed too much zeal in applying himself to studying the 'Art of War' was regarded as a freak by his comrades.

There were a few simple examinations which officers up to the rank of Captain were expected to pass, and they generally succeeded in doing so with a great deal of kindly help from selected instructors. So long as you

didn't get into trouble, your promotion came along in
its turn and was almost entirely dependent on the
length of your service. A fatal system where old men
receive promotion because they are old, and young men
find no chance of coming to the front owing to the
block caused by the old men who in many cases have
lost all true interest in the service and have become
mere 'pension-earners'. There was an absurd idea that
they had some 'right' to promotion, whereas the only
'right' they had was to retire from the army and make
room for keener young men.

A good deal of our parade work was done in full
dress and was chiefly confined to a few simple but spec-
tacular parade movements very accurately carried out,
the Manual Exercise, and Bayonet Exercise. The latter was a really beautiful sight. A thousand men in
lines at open order thrusting their gleaming bayonets
simultaneously into the bodies of a thousand imaginary
foes. When performed to music it was capable of
bringing tears into the eyes of the onlookers.

Fierceness on parade was the order of the day, and
ferocity increased with your rank. Subalterns were
barely noticeable, their duties being confined to doing
right or left guide to the company. Captains shouted a
good deal and permitted themselves an oath or two.
Majors, mounted, swore a great deal. The Colonel
was generally angry with everybody and let them know
it.

But the Annual General Inspection reduced them
all to comparative silence, the intensity of the General's

ferocity putting all minor efforts into the shade. In these days the Annual Inspection is a helpful affair. If anything is not quite right, the G.O.C. will advise how it may be improved. Whatever criticism he makes is with a view to helping more than condemning. But in those days it was a terrible affair, and for at least a week before it all ranks suffered from a severe attack of 'Inspection Fever'.

The Inspection was carried out on lines that admitted of a great deal of eyewash, and was seldom, as it is in these days, a real endeavour to test the efficiency of a unit.

The most amusing performance at General Inspection was the Officers' Sword Exercise.

For this we fell in in two ranks wearing full dress. Ranks were opened and the front rank turned about, whereupon by word of command the most desperate battles took place between the two ranks with their naked swords.

The correct action was neatly arranged to avoid tragedy, each 'cut' from one rank being met by the correct 'guard' from the other.

But we were not very clever, and it frequently happened that when the front rank made 'cut one' the rear-rank officer made 'guard three', which resulted in the crashing of his nice white helmet — extremely amusing to the rest of us but filling the C.O. and the Inspecting General with intense rage.

After that, we generally put on fencing helmets and jackets and did some loose-play with single-sticks. This,

also, often produced amusing incidents. I remember
two Indian officers losing their tempers. Each got in
some good stinging smacks, then with violent hitting
and parrying both sticks broke. They flew at each
other, using the short sticks as daggers, then discarding
these they grasped each other round the neck and
rolled over into the ditch where they were finally separated, and with difficulty made to shake hands.

These old-fashioned ideas of soldiering were just
beginning to yield to more up-to-date methods at the
time I joined the 20th Punjabis in Rawal Pindi to take
up the duties of Adjutant. The duties of a conscientious Adjutant are absorbing and difficult at all times,
but I found my position exceptionally difficult owing to
this clash between the new methods and the old.

The 20th Punjabis, which had been raised during the
Mutiny in 1857 by Sir Charles Brownlow, had had
during the thirty years of its existence the good fortune
of seeing more than its share of active service, and like
many of the old Frontier regiments, had retained a
great deal of irregularity.

In the British Service an Adjutant's first duty was
to keep the regiment up to the mark in all points of
detail regarding regulations as to drill, dress, and discipline. The great test for dress was Guard Mounting,
when scrupulous attention was paid to the exact
method of wearing clothing and accoutrements, and
to the spotless cleanliness of the individual and his
uniform. Every button was examined and even turned
over to see that the back was polished, and every bit

of metal was expected to sparkle like a jewel. I found very different conditions prevailing in the regiment I had now joined.

The greater part of the Indian Army was at this time as regular in every way as the British Army, but the Frontier Force and some of the Punjab regiments still clung to their irregularities, especially in the matter of uniform.

We resembled no other regiment in any point, and did not even resemble each other. In full dress we wore the uniform of a rifle regiment in drab, but with the difference that most of us wore on our tunics the lavish embroidery of a full Colonel. But there was no agreement on this point and some of the senior officers had adopted the correct uniform of a rifle regiment. Thus while a Major might be wearing the small amount of lace permitted to his rank, a subaltern would be wearing a sleeve embroidered almost up to the shoulder.

At an inspection in Rawal Pindi the General remarked to the C.O., 'Your officers are well dressed and smartly turned out, but before I see them again please see that they dress alike.' We hoped that this same General would not see us again, and he did not.

In service dress we wore gaiters of Sambur skin, and scabbards covered with black asses'-skin. The Indian ranks wore blouses and a combined garment of breeches and gaiters in khaki drill, called '*tumbahs*'. On their feet they wore either sandals or shoes of varying pattern, made by the regimental shoemakers. Under these circumstances you can imagine what a

shock Guard Mounting was to a keen young officer
brought up in the school of absolute exactitude.

I well remember my first attendance at this cere-
mony. Before inspecting each man I glanced along the
line of heads and noticed several different ways of tying
pagri, but I had of course learnt by now that Sikhs,
Dogras and Pathans have each their particular way of
arranging their head-dress. Then I noticed that some
of the fringes were black, some blue, and some green,
some composed of long strings, some of little cotton
balls. Bodies and legs were uniform. But what fantasy was displayed in footgear! The first man had
plain leather sandals, the next a good blunt-toed Punjabi shoe, the next a pair of ornamental sandals with
gold thread and silk tassels, the next a pair of light
Punjabi shoes, with thin ornamental points extending
some inches beyond the toe. There were still other
varieties which I need not detail.

Without rushing things too much at first, I determined to set things right as soon as possible. That,
however, proved not to be very soon, in fact I think I
found in the end that the spirit of the regiment conquered me and I became as bad as any of them. There
is a certain charm about minor irregularities in dress
which seems to have a fascination for soldiers.

The chief obstacle in my endeavours to effect an
improvement in the direction of regularity was the
Subadar-Major, a veteran of the old school, who could
never be brought to believe that there could be anything good in a new way of doing things, and whose

invariable reply to my suggestions was: 'This is the custom of the regiment. What you suggest has never been done.'

On one occasion I met the Regimental Drum-Major going for a walk to the city. He wore on his head the regimental *pagri* with two red roses in it; on his body his full-dress tunic and medals; on his legs snowy white baggy Pathan pyjamas; and on his feet some very handsome and ornate chupplies.

I spoke to the Subadar-Major about this weird mixture of uniform and mufti, but he could not in any way realize what the trouble was about. All I could get out of him was 'I think he was very nicely dressed', which was true enough.

Subadar-Majors of those days were nearly always old men who had been in the regiment before their present colonels had joined as lieutenants. They were full of wisdom and possessed great influence.

In this particular case the Subadar-Major was a very remarkable man. Mauladad Khan, Kuki Khel Afridi, had joined the 20th on its raising, and had seen much service. He wore medals for the Mutiny, China, Kabul, Egypt 1882, with clasp for the battle of Tel-el-Kebir; and the N.W. Frontier with many clasps. He had also been awarded the Order of Merit, Sirdar Bahadur, the Medjidieh, and the C.I.E. He could neither read nor write, and regarded those accomplishments with some scorn.

The C.I.E. (Companion of the Indian Empire), which in those early days was a particular honour, he

could not understand and did not much appreciate.
He explained that there was some sense in the Order of
Merit, and in the Sirdar Bahadur, there being a money
allowance attached to them. But the C.I.E. was quite
beyond his comprehension, a very barren honour.

He had had the honour of visiting England as the
guest of Queen Victoria after the Egyptian Campaign,
there being at that time no such thing as the appointment of orderly officer to the Sovereign. Queen Victoria always took the deepest interest in her Indian
subjects, and for that purpose had actually undertaken
the study of Urdu. But Mauladad's knowledge of
that language was very limited, and barely sufficed
for any subject beyond military duties. His interview
with Her Majesty must have been interesting.

He was taken to see all the sights worth seeing, but
took little interest in them. His memories chiefly consisted of admiration for the greenness of the fields compared with the barren hills of the Khyber, and the
magnificence of the horses and cattle.

It can well be understood how great an obstacle he
was to my efforts towards regularity, being more irre-
gular in every way than any man in the regiment. He
wore his *pagri* anyhow, and had a habit of taking it off
at most solemn moments to scratch the top of his head.
In place of a regulation sword he carried an old *tulwar*,
curved like the crescent moon. He had no idea at all
of the solemnity of a ceremonial parade in which he
could see no sense, and his attempts to salute with his
tulwar in the March-past consisted of a friendly wave

and a shake of the blade in the direction of the Inspecting Officer. When the latter took exception to such a
peculiar deviation from the proper salute, it had to be
explained to him that 'It was only Mauladad', and no
more was said.

I did succeed in curing him of one of his peculiari-
ties, and that was the wearing of a coloured handker-
chief protruding from the inside of the collar of his
tunic, and fluttering round his neck, but he only gave
in to me over this out of pure friendship. In plain
clothes he was hopeless. No one could recognize in
the peculiar jumble of odd garments he wore the distinguished officer of Her Majesty's Indian Army.

About this I also spoke tactfully to him, but to no
purpose. It only made him laugh, and he told me of
an amusing adventure that befell him in this connection. He said, 'I was going home on leave once. I
started from Peshawar towards the Khyber Pass in a
tum-tum, but as this broke down half-way I continued
on foot. It was a very hot afternoon in the summer,
and as I walked I came upon a Sahib lying in the shade
of a tree, who seemed to be ill. I went up to him and
spoke to him, giving him some water and helping him
to his feet. He was very grateful, and putting his hand
in his pocket, produced a four-anna piece with which
he presented me. He evidently thought I was one of
the men employed on mending the road. I gave it
back to him, telling him who I was and that I had
plenty of money, but he did not look as if he believed
it.'

He had the heartiest contempt for all 'red books', as he called the Military Regulations, and was continually giving punishments he had no power to give, in utter defiance of the Indian Articles of War. On visiting the Quarter Guard I often found a man imprisoned by order of Mauladad, often no one knew what for, and when I spoke to Mauladad, he did not seem quite sure himself.

One morning the Colonel asked me how many men were on duty in the Quarter Guard and I told him twenty-one. The next day he had me up and said, 'You don't know much about your work. You don't even know how many men you have on duty. I visited the Quarter Guard and found twenty-four men.'

This was an unpleasant rebuff for me, but I knew I had been right. I set to work to inquire, and I found that it was Mauladad again. 'Yes,' he said. 'It was a dark and stormy night, so I put an extra sentry on the back of the Magazine.' A very wise precaution, of course, but quite beyond his powers, and making things rather difficult for me.

He had considerable influence and power outside the regiment, being well known to Lord Roberts and to many of the senior Generals, but his power did not really reach as far as he thought. When I joined the regiment he came to see me in my bungalow, and in the course of conversation said, 'You get a lot of pay as Adjutant.' I said, 'No, just at present I get nothing extra because it is only an Officiating Appointment', to which he replied, 'That is most unjust. You do the

work, and you must have the pay. I will see that you
have it.' But, alas, I never received it. The Controller
of Military Accounts holds a very strong position, and
I am afraid he was rather out of Mauladad's reach.
If they could have met in the Khyber on the other side
of the frontier, I am sure we should all have had an
increase of pay.

He knew his drill well up to the period of 1882.
Anything beyond that he refused to learn, regarding
any change as mere foolishness. About 1890 we either
had a new Drill Book, or some pamphlet of important
alterations was issued.

In order to impress the matter on the minds of the
Indian ranks, the Second-in-Command was ordered
to give a lecture on the subject to the Indian Officers.
This was very thoroughly done in a most painstaking
way, with the aid of diagrams skilfully drawn on a
black-board. At the conclusion of the lecture the
Second-in-Command really seemed to have succeeded
in explaining the new formations and movements.

Mauladad, however, had to have his turn. In a
short speech to the Indian Officers, he summed up the
whole affair somewhat as follows:

'You've all heard what the Major says, and you must
try to remember all these new changes. What they are
all about I don't know, but it is God's will that there
have to be changes. But they are really of no importance at all. In the "attack" there is only one thing to
remember, and that is "Fix bayonets and charge".'

Fine advice for frontier fighting in the days of Mauladad, but it was a good thing that our ideas had got beyond that stage of primitive fighting before we entered on the late Great War.

'Fix bayonets and charge', was his advice on all occasions.

At one inspection the General asked him what he would do if during an advance he suddenly found a body of the enemy on his right flank. His reply was, 'Fix bayonets and charge.'

'Very good,' said the General, 'and if it seemed to you that the enemy entirely outnumbered you, what then?'

'Fix bayonets and charge,' he replied without hesitation.

The General did not put any further questions to him, but turning to the Colonel said, 'That seems to be his solution of every problem, and I will not say anything to damp his ardour. I believe if I asked him what he would do if I dared to disagree with him, he would reply "Fix bayonets and charge ".'

He had a great turn for humorous criticism. A rather delicate officer was temporarily attached to the regiment at this time, who was quite unable to endure the normal hardships of a soldier's life, and generally had to 'go sick' when we had rough times. At one time when the poor fellow was really ill, Mauladad asked me where he was.

I said, 'He is ill, but I do not know what of.'

Mauladad replied, 'I know his complaint, he's got Outpost sickness.'

About the time that I was born the regiment had been stationed at a small place in the Punjab called Talagang, and it seemed that most of the regimental customs had arisen during that period. I learned to hate the sound of the word 'Talagang'. Whatever change I suggested in any regimental matter with a view to introducing a little regularity, was always opposed because it had not been done in Talagang. And Mauladad would explain his way of doing it 'as we used to do in Talagang.

And the Colonel was almost as bad as the Subadar-Major. When I put any matter up to him, he would send for Mauladad and ask him, 'What used we to do in Talagang?'

Under these circumstances if I had not been very young, I might have given up hope, but youth lives on hope, and I lived to see a great many of the desired changes tactfully introduced.

CHAPTER VII

INDIAN SOLDIERS

WHILE I was fighting against the spirit of the regiment, I was myself becoming unconsciously imbued with it, and by the time I had served thirty years in the Indian Army I was somewhat like Mauladad in my dislike of new notions.

But this tendency to do things in a certain way because our fathers did them in that way, is of course ruinous in all affairs of life, and if it were permitted to any extent in the army would result in hopeless inefficiency. So while I smiled at Mauladad's constant reference to the custom of Talagang, and treated it as a joke, I succeeded in my own time in getting my way in matters of importance.

Later on in life, as a senior officer, I managed to keep my conservative spirit entirely for matters of uniform, and not for questions of training or drill, but I was very jealous of any interference with any of our small irregularities in uniform, though in the end they had to go.

I could not, like Mauladad, baffle the Inspecting General by referring him to the practice of Talagang, but whenever I was asked 'What authority have you got for the men to wear that extraordinary thing?' my invariable reply was, 'It's an old custom of the regiment, sir.'

In this way I got rather badly caught out on one occasion. I can't remember when the fashion was introduced of officers in khaki wearing a coat with turned

97

D

down collar showing a khaki shirt and collar and tie, but I suppose it began gradually after the Boer War, and by 1910 had become quite universal, though up to that time there had been no regulation permitting it.

We took to it as a regiment about 1906, and instead of wearing a black or khaki tie we decided to start a brilliant emerald green one, that being the colour of the regimental facings.

This caused trouble on more than one occasion, but we managed to cling to it till 1908 when I was commanding the regiment in Jhelum and we were inspected by Sir Alfred Martin, who at once spotted the remarkable tie – he couldn't help it, you could have seen it a mile away.

He promptly asked, 'Where on earth did you get that thing from? It's not regulation.' Without pausing to consider I gave the usual reply, 'It's a very old custom of the regiment.'

I saw the slip I had made, and could not help smiling. The General smiled also, and without troubling himself to remind me that the open-collar coat had only been introduced a year or two ago, took the line of 'direct action', by ordering me to discontinue its use at once. And that was the end of the green tie.

If Mauladad had been in my place he might have won the day, by insisting that though the coat had only been recently introduced, the tie itself had always been worn in Talagang. Owing to the fact of his being Subadar-Major and also of his splendid career in many campaigns, Mauladad was, of course, the most import-

ant man in the regiment, but all the other Indian
Officers, Sikh, Dogra and Pathan, were of a like spirit.

There were no direct commissions in those days,
and consequently no young Indian Officers. All the
Indian Officers were men of proved merit and ability
who had attained their present rank after years of struggling from recruits upward. This made a great weight
of opinion against me in all matters of change and I
almost wonder now that I dared to stand up against it.

It was a difficult task for a young man of twenty-five
with no war experience and consequently no medal on
his breast, to suggest new methods to old men who had
been soldiers long before he was born, and whose
breasts glittered with medals and decorations, and that
too in days when medals were not given as easily or
as plentifully as in these present times. A man who had
taken part in six arduous expeditions on the frontier,
would have only one medal with six clasps to show.

I felt my position acutely, and I hope I was tactful
enough in my endeavours to have my own way. It is
certain that I was always the best of friends with these
old heroes, and retained their friendship after their
retirement until they were one by one removed by
death. As far as I know, only one of them remains
alive, Captain Arsla Khan, Sagri Khattak, of whom I
had news a year ago, still active and exercising a bene-
ficial influence in his village on the Indus.

I am glad to think now that at that time it never
once occurred to me to take comfort from the knowledge of superior education. If I had said to Mauladad,

'You cannot even read or write whereas I am an accomplished scholar, with knowledge of mathematics, several languages, and many other things;' he would probably have replied somewhat to this effect:

'With all that school learning you ought to be the regimental clerk instead of being Adjutant: Arithmetic won't teach you to shoot a man, or push a bayonet into his stomach.'

Mauladad retired on a very handsome pension a year or two later, his place being at once taken by an equally unprogressive officer, and a year or two later the old hero died.

I had some trouble in regard to physical training of which the regiment had had till recently no knowledge, but which was now being strongly urged by Army Head-quarters. Before the men could be taught I had to put the N.C.O.'s through a long course of training in order to fit them to instruct their sections. This did not actually cause a mutiny but it was not far off it.

One N.C.O. asked to be allowed to speak to me after parade. He said, 'Sahib, I have seen much service and have fought in several campaigns. I know well how to use rifle, bayonet, or *tulwar*. What more does the Sirkar want? Am I to frighten the enemy by behaving like a monkey instead of using my rifle. I feel ashamed of myself at being made to bob up and down in this way in front of everybody?'

It was hard to soothe him, but I explained that he was not going to be called on to do these things himself, but only to learn them sufficiently to be able to teach the young soldiers. And I then flattered his vanity by saying, without much truth: 'There was no need for these things in the days when the Sirkar could get fine strong recruits like you were, but see what poor things we now get in comparison, and you will agree that it is necessary to do these things to strengthen their limbs before they can make proper use of their weapons.'

As a matter of fact, up to the time of my giving up the command of my regiment in 1914 we were getting just as good youths as recruits as ever we got, but the old soldier always likes to think he is a better man than the soldier of the present day.

The enlistment and training of recruits was the most interesting branch of the Adjutant's work. What splendid material passed through one's hands – it would be hard to find any agricultural class in the world to beat the farmers' sons from whom we enlisted our men. Apart from their high military qualities they compelled one's admiration chiefly in their capacity as farmers.

In England the farmers' claim to our sympathy is admitted. He grows turnips in one field and wheat in the other, and the weather conditions that suit turnips don't suit wheat, so he remains in a perpetual dilemma.

The clever rhyme in the child's book of poetry (I am sorry I forget the author's name) says:

'The farmer will never be happy again,
    He carries his heart in his boots,
For either the rain is destroying his grain
    Or the drought is destroying his roots.

In fact if you meet this unfortunate man
The conclusion is only too plain
That Nature is just an elaborate plan
To annoy him again and again.'

But think of the Indian farmer who faces not only drought and flood on a scale of intensity unknown in Europe, but has also to contend against locusts and other pests. He lives in a village that swarms with flies, mosquitoes, sand-flies, hornets, wasps and white ants. The latter cause immense destruction by eating nearly everything except porcelain and metal.

His house and cattle sheds are alive with scorpions. In the long grass through which he finds his way to his fields lurk cobras and other deadly snakes, while in many parts of India there is the added risk from man-eating tigers. Plague, cholera and malaria are always with him.

In spite of these terrible conditions and of a climate that roasts you in summer and freezes you in winter, this brave fellow holds his own, and faces the world with a broad smile, having apparently more capacity for the enjoyment of life than other people who live under far happier conditions.

It was a pleasure to have young fellows from this class to train, but it was not an easy task in the early stages to guide their rustic minds from agricultural considerations to the rudiments of the Art of War.

An Adjutant would have had a full day's work if he had had only his recruits to attend to, but in a large garrison like Rawal Pindi we were not often left in peace, and frequent Brigade parades made regimental training difficult. There was rather a run on 'Ceremonial', and as we had never excelled at that branch of the military art we had to waste a good deal of time over it, and with all our efforts it was a long time before we could really do ourselves credit in the march-past.

Our band was not particularly good for the reason that our chief interest was centred on our subsidiary band — the *dols* and *sarnais*.

The latter are the simple musical instruments of the Pathan tribes, the *dol* being an ordinary light drum and the *sarnai* a reed instrument like the chanter of a bagpipe. They only play native airs, but the music is very stirring and they are splendid things to march to.

Our march-past tune was 'All the blue bonnets are over the border', and the C.O. wished to change this. As I was supposed to have musical tendencies I was consulted and quite seriously suggested 'The man that broke the bank at Monte Carlo'.

They thought that I was trying to be funny, but I was not so in the least. Although the latter is a ribald music-hall song, it has a fine swinging tune and would make a splendid march — the silly words would by now have been long forgotten, and if my proposal had been accepted I could easily have written a couple of verses of a martial nature and rechristened the tune 'The way we stormed the heights at Lundi Kotal'. Having got as far as that it would have been a simple task to weave a legend or two to fit in with the verses.

But an Adjutant finds little time for writing poetry —
in fact, no day is long enough for all the things he has
to do. His work is hard and unceasing, but it is extremely interesting, he is well paid for it, and he escapes,
as a rule, all the wearisome attendance at boards, com-
mittees, and courts martial which are the bane of other
officers' lives.

But he does not always escape. I had, for certain
reasons, to attend a committee in the barracks of a
British Infantry unit, and I took a great dislike to the
very fussy Colonel who was commanding this particular
battalion and who seemed to think that because I was
in what was quite rightly called 'a Native regiment' I
couldn't possibly be a proper sort of white man myself.
This sort of silly idea was prevalent then, and, for all I
know, continues to the present day.

Consequently, I cannot say I was sorry when I heard
the following sad story of his being let down through
his fussiness.

On visiting the coffee-shop one day he asked what a
soldier was to do if he had any complaint or suggestion
to make. The answer not proving satisfactory he said,
'The men must have a proper way of expressing their
needs. Put up a notice board with "wanted" on it so
that a man can write whatever he has a fancy to.' It
was pointed out that the men might make a misuse of
such a privilege, but he insisted and the board was
accordingly made and displayed.

'Anything written on the board?' he asked on his
visit a few days later.

'I think not, sir,' replied the attendant.

'Bring the board here and let me see,' retorted the Colonel. The board was accordingly brought and beneath the word 'wanted', the old gentleman read 'A new Colonel'.

While stationed in Rawal Pindi the regiment took part in some very fierce manœuvres at Attock in 1890, in which the following amusing incident took place. Indian Officers, especially trans-frontier ones, generally take manœuvres very seriously. In this case a great deal of excitement was caused by one who took up with fierce determination the attitude of 'the boy stood on the burning deck'. He was placed with a small body of men at night to guard a pass by which the enemy might endeavour to turn the position, and he was given some fireworks – blue lights – with orders to light one of these as a signal if he were driven from his post. He had only about forty men under his command and in the middle of the night a whole brigade of the enemy advanced on the pass. He thereupon correctly decided to display a blue light before retiring, but the fireworks were damp or went wrong in some way and he could not get them to light.

Meantime the opposing brigade began to get angry and umpires were sent forward to order his retirement. But to these his only reply was to order his men to fix bayonets while he explained that his instructions were to retire *after* he had fired a blue light, and consequently he could not retire *before* he had fired a blue light. His fierce obstinacy could only be overcome when the enemy brigade were induced to lend him a blue light of a better description from their own supply, and when the umpires had helped him to light this he retired after having held up a whole brigade for two hours.

In Pindi I had two interesting friends — a Pathan poet and a Persian scholar. The former improved my knowledge of Pushtu very much by spouting from memory unending odes of his own composition. The time-honoured reward for a poet in the East is the bestowal of a robe of honour. As I could not quite rise to this I gave him two part-worn tweed suits which he fashioned to his own shape and wore with some distinction — but I felt more keenly than he did the degradation involved by his wearing this most unpoetic garb.

The Persian was a suspicious character from Tabriz — either a Russian spy, or a criminal escaping from justice. In his sober moments he taught me Persian, and when he was drunk he was often rather amusing.

In my moments of leisure I found time to take part in amateur theatricals, and I also acquired some renown as a singer of somewhat vulgar music-hall songs.

In 1891 we marched to Mian Mir and in the summer of that year I had the good fortune to be bitten by a mad dog, which resulted in my being sent to Paris to be treated by the famous Doctor Pasteur with his inoculation against rabies which was a recent discovery at that time.

As I had no money at all in my pocket my expenses

had to be defrayed by my father, and take it all round I
felt I had good reason to be grateful to the dog for
a very pleasant holiday. The treatment, which was
directly under Pasteur's own supervision, varied little
from present-day methods except as regards the régime
recommended for the patient.

I believe that a quiet life and abstention from alcohol is now advocated, but all I was told to do was to
'eat, drink, and be merry'. And I did all three with
gusto.

An Irish carpenter with ginger whiskers from Dublin was the only other representative of what was then
called the United Kingdom and he and I chatted
pleasantly while waiting our turn to be pricked. About
the fourth day he confided to me that he did not mind
the treatment itself but that he found the daily restraint
very trying.

'How is that?' I inquired.

'Well,' he replied, 'for a man who's been accustomed
to a drop of something good every now and again just
to keep him cheerful, to be told he mustn't go near the
bottle is trying him pretty hard.'

'But,' I hastily interjected, 'they haven't cut your
drinks, have they?'

'They have so,' he mournfully informed me, 'they
told me that if I even got the smell of it, the chances
were I'd be a dead man in the twenty-four hours.'

I did not think it necessary to tell him that I had
been assiduously pursuing a quite different line of conduct. I felt that my case must be quite desperate. I

had misunderstood my instructions, and the good wine I had been imbibing was to prove the death of me. I passed a most uncomfortable hour until I was able to secure an interview with the operating surgeon who, to my intense relief, repeated the original formula 'eat, drink, and be merry'.

When I referred to the case of my Dublin friend he smiled and explained: 'We received a special warning with that man that if he had a drop of liquor in him, he'd turn Paris upside down, so we gave him to understand that one drop of spirits would cause his instant death, and that has kept him quiet.'

From Paris I returned at once to the regiment without even having had the chance of visiting my own country from which I had now been absent seven years. During all this time in India I used to have a bout of malaria every year in the autumn. For this I can blame no one but myself, I took no precautions at all and often slept out on summer nights with practically nothing on and no mosquito curtains, offering myself a juicy prey to the fierce mosquitoes for which Mian Mir is justly famous.

And I am afraid I was never guided by any health rules. I can only attribute my having survived to the great age of sixty-two years by my having started life with a very robust constitution. Or perhaps it may be because I had no health rules!

In those hectic years from 1890 to 1894 I freely burnt the candle at both ends, having hard work all the day, and social pleasures amid the gaieties of Lahore that kept me up most of the night. At the time I did not bother at all about these attacks of malaria, but in 1903 the accumulation of microbes in my blood very nearly brought my promising career to an end.

In spite of many occupations I found time to write occasional short articles which were kindly printed by the *Civil and Military Gazette*, and by this means I was able to add to my income which, though ample, did not suffice for my many extravagances. At that cheerful and reckless period of life I do not think any income would have been large enough for me.

CHAPTER VIII

YOUTHFUL CONCEIT

DURING my stay in Paris I made many friends of many nationalities. Among others I formed the acquaintance of a very lovable and remarkable character — Sigismond de Justh — a Hungarian nobleman, a writer and a musician.

When the regiment was settled down in Mian Mir I persuaded him to come out and spend the winter with me, and it was through him that I made the acquaintance of Sir Aurel Stein who was then working with the Lahore University. In this way a kindly providence furnished me with a life-long friend. Providence had to bring my Hungarian friend all the way from Buda-Pesth to the Punjab just to perform this task, because normally, professors of universities and disreputable subalterns seldom meet.

De Justh was about 30 years of age, very delicate, and of an extremely sensitive disposition. It appals me now to think of what he must have endured during those four months in a British military Garrison. He and I were, of course, the best of friends, and he readily forgave my many shortcomings, but he was not quite so ready to forgive the transgressions of the general public, which were numerous enough. He did not even object to my atrocious singing, regarding it, from an artist's point of view, as being suitable to its surroundings.

I may say for myself, too, that I was capable of

appreciating beautiful music and could never have been guilty of the hideous bad taste of interrupting his performance at the piano to suggest a change to the vulgar compositions of the music hall. Yet this was actually done at a dinner-party in Lahore to which we had both been invited. De Justh never cared to perform at dinner-parties merely to provide a medium for blending the conversation, but he was always polite and, on this occasion, yielded to his hostess's importunity, and seating himself at the piano was soon lost in a dream of music. Suddenly, without any warning, the host walked over to the piano with a roll of music in his hand, and bending over de Justh, said, 'I say. I wonder if you could play the accompaniment to "Where did you get that hat?" – it's a ripping song and we'll all sing the chorus.'

De Justh stopped playing and looked up at him with a dazed expression, as he gasped, 'Yes, I think I could play it.' He made no further comment, but as soon as we got outside he said, 'I must leave to-morrow. I cannot live among these people.' He did not leave, however, but stayed to endure many similar agonies.

Another thing that made him rather unhappy was the tendency of not very well-educated Englishmen to regard all non-English people as 'foreigners', grouping under this term all the nations of Europe who were supposed to have some common tie. Many distinguished foreigners visit Lahore in the winter season, and from whatever country they came it was nearly always assumed that it would be a pleasure for my

'foreigner' to meet the new-comer. This filled my
proud and blue-blooded Hungarian with intense rage.
I once heard a lady say to him, 'Oh, Mr. de Justh,
you are a Hungarian musician and I know you will be
glad to meet a friend who is coming to stay with us
next week. He is a German professor.'

But de Justh was happy enough in the Mess, and
enjoyed life thoroughly. He gave himself no airs and
not only played the accompaniments to our ribald songs
but joined heartily in the choruses.

He was delighted to find a fellow country-man in
Lahore in the person of Dr. Stein, and brought about
our mutual acquaintance, I believe, with a view that
when he should have returned to Hungary, I should
have some influence to counterbalance the rougher side
of my character. He died two years later of consumption.

At the risk of boring the reader I would like to try
and give some idea of what I was like at that time, so
that it may be understood what my highly strung and
delicate friend had to endure.

Life in Mian Mir was far from being dull. Mess
dinners, especially on guest-nights, were lively affairs,
as I dare say they still are. After dinner our amusements were varied. The more sober ones (I don't mean
in the narrow sense) settled down to whist, while the
remainder sang songs with banjo accompaniments in
the ante-room, or played pool and gave performances
of athletic stunts in the billiard-room. Athletic stunts
and simple games constituted wholesome amusement,

but even Ring-a-Ring of Roses becomes a fairly dangerous game when played by a lot of grown men, and casualties — sometimes serious ones — were pretty frequent.

One could always raise some excitement on a dull evening by appealing to the rivalry that existed between those officers who had entered the service through the Militia, and those who had come from Sandhurst. On one occasion I entered the billiard-room noting that I was the only Sandhurst man against six militiamen. It was a hot evening and there was an air of depression about. So I thought I would cheer them all up by saying 'To St. Helena with the Militia', or words to that effect.

I was prepared to be felled, and also perhaps to bear the weight of all six of them on my prostrate form in the scrimmage that would ensue, but I did not calculate on catching my foot on the step of a billiard-room settee and so receiving the 70 stone odd of militiamen on my suspended leg. Something went off with a crack and I had to withdraw from the competition. What exactly happened I don't know. I had not broken my leg, but my ankle was very painful and I was on crutches for a long time afterwards.

Being laid up was a tedious affair, but it enabled me to make up arrears of office work. Half the pleasure of my being Adjutant was cancelled by the burden of pen and ink to which I had a long-standing aversion, but there was sometimes opportunity for a smile even in the performance of this dull duty.

The smile was generally caused by my native clerk's efforts at the English language. Indian babus have as a rule reached a fairly high standard of perfection in the use of English both written and spoken. They often amuse one, however, by the use of expressions or phrases that are grammatically quite correct, but are otherwise quaint and unusual.

My clerk cheered the uneventful hours I had to spend in the office by frequent effusions of this nature. I told him one day to make out a permanent shooting pass for one of the Indian Officers. He returned with the pass prepared for my signature. It was worded in quite correct, though unusual, English, and ran as follows:

'Jemadar Punjab Sing has permission to be absent from his quarters for the purpose of playing hunting with himself for ever.'

Needless to say I did not sign this literary gem, but gave it a place of honour in my collection of curiosities.

Another effort of his was a charming little note which he left for me one day on his table to excuse his absence from office.

'DEAR SIR,

I did try very hard, but the pain made it impossible for me to stay.

Yours faithfully
ALI BUX. Head Clerk.'

Mian Mir, famous for its special breed of mosquitoes and the consequent prevalence of malaria, has

been called 'The White Man's Grave'. A little unfair,
I think, but the cemetery is pretty full, and a good
many comrades of the old days lie there. In these days
with improved sanitation and the alteration of its name
from Mian Mir to Lahore Cantonments it is probably
a renowned health resort.

I had an attack of malaria every year I was there,
but it was chiefly due to my own carelessness. I did not
particularly mind a fierce bout of fever and infinitely
preferred it to the daily burden of taking precautions.

Nothing could have been gayer than the life we led
in 'the white man's grave'. Lahore was only three to
four miles away and the civilians of Lahore clung to the
spacious ideas of hospitality that added so much to the
charm of life in India in the old days.

Some of the happiest hours of my life were spent in
their society. I was fairly popular and had achieved
great renown as a comic singer. The result was that I
dined with friends in Lahore nearly every night of the
week, except on our own guest-night. After dinner I
was generally expected to help to entertain the guests
with selections from my repertoire.

On one such occasion when a song of mine had been
greeted with considerable applause I was accosted by
a charming lady who said, 'You sang that so well. But
what a nice voice you have. It seems a pity to waste it
on such poor songs. You ought really to give us some
good sentimental songs.'

This touched me in a very weak spot. Sentiment is
the key of my nature. I am a mass of sentiment. It is

for that reason that I sang comic songs. It was for that reason that I preferred parodies to the sentimental songs themselves — the latter fall so far short of my sentimental yearnings.

It was for that reason that in those early days I could not bring myself to sing 'White wings that never grow weary', preferring the barrack-room version of 'Why twins? They might have been triplets'.

However, urged by my discriminating lady, I made an instant resolve to abandon comic songs, and set myself to work at 'I'll sing thee songs of Araby', 'Alice, where art thou?' and 'Her bright smile haunts me still'. I had no sooner perfected myself in these than I received an invitation to sing at a concert in the Montgomery Hall in Lahore.

I chose two songs of my new selection and duly appeared on the stage. My first song was received with deafening applause, and I realized how right Lady X. had been with her kind advice. I felt quite pleased with my effort and in response to an encore sang another of the same brand. I rendered it with even greater effect than the first one, but alas, on its conclusion there was no sign of grateful enthusiasm on the part of the audience, in fact beyond the feeble clapping of a few polite friends, I left the stage in silence. In modern parlance I should say that I 'had got the bird'.

But why?

The mystery was briefly explained by Lady X. whom I met immediately after quitting the stage. She said, 'You sang that first song very nicely. But those songs didn't suit you a bit. And we never thought you would have two of them. We only applauded the first because we felt sure that you would give us one of your comic ones as an encore.'

Oh, the deceitfulness of women! She had obviously forgotten her remark on the previous occasion which had decided me to alter my style. That remark had merely been made just to pass the time and to say something that would please me.

I was also a great hand at sporting songs. Nothing could equal my rendering of 'Drink puppy, drink' (on which all the puppies drank), or 'The boar, the mighty boar's my theme'. It's odd how non-sporting fellows can sing these songs just as they ought to be sung, while the sporting ones are generally mute.

I really feel certain that for one reason or another I must have been very popular at dinner-parties, because I had certain tricks which would otherwise have made me an intolerable guest.

In most ways I consider myself an ideal guest — even at the present day. I take whatever is offered me and thoroughly enjoy good things. I never want a second helping of anything, but I will always take one to please my hostess if she insists on it. I have no fads, and do not have to swallow surreptitiously little tabloids to aid my digestion or to counteract the ill-effects of bad cooking or poor wine. As a conversationalist I have a stock of harmless anecdotes, and a smattering of knowledge of most subjects in vogue, and I generally agree with whatever other people say.

But I am a very late sitter. I don't want to go out to dinner, but once I get there I never want to go home again.

This evil trait in my character was at its worst in the Lahore days, and, as I said before, I must have been very popular on other grounds, to enable people to put up with it. I used to keep my hosts up pretty late, but I always felt I was leaving early if I got away before daylight.

My faults in this respect were brought home to me at one dinner-party. All went well till about midnight, by which time all the guests had departed except myself, and I was left confronted by my host, hostess, and their daughter — obviously very tired and sleepy.

But their frequent and ill-concealed yawns did not in the least damp my ardour. I felt I was at the top of my form and reeled off yarn after yarn till my host took a mean advantage of my being out of breath for half a moment and managed to suggest a '*final* whisky-and-soda', laying tremendous emphasis on the word '*final*'.

To this I readily assented, and gaining fresh inspiration from the refreshing beverage I started an entirely new series of anecdotes, undeterred by the alarming frequency of family yawns.

At last, in another unwilling pause, my host managed to interject 'Won't you have a whisky-and-soda *before you go?*' That really was putting it rather bluntly, but I was not offended. I gladly accepted the proffered refreshment and was beginning a new series of comments on life in general, when I thought I noticed an ominous gleam in my host's eye which, coupled with the unmistakable stress he had laid on those words '*before you go*', seemed to me to indicate a desire for my departure, so I said I thought that if they wouldn't think it rude of me I ought really to be off. And they didn't think it rude, so I went.

But what makes me sure of my popularity is the fact that these kind people actually asked me to dinner again. I treated them better on the second occasion.

Of course they were hampered by the silly rules of polite society. My bachelor friends did not allow any such rules to cramp their style and never hesitated to express their opinion of this objectionable habit.

The frivolities of life were made all the more piquant by not infrequent minor tragedies. One of the worst of these was an occasion when I was run in for stealing a horse and trap belonging to a senior officer. A very serious charge with a prospect of imprisonment for life or such less punishment as the G.O.C. might think fit. I really had no intention of actual theft, but I must plead guilty to having borrowed the conveyance without the owner's permission. Intention is the essence of crime, and I was able to convince the G.O.C. that whatever I did, my intentions were rather amiable than criminal.

The fact of the matter is I had promised to drive home three brother officers after a late night at the club. When we got outside the club I found my trap had disappeared but another one was conveniently waiting.

Probably affected by the moonlight or the freshness of
the midnight air, I determined to make use of the
conveyance that Providence had so kindly put in my
way, without reflecting on the question of ownership.
Having got rid of the syce by a simple ruse, we climbed
into the trap and I drove my friends to their various
destinations.

In order to get rid of the horse and trap at the end
of our journey I asked the last of my companions whom
I had safely delivered at his bungalow to hold the horse
a minute while I lit a cigar. As soon as he had hold of
the horse I jumped out and walked hurriedly away,
leaving him to deal with the situation as he thought
best. Unheeding his vociferous protests I reached my
own bungalow a hundred yards away, and dismissed
the whole trifling incident from my mind.

But on awakening the next morning I found the
matter was not at all trifling. My dull-witted friend
had not been clever enough to take the next move and
pass the horse and trap on to some one else. He was
caught red-handed and at once hauled before the
General by the indignant Colonel who owned the turn-
out, with the natural result that I had to confess that I
was the culprit.

It was a silly thing to have done, I thoroughly admit,
and I do not record it here as being either a clever or
an amusing joke, but just to show what stupid things
young fellows can do. Before the G.O.C. I pleaded
my youth and inexperience, I offered an ample apology,
and to make any amends in my power. The General,

who had once been young himself, was inclined to
dismiss the affair with a reprimand and a warning.
But the Colonel, who had never been young himself,
was not at all satisfied with this and wanted to take the
matter into the civil courts. He was fortunately prevented from doing so, and I was still permitted to
retain my Commission in Her Majesty's Army.

Soon after this I became possessed of a wild Waziri
horse – one of the best I ever had – in rather a peculiar
way. He was given to me for nothing by his owner in a
fit of temper.

The horse had bolted with him and ended up a mad
gallop in my compound where my friend dismounted
and handed me the reins with the remark: 'You can
keep the beast or shoot him – whichever you like.'

I kept him with pleasure and rode him for the next
five years. He was christened 'Tezwala' – or 'Swift-one'
in the regiment, and he lived well up to his name – just
the sort of horse for an Adjutant who is always in a
hurry.

In 1892 a cholera epidemic broke out and Professor
Haffkine visited Mian Mir to inoculate the troops
against the disease. The Colonel told me to persuade
as many men as I could to volunteer for the operation.
I passed the order on to the Native Adjutant, who
reported to me the same evening that there were no
volunteers.

I said that that would not do at all, the regiment
next door had produced fifty volunteers, and we could
not allow ourselves to be beaten by them, so we must

have at least 100. On the next day exactly 100 volunteers paraded outside the hospital. The Professor had his apparatus ready in the verandah of the hospital and started by explaining that the operation was quite painless and undoubtedly efficacious.

I translated this to the men who looked very woebegone, and then the Professor caught me on the hop by suggesting that I should set an example. As there was no way out of it, I submitted very unwillingly to the two punctures, while the men looked on with awe.

Having set the example I was prepared to smile at the other victims as their turn came, but when the Professor was ready not a man could be persuaded to budge, so I passed down the ranks saying a few words to each man with a view of instilling a little courage into them.

The Native Adjutant objected to this, saying, 'It's no use talking to them. Just let me give the word of command "right turn, quick march, left wheel" and they will all pass before the doctor and be done according to your order.' But curiosity impelled me to talk to them and I found that not one of them had had any intention of thwarting the laws of Fate by taking the precaution of inoculation.

The first man said, 'I was told it was a hundred yards' race, and that's what I put my name down for.' The next said that he had been told it was a cure for sore feet. Others had been induced by the crafty Native Adjutant to put their names down for various athletic competitions or for the cure of coughs, colds or stomach-ache.

It was obviously a moment where hesitation would be fatal. I could not endure the thought of being the only victim, so I adopted the Native Adjutant's plan and in a very short time all the athletes and the petty ailment men had passed in procession before the Professor and had each received his full dose of cure-all mixture.

The Colonel was very proud that we should have had twice as many volunteers as the regiment next door and said it showed a good spirit on the part of the men. It did.

I spent one leave period in the Kangra Valley in the country from which we enlisted our best Dogras. I enjoyed a very amusing month there with the tea-planters, but it was rather a wild time. Tea was entirely barred as a beverage and we commenced the day with the strongest potions procurable for 'chota hazri'. It was not a healthy way of starting the morning's work, but the fact that the whole day was spent in the open air, and half the night riding from one estate to another, helped to counteract the ill effects. But I think I had better not dwell too much on this period.

Another interesting leave I took was, in 1893, when I wandered through Kulu and Lahoul into Ladakh, returning to India by Leh and Srinagar.

I had intended originally to spend the whole two months in Kulu, but I was driven out of that delightful valley by cholera and so moved into Lahoul. Having got so far, I did not want to turn back, so we pushed on to Leh. We had rather a rough time as I had made no preparations for warm clothing and supplies, and the long march at great heights, often over 15,000 feet, was very trying to my servants.

In the summer of 1894 I found time to look into my accounts, and was horrified at the size of the debit balance. My father had, quite rightly, stopped my allowance a year before, and I would not in any case appeal to him again. Moreover, I was disappointed in not having seen any active service so far, and so I resolved to leave the army and start a new career in South America – a land that had always had a fascination for me.

A friend who was a Manager of a Bank, hearing of my intention, invited me to come and see him and talk it over. The result of our interview was that he squared all my debts through the Bank and made a reasonable arrangement by which I could gradually repay the amount. I am grateful to him, though even now I rather hanker after South America.

CHAPTER IX

THE WANO NIGHT ATTACK

My weary period of waiting for an opportunity of seeing active service was at last about to come to an end. In September 1894 the regiment was ordered to proceed to Dera Ismail Khan to join the Brigade under General Turner that was to proceed to Wano in Waziristan for the purpose of delimitating that portion of the frontier. The other units were the 3rd Sikhs, the 1st Gurkhas, a squadron of the 1st Punjab Cavalry, and an Indian Mountain Battery. The expedition was supposed to be a peaceful one, the leaders of the Wazirs and the Mahsuds having agreed to a discussion of frontier questions, but in the end it resulted in a good deal of hard fighting.

We crossed the Indus by the Steam Ferry in September during a spell of very hot weather, and joined the Brigade in Dera Ismail Khan, and towards the end of October we marched up the Gomal valley and camped on the Wano plain.

The civil authorities still maintained that it was to be a peaceful affair and the troops were warned to be careful not to arouse the resentment of the tribes. But as usually happens on these occasions the tribes thoroughly enjoyed arousing the resentment of the troops, and we objected very strongly, but without retaliation, to their playful habit of showing their friendliness by firing into the camp at night.

The site we took up for camp was about a mile out

on the plain, front and rear on nullahs and the flanks
on open ground. The left flank appeared particularly
vulnerable.

This flank was held by the 1st Gurkhas, the right
by the 3rd Sikhs, while the 20th Punjabis held the
centre front and rear, an arrangement that made the
exercise of command, in case of trouble, very difficult.

A certain portion of the front was allotted to the
Cavalry and Artillery, which is also inadvisable. If
there is an attack the cavalry must necessarily look after
their horses and they are apt in consequence to be too
thin on the front line.

The whole perimeter was so large that it was difficult to man the front line without absorbing reserves.
This is generally the case in perimeter camps because
the fighting troops are obliged to take up space not,
as they would wish, influenced solely by tactical considerations, but by the necessity of leaving sufficient
interior space for the various non-fighting units. In
this case we had our transport of mules and camels, a
supply unit, and the Civil Commissioners' Camp to
accommodate in the area.

There were no hills close to the camp, which was
protected by a circle of picquets.

Firing at the picquets and into the camp at night
continued to be a source of amusement to the tribesmen, but their leaders apologized and said that these
things were done by a few irresponsible 'badmashes'.
We were still supposed to be friendly, and I actually

had tea one afternoon with one of the leaders, both he
and I being the guests of an Afridi officer, an old friend
of mine. We sat on the ground in a small *tente d'abri*
and drank green tea with much sugar and cardamum
seeds in it. After all the tea was finished my friend
emptied the tea-leaves out of the pot into a saucer,
sprinkled them with sugar, and offered them to the
Mahsud, who ate them all with great gusto. This fact,
more than anything else, impressed that tea-party on
my mind.

In the first week in November a havildar of ours,
Nek Awaz, commanding the Quarter Guard, walked
out of camp by night and joined the enemy who was
still supposed, however, not to be an enemy. On the
next day we had reason to believe that trouble was
brewing, and precautions were taken accordingly. An
hour before dawn on the following day, a fierce attack
was made on the front and left flank of the camp, by
two very large bodies of tribesmen.

The full account of this night attack is given in the
official records, but a few words from a personal point
of view may be interesting, and as it was my first introduction to real fighting the events are naturally deeply
impressed on my memory.

I remember noting in my diary how important it is
to put down all records in writing at the very first
opportunity. I had done that myself, and I was able to
state the share taken by every one in the fight with considerable, but not complete, accuracy. One cannot see
everything oneself in a fight, and all I could do was to

record what each person said of events in which he had been the principal.

What astounded me afterwards was to find these same people a few days later giving quite different accounts of the affair. This was not due to their desire to state anything that was not true, but merely to a common trait in human nature — inability to remember exact details for any length of time, and liability to confuse in one's mind what one actually saw or knew and what the mind had unconsciously received later from statements of other people. Instead of being just what one knows, it becomes a mixture of knowledge and hearsay.

The conversation in camp on the evening before the attack was chiefly confined to discussions as to the probability of its coming off, and the general opinion was that nothing would happen. If we had really believed that an affair on a large scale was imminent, we should have taken more interest in our stone parapets, which, when the enemy really did attack, proved no obstacle at all. Both officers and men were disinclined to take much interest in the building of parapets which was looked on as an unpleasant fatigue.

What a change came over us after the attack was over! Then, when there was very little need for it, every one took the deepest interest in wall-building. I never saw such zeal. A few days after the attack I actually found a non-combatant officer attached to the force quietly engaged in adding a few stones here and there to the parapet in the neighbourhood of his own tent.

To return to the account of the attack. I went round the guards in the early hours of the morning, probably about 4 a.m., and found all well. There were no signs or indications of any movement on the part of the enemy. I returned to my tent and lay down as I was, to get a little sleep.

A very short time later, about an hour before dawn, I was awakened by a tremendous din – sounds of firing mingled with fierce yells.

I was out of my tent in a moment, and at my post near the Quarter Guard a minute later finding the regiment and all officers present and prepared. In the darkness nobody could quite know what was happening, but a body of the enemy on our front, after firing a volley, seemed to be advancing on us, while the Gurkhas on the left flank appeared to be heavily engaged.

In a very short time the artillery fired off some star shells, which gave an excellent illumination and made matters quite clear. The enemy were advancing in two lines in great strength on our front, while a fierce hand-to-hand fight was proceeding on the left flank, and there appeared to be some disturbance in the centre of the camp.

What had actually happened was this. The tribesmen had determined to attack the front and left flank, and had managed to creep up to the first picquet on the left flank without their movement being detected. They attacked and overwhelmed the picquet, then, firing a volley, charged down on the Gurkhas. As the

E

picquet was only about 600 yards from the camp, the tribesmen must have reached the parapet (a very trifling one) within two minutes of the first indication of their movement and before the troops could have time to fall in on their posts. There were no obstacles at all on that flank, it was just an open run for them.

Their first line swept straight into the centre of the camp, and had they been followed by the succeeding lines, all would have been lost. But before their main body could reach the parapet our line had been restored, and a company, sent under Colonel Meiklejohn from the Reserve of the 20th Punjabis to reinforce the Gurkhas, strengthened that flank sufficiently to ward off the several successive charges that were made there by the determined enemy.

Meantime the tribesmen who had penetrated into the centre of the camp were naturally under the impression that the victory was theirs, and employed themselves slaughtering mules, domestic servants, and other followers (the baker saved his life by getting into his oven). But it soon became apparent to them that their enterprise had failed and that the Sirkar's soldiers were more than holding their own. It then became a difficult question for them how to escape from the camp. This most of them succeeded in doing by separating and acting independently, leaping over the parapet from the inside in any convenient space left by the troops. A good many were shot down in this way, the more fortunate ones broke out successfully in rear where there were few troops, and a considerable number were

killed in the centre of the camp by a company sent
with orders to use bayonet only. This is a terribly
dangerous proceeding, of course, but it had to be done.
In the dark it is hard to tell friend from foe, one has no
time to parley, and one may in this way kill more of
one's own friends than of the enemy.

At tragic moments, comedy is always at one's elbow.
During the fighting the bandsmen were as usual in the
ranks. A cornet-player was close to me and he was hit
on the trigger-finger as his rifle was 'at the present'.
He made little fuss about the pain, but I heard him
muttering, 'There goes my thousand-rupee finger, my
thousand-rupee finger.' The poor fellow would never
be able to play the cornet again.

The star shell gave splendid light and we were able
to see the flashing swords as the enemy advanced in
successive waves on our front, led by a brave old
Mullah, mounted on a white horse. Line after line
came on with undaunted bravery, but now that the
perimeter was held in force they had no chance of success, and just before day broke they decided to retreat.
This was of course the moment to render their defeat
decisive by a vigorous pursuit. The cavalry were on
their heels in a very short time, and the infantry followed a little later, driving the last stragglers as far as
the Inzari Pass, whence the troops returned to camp.
Casualties were heavy on both sides, but those of the
enemy were probably at least ten to one of ours.

It was a gallant performance on their part and well
conceived, and was within an ace of success. A delay

of two minutes in reforming the line on the left flank would have resulted in the whole force being wiped out. The affair was planned and organized by the Mullah Powindah, a famous and inspiring leader. But like most leaders, he led from behind and was not among the casualties.

It was a hard fight and the troops behaved splendidly, but we received little credit for it as it was apparently assumed that we had been caught napping and narrowly escaped disaster – the latter was certainly true.

My regiment was in disgrace on account of the desertion of Havildar Nek Awaz. He was supposed to have led the enemy in the attack, but he did not do so as no leaders lived and he was known to be alive long afterwards. But it is likely that he gave them useful information. As a punishment when the force advanced later into the Mahsud country, we were left behind at Wano, much to our chagrin.

Some amusing events occurred with reference to looting of which there was a certain amount. The body that penetrated to the centre of the camp had opportunities for loot, and many of them carried off such things as they could lay their hands on. One man is said to have removed a promising-looking box from an officer's tent and carried it some distance before he found that it was not only valueless but unclean.

This sounds too good to be true, and one naturally asks how there could be any evidence on the subject. The answer is that the box in question was found several hundred yards outside the camp at daylight and it could not have conveyed itself there.

Horses broke loose, and getting out of camp were picked up by the tribesmen. One officer, who had lost a charger, appeared before the Committee appointed to inquire into individual losses, claiming a large sum for his horse which from his description appeared to be one of the most valuable animals in India.

He stated its value at a very high figure, which the Committee had no power to sanction. They therefore awarded him the maximum permissible, which he was obliged to accept, with apparent reluctance.

A few days later a parley was held with our late enemies at which they agreed to return articles looted from the camp. As might be expected they regretted in the case of articles of value that these could not be traced, and contented themselves with returning things of no great use.

Among these, to the despair of the unfortunate owner, they returned the stolen charger, an old Arab horse that had been of some value ten years before, and had obviously been in a state of chronic lameness for some years past – an animal that no one would dream of accepting as a gift.

There was a good deal of amusement at his discomfiture, and he had to endure many congratulations on his good fortune in recovering his horse. He stoutly maintained, however, that he had not given a false description but that the present state of the animal was solely due to the malign influence of the Mullah Powindah during the few days the horse had remained with his followers.

After the great night attack the Brigade was for some time in a dangerous position, and had the enemy made a second attempt with equal vigour things might have gone badly for us. But fortunately the tribesmen are seldom able to make an effort on a large scale immediately after suffering a serious defeat. They attack with great courage, but soon lose heart after a first failure.

We were cut off from India, having no lines of communication, and we had expended a great deal of ammunition, and if hostilities continued it would have been difficult to obtain fresh supplies.

A battalion of the Border Regiment was on its way up to reinforce the Brigade, and with them we should receive our necessary munitions.

For some time after the attack we suffered from 'false alarms'. A fierce attack was made by the enemy one evening about nine o'clock. They were advancing again on the left flank. A heavy fire was opened on them. On running to the parapet I was met by one of the Mess servants in a state of panic. I asked him what was up. He replied, 'The enemy are attacking in great strength. I have seen with my own eyes about 4,000 of them, with banners, swords, and rifles.' During a lull in the firing a chorus of voices was heard in the distance: 'We are the Commissioners' camels returning to camp. Do not fire on us.'

It was fortunate for them that firing in the dark produces little result. They came happily into camp a few minutes later with no other casualty than one camel wounded in the neck.

When the officers were at the dinner-table in the Mess tent in the evening, a passer-by would slam down the lid of an empty box with a bang which seldom failed in producing a temporary alarm, amusing on one side, annoying on the other.

Sleeping one night fully dressed in my tent, I was awakened by an officer who whispered hoarsely in my ear: 'They're on us.' I was out of the tent in a bound. Once outside he invited me to listen to the sound as of a large body of men hurrying down the nullah in front of the camp. Just such a noise as would be made by men hastening over the rocky ground in grass shoes. But on investigation we found a group of our camels a few yards away, and this peculiar sound was produced by the crushing of gram with their teeth as they consumed their evening ration.

The arrival of the Border Regiment with supplies put an end to any cause for anxiety. The day after their arrival the Adjutant, an old friend of mine, was having breakfast with me, when suddenly the alarm sounded. Alarms were new to him but not to me. I warned him that he would be disappointed.

Coming out of the tent, I was met by an excited Staff Officer, who reined in his horse in a dramatic manner and yelled, 'Turn out your men!' I said, 'Where are the enemy?' and he replied as he galloped off, 'Look up on the hills there.' I looked up on the crest-line of the nearest hills and there sure enough they were, line upon line of tribesmen in the usual crouching attitude, showing only head and shoulders.

Three points of view instantly flashed through my mind: (1) Tribesmen never have attacked at breakfast time and never will; (2) Tribesmen do not prepare for an attack by lining up on the sky-line; (3) If they really are coming, they are some way off and we have plenty of time. Under such circumstances they are welcome.

However, orders must be obeyed, and in a few minutes we were all at our posts. As soon as we were ready the enemy flapped their wings and flew up into the sky, reminding one of combats in the ancient days of the Mahabharat. They were vultures, the large carrion-eating birds well known in the mountains and plains of Northern India. It was really a very foolish affair, but it amused us to laugh at ourselves, and to make the usual witty references to the Staff.

When the Brigade moved off a little later to enter the Mahsud country, we were, as I said, left behind at Wano, which was very disheartening for us, but not particularly so for me, as I was laid out with my second go of rheumatic fever, and I should have had a poor chance of recovery in a Field Hospital on the march.

The winter had been very cold, with some snow on the surrounding hills and a little in camp, and sleeping in wet clothing had brought back the rheumatism of which I had laid the seeds in Suakim in the first year of my service.

I was pretty bad and not expected to pull through, so it was fortunate for me that with the departure of the Brigade we were ordered to occupy the small village of Wano, and I was comfortably stowed in a small cowshed at the foot of the main tower.

Lying in a camp-bed with this painful disease was not a very cheerful affair, but the tedium was relieved by frequent visitors when I was well enough to be able to talk to them. Among these none was more welcome than Subadar Alim Khan, a Kambar Khel Afridi. The Afridis – Mahomedans who live in the barren rocky hills of the Khyber Pass – are subjects of neither King George V nor of the King of Kabul. They are under no rule but that of their tribal leaders and have no laws except a short unwritten code dealing with the honour of their womenfolk and agricultural rights. They are all involved in unending blood-feuds and only a small proportion die in their beds. This particular man died mysteriously at his home in 1900, his two sons died a year or two later, and his only grandson a few years ago – it is improbable that any of them died natural deaths. I remember another case which we would think tragic, but which was told me as a funny story. Our leave men had returned from their homes and, as usual, I asked for news of old friends who had gone on pension. I inquired for Havildar Mehr Kalim.

'Oh, he's dead.'

'I'm sorry to hear that. What did he die of?'

'He was shot by his only son.'

'That is a bad affair.'

'Not particularly. You see, he was an only son, too, and he had shot his father.'

From this it may be gathered that these hardy mountaineers look on death from quite a different point of view to ourselves. With Alim Khan it was an unending topic, which might have been depressing for me if I had not been able to see the funny side of it. He used to sit by my side and tell me long stories of blood-feuds in which I generally knew the participants. Then he would stop and the conversation would continue something like this:

'I'm afraid you're going to die, too.'

'Not a bit. I feel better to-day.'

'Yes, you feel better. People who are going to die always get that feeling.'

'But I'm not going to die – why should I?'

'Well, you've got a sort of glazed look in your eyes, which is a certain sign. I have never known it fail. I am sorry you should die. You've been a good Adjutant and a good friend, I shall miss you.'

On another occasion he proposed to take over my cure himself. He said:

'These doctors are no use. I have seen your disease before and I know the only way to cure it. Ask the doctor to let me try.'

'What is the method?'

'I shall buy a big sheep and have it blessed by the Mullah, then cut its throat, skin it, clap the skin on to you while still warm and sew you up in it. You will

stay like that for ten days and then, if God wills, you
will be all right. There is no other cure.'

I preferred the risk of death to the undergoing of
such a smelly remedy, and in spite of Alim Khan's
gloomy forebodings I made a good recovery in time to
accompany the regiment when it was ordered in the
spring to march back down the desolate Gomal Valley
to Tank, thence to Bannu and up the hitherto unex-
plored Tochi Valley, rejoining the Brigade *en route*.

There was very little opposition to our advance, and
the regiment proceeded as far as the Afghan frontier,
where we enjoyed interesting experiences with the
Survey Party in Birmal and Shawal. On our return
from this duty we settled down to spend a very hot
summer in the valley, with little to do beyond escorting
convoys.

In cantonments officers and men can find some sort
of amusement in bungalows and barracks to help
them pass away the long weary hours of an Indian
summer's day, but in tents in this remote valley one
could do little but read and eat and drink and ponder
over deep problems.

In strict justice to Government, who paid us our
salaries as soldiers, these problems should have been
exclusively of a military nature. But they were not.

All the Sikhs and Dogras were turning over and
over in their minds the following themes:

'When shall I get leave?' 'I wonder how the crops
are this harvest?' 'I have only one lawsuit on at present, which is held up because I cannot persuade a

friend of mine to make a statement directly opposed to facts. Can I not think of some more lawsuits I could start for the honour of my family?'

And every Pathan was thinking: 'When can I get leave?' 'When I get home, shall I get a chance of shooting the next man in my blood-feud? How can I get back to my village without giving him a chance of shooting me?'

And I was wondering: 'Why did the All-wise Creator send flies into the world?' and 'Why such a lot of flies?' and 'Are all the flies in the world in this particular spot?' and 'Where do they come from?'

There were millions of flies in every tent, rendering sleep by day impossible, and making it difficult to eat one's food without getting some of them into one's mouth. As a rough guess one may say that there were a hundred million flies. And all these flies were making a happy living out of us. The question is: 'If the Brigade had not been there would those poor flies have died of hunger, or would they not have been there?' And this brings us back to the question, 'Where do they come from?'

Beginning work at about 5 a.m., we had to get through fifteen hours of daylight, of which seven were too hot to do anything out of doors. The heat in one's tent was perhaps greater than the heat in the open, but the canvas at any rate formed some protection from the direct rays of the sun.

Somebody instructed me in the game of Patience and presented me with a pack of cards, and I found it helped to pass away half an hour of idleness when I was tired of reading.

I was playing this foolish game on the floor of my tent one afternoon when an Afridi friend came to see me. He asked me what I was doing and I explained, but he did not believe me.

He said: 'I know you gentlemen often play cards together for money in the Officers' Mess, and I can guess quite well what you are doing. You are practising tricks which will help you to win more money from the other officers when you go on leave to the hills.' An ingenious suggestion, and nothing that I could say would persuade him that I was telling the truth. He said: 'One person cannot play a game at anything, and if you could you would not waste your time like that.'

I had an illustrated paper by my side with a picture of Charley's Aunt in a fantastical get-up, displaying a splendid set of teeth in a wild burst of laughter.

My Afridi caught sight of this and, wagging his head, solemnly said: 'I know who that is.'

'Who?' I asked.

'Queen Victoria.'

I saw the last of the Tochi Valley in August 1895, when I proceeded to join a garrison class at Chakrata to pass my examination for promotion to the rank of Captain.

CHAPTER X

GERMANY AND RUSSIA

FROM Chakrata I obtained leave to England, returning for the first time to my native land after eleven years' absence.

I went first of all to Germany, to visit Wiesbaden, famous for the cure of rheumatism, and also to learn the language.

My father had at that time a house in Heidelberg, where he frequently entertained the officers of the garrison, and his many friends among the University Professors and other civilians. I was made an honorary member of the Officers' Mess of the Badische Grenadiers, and we usually dined there once a week on guest nights.

I formed also a great friendship with a young Englishman about my own age – Clement Harris, a musical genius and a man of most attractive personality. Had he lived, he would undoubtedly have made a place for himself in the ranks of the great composers, but he was killed the next year in the Græco-Turkish War. His romantic love for the Greeks induced him to throw up his musical studies and offer his services to them in their struggle for freedom.

Through him I was introduced to the interesting student life for which Heidelberg has always been famous, while through my father's influence I gained a thorough knowledge of the military side of life.

So I learnt my German very comfortably and happily, imbibing enormous pots of light and wholesome beer and eating great quantities of sausage and sauerkraut. Food and drink are almost part of a language. To get the 'spirit' of a language one must live as the people do, and eat and drink what they eat and drink.

I made this very good excuse for the vast quantities of beer I consumed in Germany, as I made it later for the incredible amount of vodka I imbibed in Russia. It is a good excuse and there is a lot of truth in it.

My rheumatic cure in Wiesbaden was quite a pleasant adventure. Wiesbaden is a delightful town, the Kursaal was always gay, and my cure not at all irksome. I lived in a very good hotel on a 'strict' diet, which, however, allowed me plenty of the things I liked most to eat, and a bottle of Rhine wine every now and then. I am not sure now whether I had to pay the doctor an extra fee for such a good prescription or not.

I had to get up early — which in the bright summer days was a pleasure — and walk to the hot springs, sip some hot bad-egg water to the accompaniment of an excellent band, return to the hotel and have a hot bath and massage, and spend the rest of the day in placid and lazy enjoyment of life. I made many acquaintances among all nationalities at the Kursaal, and shortly succumbed to 'love at first sight' in the most literal sense.

By an extraordinary coincidence the lady who gave rise to this novel sensation in my breast — at a time when I had no reason even to think that she was English —

turned out to belong to a Devonshire family well known to all my people except my wandering self, and connected with my old school at Westward Ho.

Under the benign influence of love the male is supposed to pay particular attention to his wardrobe and endeavour at all times to look his best. I suppose I had some subconscious idea of this sort in my mind.

I was therefore much gratified one morning at observing, as I took my daily walk at the hot springs, that every girl I met smiled sweetly at me. My thoughts were concentrated entirely on one girl, still, I must admit I was grateful for this little tribute from the others. Such is masculine vanity – old Pepys is a type of us all.

On my return to my hotel I sat down at the break-fast-table, and the waiter said to me, 'Sir, you have forgotten to put your tie on.' Strange that such a trifling omission in one's dress should attract so much attention.

Returning to Heidelberg, my charming voice was again noticed, and I was begged to have it properly trained. I nearly always do what I can to oblige, so I agreed and was introduced to a very renowned singing-master. The interview was a very painful one – for him. He said, 'I should like to hear your voice. Sing something.' I demurred, saying that I could recall nothing but degrading barrack songs, but he insisted.

For the life of me I could think of nothing but 'Duckfoot Sue', of which I trolled out one verse:

> 'Oh, her face was the colour of a ham,
> She'd ears like a Japanese fan,
> She could talk for an hour
> With a forty-horse power,
> She'd a voice like a catamoran.'

Having got into the swing, I could have carried on for any length of time, but my rhapsody was cut short by the Professor who, I noticed, was holding both hands to his ears and breathing heavily. When calm was restored he said that I had the making of a good voice, and that if I would promise never to sing drivel of that sort again he would undertake my training.

We made a fair start the next day, but after a fortnight's conscientious endeavour I felt a hankering for the old form of song, and cancelled my agreement.

While learning German I came across a Russian student in Heidelberg University who was very hard up and wished to make a little money by giving lessons in his language, so I decided to take that up to pass the time.

At this time India was constantly threatened by the Russian advance in Asia, and it seemed probable that we and the Russians would one day find ourselves at war. So it was obviously a sound proposition to study the language of our future enemies.

I returned to London in October 1896 and passed the examination in both German and Russian. I was then sent to Russia 'on duty' to perfect myself in the language.

Arriving in Petersburg in November, I determined to lose no time in getting a thorough knowledge of the people. I lived like a Russian among the Russians and learnt to admire their many good qualities, forming friendships which last to the present day.

Whatever grievances we may have against Russia as a nation, one must admit that Russians as individuals have many charms that other nations lack. Their chief faults are a lack of order, both in private and public life, and a sad trait of fatalism that leads them to fold their hands when trouble comes and say, 'It is God's will'.

On the other hand, they possess so many virtues. Nothing could equal the kindness and generous hospitality I enjoyed while I lived with them. In the East it is a form of politeness to say 'Whatever I have is yours', but I found that when a Russian said it he really meant it.

War with Russia has not yet come, and will not come in my lifetime, but my knowledge of the language has not been wasted. I found it very useful during the Boxer War in China, 1900, and in the Great War — on both of which occasions I had a good deal to do with Russians.

The country has undoubtedly changed a great deal since the revolution as regards its system of government and general conditions of life, but there is no reason at all to suppose that any fundamental change has taken place in the national character — in fact, it is quite certain that it has not.

A false idea of Russia has grown up among those

who do not know the country, because it is difficult for them to realize that the present Bolshevik government in no sense represents the Russian nation.

What has happened in Russia is that an inevitable revolution destroyed the monarchy and the aristocracy, and, before a reasonable form of government could be evolved, a group of extremely capable and determined men took advantage of the state of disorder to seize the reins and carry out an experiment in government on communistic lines, with an avowed intention of fomenting world-wide revolution – an international and not a national programme.

The experiment failed from the outset – as far as the introduction of true Communism went – but the communist group, suffering no indigestion from having eaten every one of their principles, remain in power. This government, therefore, not only does not represent the country governed, but does not even represent what they set out to demonstrate – a system of communistic rule.

But the whole world is grateful to them for their splendid demonstration of the futility of Marxian theories when put into practice. It was an experiment that had to be tried somewhere some day, and, from many points of view, Russia was the most favourable ground for the operators; but as Russia is a peasant land to a greater extent than any other country in Europe, the experiment was doomed to failure from the outset. One might conceive some possible success for Communism applied to industrialism, but never

when applied to land. The peasant hungers for land.
It was this desire to own land *for themselves* that led
the Russian moujiks to throw in their lot with the revolution. To oust the landlords and possess their lands
– not to oust the landlords to till their lands for the
benefit of industrial comrades. As soon as communistic
ideas were applied to them, they just stopped cultivating
their land, sowing enough for their own needs and
leaving nothing for the share-out.

In spite of the tragic events of the past ten years, it
is doubtful whether any change whatsoever has taken
place in the character of the Russian people.

I started life in Russia in the bosom of a hospitable
family who occupied a flat in one of the big mansions
of the Vassilievsky Island in Petersburg. I went to
them with recommendations. The widow informed
me afterwards that had it not been for those very strong
recommendations from a very dear friend (my Russian
student) she would never have taken me in.

They had never seen an Englishman before, but
had heard wild accounts of their terrifying and drunken
habits, just as we have heard of Cossacks eating babies
and consuming candles as sweetmeats. So when in our
first interview, in response to her question, 'What do you
drink?' I replied 'Whisky', she felt that all was lost.

Breakfast was running in her mind and she was
thinking of 'tea, or coffee', and my reply of 'whisky'
conjured up visions of a drunken Englishman smash-
ing the furniture. However, for the sake of her old

friend, she took me in, and described all this to me later when I had astonished the family by the mildness of my behaviour; I'm not sure that they weren't just the least bit disappointed.

A winter in Petersburg in the old days was a very gay affair, and I thoroughly enjoyed my introduction to Russian life. Beyond calling at the Embassy and dining once or twice with a charming English family, I lived entirely among the Russians and never spoke a word of English.

I had arrived in Russia with a good vocabulary and a fair working knowledge of the language, but it took me some little time to learn the 'song' wherein resides the spirit of the language. Every language has its own peculiar little song in quarters of semi-tones; and correct grammar, idiom, and pronunciation help one very little towards perfection if one has not caught the song. It is also for this reason that one finds difficulty in understanding the language spoken between two natives even when one can speak it fairly well oneself.

For two weeks I sat at table listening to the chatter of the ladies, and barely catching a word or two here and there. They talked very freely among themselves, realizing my mental deafness, but one day the song suddenly came to me and from that time forth I had the key to the language. The widow was saying to the niece that she liked hers rather long with lace frills at the end – or something of that intimate nature – when she caught my eye and blushed. She said to her niece, 'He understands too much now, we must be careful in future what we say.' I felt sorry I had not been able to keep up my appearance of ignorance.

It took me a little time to get accustomed to the habit of masculine kisses, one on the lips and one on each cheek, but in the end I ceased to shy at it.

Easter was a wonderful time, with all the mediæval splendour and pageantry of the Russian Orthodox Church. On Easter Eve the churches are draped in mourning. Every one goes to the midnight service, and as the clock strikes twelve a joyful cry goes forth, 'He is risen!' Every bell throughout the length and breadth of the land peals forth the good news, and every one says to each passer-by, 'Christ is risen!' to which the other responds, 'Verily, He is risen.'

This salutation continues on Easter morning, accompanied by the three kisses. The custom would be quite pleasing if one only met pretty girls; but the girls are rather difficult to meet accidentally and one receives most of one's embraces from the lips of aged professors with profuse hirsute adornments — in other words, full moustache and beard. I got quite tangled up with some of them.

Although Russians have not a great reputation for thoroughness in their work, no one can deny that they hold the record for excess in pleasure. Among many such incidents I can recall one occasion on which I attended a ball which began at 8 p.m. and ended at an hour that made me late for lunch on the following day.

I made many visits to the Naval Head-quarters at Cronstadt, where, among other notabilities, I made the acquaintance of Admirals Makarov and Rojestvensky. The former was killed at Port Arthur when his flagship, the *Petropavlovsk*, was blown up during the Russo-Japanese War, and the latter commanded the unfortunate Baltic squadron which the Japanese entirely destroyed in the battle of the Shushima Straits. The Rojestvenskys were particularly kind to me and I enjoyed many happy evenings in their society.

To give an idea of the lavishness of Russian hospitality, I may mention the occasion of my first formal visit to this family. I arrived in a frock-coat at the correct hour in the middle of the afternoon, and I stayed for *two days*! A tooth-brush I was able to buy, and other things were lent to me by my host.

All this time I was working at the language under the guidance of a young man who was studying at the Engineering College. When spring-time came and people were making their arrangements for summer holidays, he suggested that I should come into the country and stay with his people.

In Russia the summer is as oppressively hot as the winter is incredibly cold. Nobody who can possibly help it remains in the town during the summer months. But as the entire country is as flat as a pancake, people cannot go to the hills as we do in India. Instead of this they resort to wooden summer-houses called 'dachas', which are dotted about all over the country.

I accepted my friend's suggestion and hired a small 'dacha' from his parents, who lived at Narishkino, a little village some distance south of Moscow.

My wooden hut was situated about a hundred yards from the Stukachoffs' family residence, at the edge of a small birch wood. I slept, of course, with my windows open, which rendered me a victim to various biting insects, but this discomfort was balanced by the wonderful singing of the nightingales. I should think the province of Orel must be the nesting-ground of nearly all the nightingales in the world.

I was very happy with my humble friends, the Stukachoffs. Our mode of life was rather rough and uncouth, but most enjoyable. I ate the weirdest of food, and I gained a very powerful addition to my vocabulary.

At dinner-time we ate our most excellent Russian soup of 'Schee' flavoured with sour cream, with wooden spoons. Our meat-dish was placed in the centre of the table where each could have a fair chance at it. We selected likely-looking morsels and, if we did not like them on closer inspection, we put them back and chose others. Our usual drink was 'Kvas', a very light and harmless beverage, a little resembling beer. I ate and drank bravely whatever was put before me, with one exception. Cows' udders I could not manage. I tried my best, but they were like india-rubber and when you bit them they bounced back again.

I was quite contented with this rustic existence and was not altogether pleased when I was gradually 'discovered' by the neighbouring nobility.

The first to discover me was Count Pavel Evgrafovitch Komarovsky, who owned a beautiful château with vast estates a few miles away from Narishkino.

He refused to allow me to stay any longer with my humble friends and carried me off to his place, where I spent the remainder of the summer.

Through him I was introduced to most of the good families in the district, and I spent my time visiting one estate after another.

Here I might have found my lack of skill at games a great drawback; but as I can play most games moderately well, and the Russians were not very skilful – except at riding – I was quite able to hold my own.

As an Englishman I was supposed to be an authority on every game from croquet to polo, and I was often severely put to the test. I am not a good rider because I have bad hands and a bad temper, but fortunately I can stick in the saddle all right.

On my arrival to stay a few days with the Barbarikins, I was told that they had been looking forward to my visit with especial pleasure because they had a fiery untamed steed which nobody cared to ride, and they felt sure that it would now meet its master. I did not feel at all so sure about that, but I could not let my nation down by backing out of the engagement. So I had to go through with it. I had a very rough time, but the fierce animal and myself started out together and came home together, which is all I need say about my prowess. I think nothing could have kept me in the saddle with that dreadful quadruped but the realization that I bore the credit of my nation on my shoulders, coupled with a fierce determination to keep the old flag flying.

I really had rather a desperate time of it in those three summer months of 1897. Not only was I put to frequent tests in a normal sort of way, but my friends went out of their way to invent tests, to see what I would do.

One morning the Count went off on business, and I was standing after lunch with the Countess on a balcony overlooking the drive in front of the house, when a drunken peasant appeared, a burly fellow playing a concertina and dancing and singing, and apparently inclined to be rather objectionable. The Countess told him to go away, but to my surprise he answered her in a most impertinent way. The conversation continued, and at last the man became positively abusive and insulting. A look from my hostess indicated the necessity for action on my part, so I descended to the hall to arrange for the removal of the offender.

My idea was to hand the matter over to the butler or one of the footmen, but I rang bells and searched in vain. There was no sign of a man-servant anywhere.

Meantime the peasant had advanced to the doorway – the door being open – and seemed actually to be about to enter the hall. Further indecision was impossible, so – much as I dislike a brawl – I closed with him, and, like most naturally mild people, I must have done so with extreme ferocity, because as soon as the first blows had been exchanged the peasant tore off his red whiskers and other disguise and stood revealed as the Count himself – begging for mercy.

It had all been most carefully arranged – to see what

an Englishman would do – and of course the Countess herself had been in the plot. The men-servants were purposely sent out of the way to leave me a clear field.

The Komarovskys generally had a large party staying in the house and had frequent dinner-parties. I was the life and soul of these entertainments, not because of my natural gifts, but on account of the rich vocabulary that I had learnt during my stay with the Stukachoffs. They were always wondering what I was going to say next, and I am sure I must often have used the most shocking expressions.

The Countess very kindly put me right in the matter of all my *faux pas*, until in the end I was able to discard my earlier vocabulary with its rich expletives. But this, instead of gaining me applause, seemed to produce disappointment. I found I wasn't half as popular now I spoke correctly as I had been when I was frequently saying the most shocking things.

As one example out of thousands of the extreme kindness and generosity of Russians, I would mention the gift I received from Count Komarovsky when I left Gorodishtche to return to Petersburg.

A popular breakfast dish in Russia is a sort of porridge called 'Kasha'. The day before I left I happened to mention that I liked this very much. When I got to the railway station to take my ticket for Moscow, a man turned up with the Count's compliments and two sacks of Kasha weighing at least 160 pounds. A nice sort of addition to one's luggage on a train where there is no free allowance and you have to pay so much a pound for the whole weight. Still, it was a genuinely kind act.

On another occasion, when dining with some people in the country, my hostess asked me what I thought of the port. I said it was very good. Later I also praised the butter. When I got into my carriage to drive home I found a box rather in the way of my feet. On my arrival home I found it was a present for me, and contained six bottles of port and four pounds of butter.

In the autumn of this year, 1897, while I was still on duty in Russia, serious trouble broke out all along the North-West Frontier of India, and I read in the Russian papers an account of the action against the Mohmands at Shabkadr in which my regiment had taken part. It was only the usual frontier scrimmage, but the Russian newspapers described it with much exaggeration as a very serious affair and a great defeat for the British.

I returned to London in October and passed the Interpreter's Test.

CHAPTER XI

FRONTIER SERVICE AND JOURNALISTIC ADVENTURE

HAVING successfully disposed of the examination, my mind was now free to contemplate the bliss of approaching matrimony. We had been engaged for a whole year, but having been separated during nearly the entire period, I felt a little nervous at the prospect — no doubt my future bride felt more so.

I was due to sail for India before the end of November, so the date for the wedding was fixed early in that month to give us time for a short honeymoon in Devonshire before embarking.

We were duly married at Bishopsteignton on November 9 — a real old-fashioned village wedding — and sailed for India twelve days later, arriving in due time at Bombay.

It was rather a rough start in life for my wife, and it was perhaps made rougher by the fact that I was not at all cut out for the rôle of the kind, thoughtful, protecting husband.

I was delighted to find myself married, but I also had a sort of sensation of surprise, and it took years to dawn on me that, however much young people may like to talk of a wife being a 'pal', she is something a good deal more than that, and treatment on terms of mere equality is not at all what she wants.

My idea was that, whereas I had hitherto had one of everything, I would now have two of everything. If she wanted anything else she would ask for it. That's where I made my mistake – they don't like to ask for it, they like to have their wants foreseen.

We stayed for a couple of days with one of my sisters at Malabar Hill in Bombay. While here I received a telegram from a married officer commanding the regimental depot in Peshawar, offering us accommodation on our arrival.

This kind offer I rather ungraciously refused. The officer was a stranger to me, having been transferred to the regiment as second-in-command during my absence in Russia, and I thought my wife would be happier in a nice hotel than as a guest in a strange house.

I never made a more stupid decision in my life. The railway journey to Peshawar from Bombay is not much under 1,500 miles and the trains were fairly comfortable, but slow. At the end of the first day my wife was rather wishing she had never come to India, but I cheered her up with visions of luxury and comfort in a nice hotel at the end of the journey.

I had not been in Peshawar for many years and I naturally assumed that in a town of that size and importance there would be a choice of decent hotels. But I was soon to find out that my assumption was entirely wrong and that there were no hotels at all.

We arrived at our destination in the dark and got into one of those weird two-horse conveyances called ticca-gharries. I told the driver to take us to the hotel. I was horrified when he replied that there was no such thing, but in all fair-sized towns in India Government provides a rest-house for travellers, called a 'Dak bungalow'; so I told the driver to take us there, explaining to my wife that it was quite all right and the Dak bungalow was only another name for a kind of hotel.

On arrival at the Dak bungalow we found its three rooms already occupied by seventeen persons! The only choice now lay between sleeping in a ditch or eating humble-pie and asking for shelter at the house of the kind people whose invitation we had refused.

I have never felt such a worm as I did when I presented myself before the lady of the house and explained our pitiable plight. What secret emotions stirred her breast, I do not know, but she showed no signs of rage, contempt, or even merriment.

It appeared that, on our refusal, the only accommodation in the house had been given to some one else, and there was now no room vacant. But by some rearrangement a very small sort of dressing-room was made available for us, and my unfortunate wife was able at last to feel that she had 'arrived', and also doubtless to wish that she had never left her home.

As soon as she was settled in with our kind friends I rushed off to rejoin the regiment, and caught it up at Hoti Mardan, where it formed part of the force under General Sir Bindon Blood.

In January 1898 the force advanced into Buner by the Tangi Pass. The pass itself is an easy one, but as a military position a difficult one to attack, being flanked by high hills, those on the north-west being rocky and precipitous, forming the enemy's right flank.

The task of turning this flank was allotted to the 20th Punjabis. It was a hard climb and, as the cliffs were held by the tribesmen in considerable force, we expected a desperate fight. But the Bunerwals were not in the mood for serious resistance and by noon we were in possession of the heights, with few casualties, capturing two standards and putting the enemy to flight.

The main body was now able to move up the pass and the whole force advanced into the Buner country, bivouacking for the first night near the village of Bampokha.

As we moved forward down the hill-side we met small bodies of the enemy, who were soon put to flight. I was with one of the leading companies, and on entering a rocky nullah found one of the tribesmen hiding behind a rock, having apparently twisted his ankle in his headlong flight down the hill.

Some of the men raised their rifles to fire, but I stopped them, as there was nothing to be gained by slaughtering this old man in cold blood. He was persuaded to throw down his arms, and we took him into camp as a prisoner. He was set free on the following day by the General's order, and said good-bye to me in the most friendly fashion.

Advancing farther into the country, we found ourselves at the village of Kinkargali, a section of which village was allotted to us for quarters. In this section we selected a fine substantial house for the Officers' Mess.

There were about twenty chickens concealed in one of the inner rooms, but they betrayed themselves by clucking, and soon found their way into the kitchen.

Coming out of the Mess next morning, I was surprised to meet at the door my old friend the prisoner of the first day. He greeted me with friendly smiles and explained that this was his house, begging me with true Pathan hospitality to make use of anything we needed. He then informed me in a whisper that there were twenty fowls concealed in one of the inner rooms. I did not trouble to tell him that they were no longer there.

It is impossible to expect tribesmen to understand the principles of regular warfare, and he quite failed to realize that though he had been captured and released he still remained one of the 'enemy', that his village had been taken in war, and that his house was no longer, for the time being, his own property.

However friendly his feelings, we had to explain to him that he must go away or he would run the risk of being shot. I was really very sorry to say good-bye to him, but friendly enemies are apt to give information to others, and must consequently be regarded as spies, intentional or otherwise.

Dr. Stein (now Sir Aurel Stein) accompanied our column with the intention of visiting some ancient Buddhist sites known to exist in Buner, his interest being obviously purely archæological. In order to

F

safeguard him during his explorations in the surrounding hills my regiment furnished him with an escort of Pathans.

On his return one day he told me that the day's work had been most interesting and successful; in fact, he was quite pleased with the results. A short time later I met the Pathan N.C.O. who had commanded his escort. He said to me, 'The sahib has no luck. He found nothing. I knew he would not. The Bunerwals have dug up those old places over and over again. There is no gold there. Why does the sahib go on wasting his time?'

I said, 'He is not looking for treasure. He is simply interested in ancient things, trying to find out how men lived two thousand years ago.' To which my friend replied, 'Nonsense, he only pretends that. If people dig in old ruins, it is to find treasure and nothing else. Every one knows that. How can you find out how men lived 2,000 years ago by digging in the ground? And who wants to know how they lived? For myself, I would sooner find a bag of gold that would help me to live.'

Buner was not at all the sort of country where one would hope to find bags of gold. Though comparatively rich from the agricultural point of view, there was nothing to tempt the soldiers to break the strict regulations regarding 'loot'.

People who know nothing about the conditions on the Indian frontier often talk about 'loot'. Of course troops are on all occasions forbidden to indulge in this pastime, but when inhabitants have fled, leaving rather nice things behind them, it is difficult to prevent the men from acquiring a few 'souvenirs'.

In Buner there was nothing of that kind except live-stock, and whatever was taken as supplies for the troops was amply paid for, but no doubt a considerable number of chickens and sheep found their way into camp-kitchens without payment. A thing that you eat can hardly be regarded as a 'souvenir', so we had not even that excuse, I'm afraid.

The country was full of donkeys, and quite a lot of these were collected by an old sepoy, Mehru. Mehru was a Sangu-Khel Shinwari from the Kabul side of the Khyber Pass, a very bad character but – as so often happens – a very good fellow. He was very popular in his company and always untiring and helpful. At the end of a long march, when the men could hardly drag one foot after another, I have seen him trudging into camp carrying three men's kits.

He was very crafty with his donkeys, but they are not the sort of thing you can easily hide. I spotted what he was doing, but looked the other way. To the ordinary observer it looked as if the animals had been hypnotized into following along behind the regiment – they seemed to have no connection at all with us, and least of all with Mehru.

Soon after returning to India, Mehru's time was up, and he drove his little herd of donkeys up through the Khyber to his home, where he developed a very prosperous business as a carrier.

But I'm afraid he was a born thief, and he eventually lost all his animals by being captured on our side of the border and sent to prison. His offence this time was stealing Government mules. He had done so well over his donkeys that ambition prompted him to go a step higher and collect mules.

When he came out of prison he came to see me and told me all about the sad affair. He had not the least consciousness of guilt. His idea was that the Indian Government had such a lot of mules that one or two less would make no difference.

I saw him last in Peshawar in 1917, when he came all the way down from his mountain home to see me and talk over old times. He was looking very sprightly, but rather aged, having just come out of prison on the Kabul side for some offence connected with his incurable propensity for annexing live stock belonging to others.

In the spring of 1898 the regiment left Buner, operations on the frontier having been brought to a successful conclusion, and marched to Jhelum. I was sent to Peshawar to command the depot and was informed that we should be there a long time. My wife therefore unpacked all our boxes and we proceeded to set up house. When all was finished the bungalow looked very smart.

Our first visitor arrived on the following day. My wife wore her hair at that time with a sort of 'bob' tied with a big bow.

The lady who had honoured us with a call inquired

her age, and when informed said, 'Then you ought to put your hair up.'

On the following day I received telegraphic instructions to remove the depot to Jhelum by train. So we laboriously packed up all our treasures and started for Jhelum. On arrival in this new cantonment we found there were no bungalows vacant, so we had to spend six weeks in the Dak bungalow there. People who know Indian Dak bungalows will gather that my bride was having rather a poor time.

From Jhelum we left with the regiment for Delhi, where we succeeded in finding a nice little bungalow and proceeded, for the second time in two months, to set up house.

This was no sooner done than my wife caught enteric fever. It was an anxious and a miserable time for me, rendered doubly miserable by the fact that I had to share my meals with the nurse – a partially-trained sort of Mrs. Gamp, the widow of a subordinate railway official.

She had been married many times and according to her account each experiment had been worse than the preceding one. They all died of drink or of weird diseases, the symptoms of which she explained to me at the dinner-table, lingering fondly over the most revolting portions.

What she and my wife talked about I don't know, but from the very few fragments of their conversation that I caught I imagine that the elder lady was warning the younger against the perfidy of men. So many whispered confidences ended up with 'Oh, these 'usbands, these 'usbands' — nothing said, but much implied.

As soon as my wife recovered and was able to enjoy seeing all her pretty things around her in her nice bungalow, I was temporarily transferred to the 26th Punjabis and ordered to join that regiment in Jullundur. We accordingly packed up our things for the third time and proceeded to Jullundur.

I liked the prospect of Jullundur — a quiet little station on the main line — and painted its charms in glowing colours to my weary wife. But the day after our arrival I was ordered to proceed to Peshawar once more to take over a detachment of the 26th Punjabis stationed in that cantonment. So we arrived back where we had started from and proceeded to set up house for the third time. This time we were more fortunate and were allowed to remain nearly six months.

As was the custom, I had in Peshawar a fierce-looking old Pathan as a 'chokidar' to guard my house at night. He drew his pay with regularity, but did little else. When I returned home late at night, he would greet me with a terrifying challenge to impress his wakefulness and importance on me, and when I was just falling asleep would disturb me by screaming defiance at imaginary intruders, every now and then letting off his pistol, and telling me in the morning that he had had an encounter with some ruffians, one of whom he had certainly wounded.

But I rather suspected that, as soon as he knew me to

be asleep, he slumbered peacefully himself the whole night long. So I set my orderly to watch him.

On the first morning the latter came to me with the old man's pistol, which he had taken from him without difficulty while he slumbered.

Before I could send for the chokidar to confront him with the proof of his negligence, he turned up himself in a state of great excitement and began to tell me a long story of a desperate struggle he had had during the night with some robbers, one of whom he had, as usual, wounded. But the other two had knocked him down and in the struggle robbed him of his pistol.

I amused myself for some time by pretending to take him seriously and to write down an account of the affair for the information of the police.

By making him repeat his story over several times I was able to record his varying statements that the three men were all tall, and that they were all short, and that one was tall and two were short, and more to the same effect, and then I gave him back his pistol and sent him about his business, leaving my orderly to continue his witticisms to complete his discomfiture.

The summer in Peshawar, though hot, was very enjoyable, and in the autumn there was good quail and snipe-shooting. I had many friends in the garrison, but things were rather dull for my wife, who enjoyed riding, but rather lacked social amenities. In the hot weather no one stays in Peshawar — with the thermometer over 120 degrees — if they can help it, and all the ladies go to the hills.

I dined out occasionally in Mess, but I must add, to my credit, that I refused most invitations, because I did not like leaving my wife to eat a lonely dinner in the bungalow.

But once out, I found it hard to break myself of my old bad habit of sitting up late. Returning very late on one occasion, I made the usual stock excuses of being unwilling to break up the party, fear of hurting my host's feelings, etc.

On the next evening at the Club I saw my wife seated under the punkah, talking with my host of the night before. I was coming up from behind them, and as I approached I heard him saying, 'He *is* a late sitter. I thought I should never get to bed. I tried to push him off at twelve o'clock, but he kept me up till three.' Silent reproaches made me resolve to mend my ways.

At the end of the year I rejoined my regiment in Delhi, and we set up house for the fourth time in a quaint old bungalow in Darya Ganj. It was built on native lines, with screened enclosures for women, and it had no plinth.

The only room we could use as a drawing-room had twelve doors, three on each side of a square, and twelve more openings on an upper sort of balcony, requiring in all twenty-four pairs of curtains.

The upper openings were to enable the ladies of the harem to look down on their lords and masters when the latter were entertaining each other. There is much to be said for the customs of the East.

Owing to the absence of plinth and the thick undergrowth surrounding the bungalow, it was rather 'snakey', and I killed a cobra in the dining-room just behind my wife's chair.

From Delhi we got two months' leave to Kashmir, enjoying some very good duck-shooting in the early winter. Kashmir in those days was a cheap enough place to live in, but we yielded to the importunities of sellers of embroidery, wood-carving, etc., to such an extent that when it was time to return to India my little purse was almost empty. But I had had the fore-thought — unusual for me — to keep enough cash for our return journey to Pindi in the usual two-horse conveyance.

At the last moment, however, a silversmith turned up with a carved bowl that fascinated us both, and for which he wanted just the sum I had put by to pay for the carriage. As my wife was determined to have it, I said, 'All right. Take the bowl if you like and walk the 150 miles to Pindi.'

So we secured our treasure, put all our things in a bullock-cart, and walked home. It was in the month of November — the non-leave season — so we had the road to ourselves and enjoyed the tramp very much.

We had one horse with us, but neither wanted to ride. A stroke of bad luck, however, compelled me to do so for two marches. I got a rheumatic ankle — the one the militiamen destroyed for me in Mian Mir — from paddling in freezing water, and I *had* to ride.

No one believes this, of course, but it is a fact. So I rode the two marches. Unfortunately, we were met by friends on the road, myself in the saddle and my wife holding on to the stirrup-leather, and the news went round that that was the way I treated my wife.

Standing too close to a bonfire one night, my wife burnt about a foot off the front of her only skirt, and we both looked disreputable tramps when we reached Pindi. We hoped to arrive unobserved, but we got mixed up in some tactical exercises and were captured by an Indian Cavalry regiment whom we knew well. They gave us a good breakfast, for which we were grateful, but we would sooner have remained undiscovered.

My wife was fond of pets and we returned from that trip with an enormous owl and three pie-dog puppies. Anyone who has been in India will remember what delightful things these puppies are, but they will also know what awful things they grow up into. My warnings were of no avail, however, and the puppies were duly collected. I remember feeling rather a fool, standing on the railway platform at Rawal Pindi with the owl balanced on one arm and the three pups twisting their leads into knots round my legs. I began to realize that I really was married.

Not long afterwards two of the pups got hydrophobia and the third I gave away (with permission) to a friend. An old Pathan acquaintance came to see me. He wanted me to give him a fire-arm of some sort. After a long conversation I ended up by saying, 'I am so sorry I can't give you a pistol just now, but here's a little dog for you.' He left the compound looking very sulky, and I expect that poor little dog came to a bad end.

We had just begun to feel really comfortable in our little bungalow when I got orders to proceed to Jhansi as Station Staff Officer. So off we went, and at the end of 1899, two years after our arrival in India, found ourselves setting up house for the fifth time.

Finding that the duties of S.S.O. did not take up my whole day, I decided to start working for the Staff College Examination. This exam. is a hard one even with the aid of a crammer, and I spoilt whatever chances I might have had by wasting my time running a newspaper which I called *The Jhansi Herald*, and which was printed for me by the *Pioneer*. The paper was not a financial success, having naturally a very small circulation, but the unlimited opportunity it gave me of libelling my friends amply compensated me for the money I lost by it.

The Deputy-Commissioner, being a great friend of mine, was among the first to suffer from my caustic pen, but he very soon succeeded in turning the tables on me. I was summoned to appear in Court to answer a charge of having published a newspaper without printing on it the name of the publisher and printer, and it was pointed out to me that I was liable to four years' imprisonment and a fine of ten thousand rupees!

There undoubtedly is such a law, but I knew nothing of it, and it obviously was never meant to apply to foolish little amateur efforts like mine. If found guilty, I probably should have neither been fined nor sent to prison. But I had to attend Court and apologize, and the laugh was entirely on the Deputy-Commissioner's side.

My little paper might even have been a financial success if only the local shopkeepers had responded to my appeal to them to avail themselves of this un-rivalled advertising medium. But none of them were inclined to venture.

However, I could not leave my advertising spaces blank, so I inserted glowing advertisements in my own phrases on behalf of all the firms I myself dealt with, and by deducting the cost of these advertisements from my monthly bills due to them, affairs were satisfac-torily arranged – at least, as far as I was concerned.

Owing to the lack of journalistic enthusiasm on the part of the garrison, I had to fill up most of the paper myself. I supplied the 'Editorial', the 'Answers to Correspondents' and 'Aunt Jane's Column'.

I also had to originate most of the correspondence to which I so wittily replied. Aunt Jane was taken quite seriously by one young lady who addressed her on the subject of 'Love', but in her last letter she said, 'I don't believe you're a woman at all'.

I had some excellent stuff from a subaltern in the North Staffords, and from one of the civilians. I in-sisted on my wife writing an article, and she complied with one that rather went home. It was called 'Dis-illusionment' and described the contrast between what a bride expected on arrival in India and what she found there.

Dealing with the local firms, I was able to furnish my bungalow neatly and inexpensively with bamboo furniture. Bamboo is particularly liable to damage by small boring insects, and can be almost eaten through without showing any outward signs of deterioration. This got me into trouble.

Being a married man, I thought we ought to entertain a little, so we started our first dinner-party by inviting the Officer Commanding the Station to dinner — a man of great weight both in military councils and in frame.

He was shown into the drawing-room on his arrival and, after greeting my wife and myself, seated himself by request in the best arm-chair, which instantly exploded as if it had been hit by a shell, while the O.C. lay prone on the floor amid the fragments.

And this chair was actually from one of our local furniture-dealers, of whom I had said in my enforced advertisement: 'Messrs. Bhagat Chand defy competition. Unrivalled furniture *de luxe* at bed-rock prices. Test our goods and see.'

I went up for my examination in the summer of 1900, but what with wasting my time over my newspaper and having no one to coach me, I did not pass.

CHAPTER XII

THE CHINA WAR, 1900

By August 1900 my wife had endured three real hot weathers in Peshawar, Delhi and Jhansi, she had set up house five times, had had enteric fever, and had contributed her first article to that important periodical, *The Jhansi Herald*.

Having started with a dislike of India, her harassed career should by now have induced her to loathe it; but women are quite incomprehensible, and this life of heat and dust, discomfort and turmoil, had, on the contrary, inspired her with a love for India. This was rather hard luck, as fate was now arranging to give us our sixth move, and this time out of India altogether.

At the beginning of this month my regiment was ordered to China to take part in the expedition against the Boxers. My wife left for England, while I rejoined the regiment on board ship at Calcutta.

We had a rough voyage and ran into a typhoon off Hong-Kong — bad enough for all of us, but terrifying for the men, very few of whom had ever seen, or even heard of, the sea before.

We disembarked at Wei-hai-wei, where we remained for a week. Things were quite quiet in this neighbourhood, but we were ordered to carry out route-marches in the country to impress the natives.

The first thing we realized was that we had come to

a land of pigs. I never saw so many pigs in my life, before or since.

In India we seldom see pigs, except as wild boars, though we occasionally enjoy a ham in Mess, imported from England.

In Mahomedan countries one has to be rather careful about pigs, because the followers of the Prophet not only regard the pig as unclean, but the mere sight, or even thought, of a pig makes them feel all-overish. Funny things human beings! I remember on one occasion, in a crowded second-class carriage, a brother officer trying to dissuade a Mahomedan gentleman from entering by showing him a silver pig charm on his watch-chain. And he succeeded.

And how our poor Mahomedans suffered here! The country was alive with pigs. Their grunts resounded from the courtyard of every house we passed; they trotted up and down the roads; Chinamen carried little live or dead pigs in baskets, and thought nothing of bumping their pork into any passer-by who happened to be in the way.

On our first route-march the leading company suddenly shot to the left side of the road, without orders, to avoid two of these monsters who were peacefully trotting down the right side of the road. But as they shied across the road they nearly knocked over a Chinaman carrying a side of pork on his back. This brought them back into the middle of the road, where they were confronted by a grinning Chinaman with four little live sucking pigs in baskets slung on a yoke.

This terrifying shock produced the natural reaction, and in a very short time the men gave up fussing about pigs, and perhaps began to regard them as not much worse than any other animal. It was a shock to our caste-ridden Hindus, too, to find themselves in a country of 350 million inhabitants who had no caste whatever.

One of the principal drawbacks of caste is in connection with food. There are thousands of different castes in India, and no caste can eat food with any other caste, or food that has only been touched by another caste.

When we sat down for our half-way halt on our first march and began to eat our lunch, a smiling Chinaman nestled up beside each of us and gladly accepted our chicken-bones when we had gnawed off as much as we could manage. Nothing wasted in this land of intensely clever people.

A disgusted Indian Officer said to me, 'No wonder there are no crows or vultures here. These Chinamen do their work for them.'

Re-embarking at Wei-hai-wei, we proceeded to Tongku, at the mouth of the Pei Ho River, to take part in an international attack on the Peitang forts. But the attack took place without us, because some of the other nations cheated by starting before the agreed time — as our allies nearly always did. After a couple of nights spent on the mud-flats by Tongku — the country alive with land-crabs that crawled into one's bedding and made sleeping on the ground very unpleasant — we were sent up the river in barges and landed at Tientsin.

In the early morning, before we got on board our barges, we thought we would cheer the men up by letting the *Dols* and *Sarnais* play a tune or two. H.M.S. *Algerine* was anchored close by, and the officers sent a message on shore to say that if the music didn't stop at once they would have to open fire. Half the officers and all the crew were suffering from abdominal pains. The Royal Navy were apparently not accustomed to 'vernacular' music!

At Tientsin we were accommodated in fairly comfortable barracks improvised from commercial warehouses. We arrived too late to take part in the relief of the Legations in Pekin, but we were kept pretty busy all the winter marching and counter-marching with a view to bringing the Boxers to a pitched battle, which they wisely evaded. We suffered little from the enemy's bullets, but we had to endure hardships from the intense cold, and from occasional blizzards with the thermometer below zero. Just as in the summer in India it was the British officer who suffered most from the heat, so here, the tables being turned, it was the men who suffered most from the cold. But they stood it very well and found drilling and sliding on the ice very good fun.

If you really want to see an amusing spectacle which even the film-producers have not yet thought of, get a company in line on the march in hob-nailed boots on the ice, and when they have got into a good swing, give the command 'Halt!' without warning. When I gave the order to halt, I had no idea of the amusing effect it would produce, and I am quite guiltless of having deliberately intended to send more than half the company flat on their backs.

As soon as I could find time I set to work to study the Chinese language, and succeeded in passing the examination in 1901, but long before that I could, of course, understand sufficient to carry on a brief conversation on simple matters. Ignorance of each other's language is the cause of half the trouble in the world, and of this I had some amusing examples.

I visited the bazar one day and found an Indian soldier bargaining with a Chinese dealer for some small article worth about 50 cents. Both sides to the bargain argued with vehemence as to the price, but each in his own language, which the other could not understand. The Chinaman was saying, 'I will never take less than 60 cents,' and the Indian was saying, 'You ask too much. I will not pay more than 80 cents.' I was able to help them to a happy conclusion.

This expedition to China was the first occasion on which the majority of the civilized nations of the world acted in combination against a common enemy, and it was on that account more interesting from a political than from a purely military point of view.

We had at this time another war on our hands, against the Boers in South Africa, which made matters rather difficult for the military authorities, but none the less, we more than held our own against the other contingents.

I think most of the Powers had rather hoped that we should find difficulty in providing the full complement of our contingent, as they were for the most part stupidly ignorant of the size and efficiency of our Indian army.

The French, who had particular reason to dislike us at this time, affected to believe that our Indian troops were not really trained troops at all. I overheard one of their recently arrived officers say how clever it was of the English to get a lot of coolies and dress them up in uniform to look like soldiers, and he added, 'they probably don't even know how to use their rifles.'

A few days later the foreign detachments at Shan-hai-Kuan got up an international rifle-meeting. They subscribed liberally and offered valuable prizes. I think it was the 29th Punjabis who were at Shan-hai-Kuan at that time — probably the best shooting regiment in India — and they walked off with nearly all the prizes.

Besides our own country, France, Germany, Russia, Austria, Italy, America and Japan sent troops to take part in the operations, but the total number of the force was not large, and the jealousies among the nations were so intense that, if the Chinese had put up a properly organized defence, we should have found ourselves in difficulties.

But the Chinese are the wisest of all races on earth and do not like fighting. They are not cowards, but deep-thinking individuals, and in a battle each man says to himself, 'If I go forward, I go to meet the bullets, and one of them may hit me. If I go towards the rear, I shall get farther from the bullets.' So he soon retires in the face of serious opposition.

At the present time China is in a state of revolution, and for some years past we have read of terrific battles fought between rival generals, resulting on most occasions in glorious victories for both sides.

But we have never seen the casualty lists. If the numbers of killed and wounded are at all in proportion to the published accounts of these terrific battles, the total losses cannot amount to less than a hundred million men. But they are probably not more than several thousand.

The period of anarchy which China is now undergoing is supposed to herald the dawn of a New China. The Chinese character, which has remained unchanged through countless centuries, is to be remoulded by the wave of a magic wand in the hands of a few graduates of Western universities.

But is this great change in the hearts and minds of more than 350 million people really taking place?

Over ninety per cent of these millions are peasants, and it is extremely doubtful whether the peasant mind is likely to be affected in any great degree by the enthusiasm of a few reformers.

Human nature and national character are subject to the laws of evolution, but evolution moves slowly in periods of thousands of years, and its progress is not appreciable in periods of time of which the century is the unit.

We are distracted by the unreal importance of events that are in themselves superficial and transient. The minds of cultivated and intelligent people are almost entirely absorbed in questions of Science, Art, Commerce and Politics, which are matters of quite secondary importance. The great matter for the world is the tilling of the soil, and it is the peasant that truly represents the race. Assuming the world's population to be 1,800 million, the tillers of the soil probably represent something like 1,400 million, and it is they who constitute the world.

Science, Art, Commerce and Politics are guiding lights for world progress, and they succeed, not by the brilliance of their own achievements, but by the extent to which they can lift up this enormous mass of toiling humanity.

And just as the occupation of the peasant has remained unchanged through countless centuries, so the peasant mind has undergone but little alteration. Human nature does not change, and the subdivisions of human nature – that is to say, those slight variations which we call racial characteristics – are almost equally unchanging.

My remarks on China and the Chinese character made with reference to the period of the Boxer War might be considered out of date with regard to the wonderful events now taking place in that country, where we are witnessing the painful birth – with too many contending surgeons and midwives – of a 'New China'. But when the child is born, he will be found to be a speaking likeness of his great-grandfather!

There is not going to be any New China, though there are undoubtedly many New Chinamen – talking European languages and wearing plus-fours and Harold-Lloyd spectacles. There is not even going to be anything new in the system of government – though various so-called reforms on democratic lines may endure for a generation or two.

People discussing affairs in China appear to me to forget two things. The first is that the Chinese are a highly civilized and cultured people, though their civilization differs entirely from our own. And the second is that their civilization is incomparably the most ancient in the world – they could almost reckon in thousands of years what we reckon in centuries. About five centuries before Christ three great teachers arose in Asia – Buddha, Confucius, and Lao Tze – and the modification produced on the Chinese character by their influence was probably the last change up to the present-day. But this was only a modification, and the mind of the present-day Chinaman still has its roots firmly planted in the days before Abraham.

In spite of his acceptance of the pure doctrines enunciated by these three great teachers, he has never ceased to be guided in all the affairs of this world and the world to come by the ancient religion of ancestor-worship and the propitiating of evil spirits.

Destroy ancestor-worship and you will have a clear

ground on which to build up a New China. But is it likely that these smart young Chinamen leading the present-day movements will be able — with the aid of a smattering of Western education — to accomplish what three of the world's deepest thinkers failed to achieve?

Another error that is made in regarding what is called the 'chaos' in China is to view it as something abnormal, whereas it is purely normal.

It has been China's way, and always will be. A Dynasty rules, and like all dynasties the royal race dies out after a certain number of centuries. Then succeeds a period of anarchy, out of which a new dynasty is born. The only difference in the present situation is that in past periods of anarchy, the Chinese were left happily free to settle their own affairs, whereas in the world as we live now there is no longer any such thing as national privacy. Facility of communications, coupled with a transient frenzy of industrialism, have brought all nations into touch with each other, and so the unfortunate Chinese are compelled to admit as spectators of their private theatricals, a heterogeneous collection of unsympathetic and un-understanding 'foreign devils'. It will easily be understood that this complicates things enormously.

But through it all the old peasant ploughs his land and sows his seed and reaps his crops, and takes no interest in the glorious victories of the Army of the North, or the Army of the South — if, indeed, he ever hears of them — and in a thousand years' time when two more dynasties will have passed away, and another normal period of anarchy supervenes, his descendants will be ploughing the same land, sowing seed, and reaping crops. He is the only thing that matters. His task is unchanging and he is unchanging.

The above facts and surmises are not to be confounded with opinions — a residence of two years in China long ago, a nodding acquaintance with the language, and a general interest in the country during the intervening years, do not qualify me to offer my opinion on the present crisis.

In an armed conflict with the present Chinese troops I can well believe that conditions would not be quite as I have described them during the Boxer War. The Chinese soldier of to-day may be highly efficient. But if he is, this is to be reckoned among the superficial changes. His efficiency will not have altered his mentality, and a very efficient soldier who has a philosophic dislike to taking risks is not the man to win victories.

The Chinese are such deep thinkers that they are apt to go on thinking till they get out of their depth and so are led to form entirely wrong conclusions from right lines of thought.

Thus on the few occasions when we came under fire at close quarters from Chinese troops armed with modern small-bore weapons, we found that as a rule their bullets whistled harmlessly over our heads, and the reason of this was as follows:

Before the war the Chinese soldiers had been in-

structed in the use of their weapons by European Instructors, and from these they had learnt, among other
things, that when you aim at an object less than 600
yards away you fire with the leaf of the back-sight
down, but for greater distances you require to raise the
leaf of the back-sight. They saw in practice that if you
fired with the leaf down the bullet hit the ground some
700 yards away, but with the leaf up it would travel
over 1,700 yards. Deep thought on this problem led
to the conclusion that the raising of the leaf must add
force to the bullet. This was obvious — leaf down
bullet only reaches 700 yards, leaf up it reaches 1,700
yards. Therefore in battle when you want not only to
hit the enemy but to hit him as hard as you can, you
must give all the force you can to the bullet by raising
the leaf. The pleasing result was that their bullets
passed harmlessly over our heads. Yet their reasoning
was very good.

Another very Chinese idea was the two-man rifle,
exactly like a Lee-Metford but about four times as
heavy and taking a very large cartridge. I suppose the
Chinese argument was that if two men could carry a
rifle four times as heavy as the ordinary rifle, they
would be twice as effective. As a matter of pure arithmetic it looks like that, but in practice these rifles
were of no use at all.

We captured a small band of Chinese armed with
these peculiar weapons, and made them give a demonstration, aiming at a high wall 400 yards away. The
procedure was as follows:

The front-rank man tied a bit of rag round the barrel about a foot from the foresight, turned his head away and shut his eyes. The rear-rank man loaded the rifle, brought the butt to his shoulder, aimed at the wall, then shut his eyes tight, and pulled the trigger. After firing a good many rounds with great deliberation we found only one hit on the wall.

In the Boxer business China had practically declared war on all the Powers by her action with regard to the Legations, and each of the Powers had therefore the right to send a contingent to show the Chinese that they were not to be trifled with. But as a matter of fact, each country sent its contingent more with a view of watching the movements of each of the rival Powers than of intimidating the Chinese.

The English and French had long been established in China on a more or less friendly footing. Russia also had been in touch with China on the north. Japan was the closest neighbour, and as a great trading nation, the most interested. Germany was pushing her interests as hard as she could in Shantung with a view of getting 'a place in the sun', though there is no more sunshine in Shantung than in Germany. Austria and Italy had no need to be there, but being in alliance with Germany at that time, the latter saw to it that they sent their contingents so as to triple her own strength. America was there, I don't quite know why, but she probably wanted to watch the Japanese. At any rate, we were glad that she was represented.

Towards the Chinese we presented a united front,

but among ourselves there was little love lost. The French hated us because of the recent affair at Fashoda on the Upper Nile, where we had got the best of an argument with them, compelling them to withdraw from that post. They hated the Germans for the defeat of 1870. The Russians and ourselves were jealous of each other's influence, and the Japanese disliked everybody in the most polite manner. In such a babel my slight knowledge of many languages was a great help to me.

In the spring of 1901 the combined armies marched through the heart of the Boxer country from Tientsin to Paotingfu. We marched in three parallel columns and I cannot remember exactly how we were divided, but I think the British Column was separate from all the others.

Between Tientsin and Paotingfu there are a considerable number of large towns surrounded with high walls of mud or brick which would render them difficult places to take if stoutly defended, but our advance was unbrokenly victorious. On our approach, the alarm would be sounded and the gates closed. Large pieces of red rag were then placed hanging out of the muzzles of the smooth-bore cannons mounted on the walls. This was done to make us believe that these were flames coming out of the muzzles of the guns and it was hoped that we would retire under the impression that the guns were firing at us.

But so far from producing that effect we did not even guess what those bits of red rag were put there

for until our Chinese interpreter told us, and so bravely
continued our advance extending for attack in the
usual way, while our artillery prepared to discharge
something more efficacious than red rag from the
muzzles of their guns.

When all was ready for the desperate encounter, the
gates of the city would open, and the leading inhabitants with smiling faces would advance on the troops
bearing gifts of eggs and chickens. This practical
joke was played on us many times till we reached Paotingfu, which city fell into our hands without much
fighting. Skirmishes occasionally took place with more
or less organized troops, but nothing in the way of a
real engagement.

The other columns on our flanks fired off a great
deal of ammunition and sent in glowing reports of
their numerous victories. I suppose that they shot the
poor old Chinamen who were coming out to offer them
the eggs and chickens, and they claimed to have themselves suffered several casualties. One man I know was
hurt by a fall from his horse, and we met one of the
foreign casualties being removed from the field in an
ambulance, but on inquiry we were told that he was
merely suffering from stomachache. I do not mention
the names of the various nationalities, as nothing is to
be gained by hurting other people's feelings.

Little of importance took place on the return march
to Tientsin, but amusing episodes in this land of para-
doxes were frequent. The fact that the European members of the Jesuit Mission and one of the Protestant

Missions wore Chinese clothing led to frequent mis-understandings.

I mentioned one day to a Pathan Officer that we were having difficulty in transporting the Mess equipment and told him that if he could secure a Chinese mule cart to help us it would be a great convenience. One evening, soon after we had settled into camp, he came to me and taking me to the transport lines showed me a beautiful Pekin cart, and a valuable mule, with very fine harness complete, asking me if this would do. I replied that it would do very well and asked him where he had got it from.

He replied that a distinguished-looking Chinaman, probably a leader of the Boxers, had been riding in it, when he came round the corner with some of his men, captured the Chinaman, but did not put him to death – although he looked a terrible villain – because he was unarmed. They therefore let him go and retained his cart for the use of the troops.

A short time later I was passing down the central street of the camp when I noticed the G.O.C. and his Staff with a group of other officers, listening to some statement that was being made by a Chinese Mandarin in his best silk official dress. The Chinaman was apparently in a state of great excitement, waving his arms and gesticulating with fury.

What chiefly attracted my attention was the fact that though I knew neither the G.O.C. nor any of his Staff could talk Chinese, and there was no interpreter in the group, they not only seemed to understand this

Mandarin but to be able to reply to him. I accordingly joined them and discovered to my surprise that the Mandarin was talking fluent French and was obviously a Frenchman.

His statement was somewhat to this effect:

'I am the head of the Jesuit Mission within this district, and when I heard that the British Column was passing near my home, I decided to pay my respects to Your Excellency. With that view I set out from my residence in my private carriage and had reached about half-way to your camp when I found myself suddenly surrounded by some of your Indian soldiers who tipped me out of my carriage into the ditch and went off with the conveyance after threatening me with their rifles.

'I have come now to ask redress from Your Excellency for this outrageous behaviour.'

The G.O.C. expressed his deepest sympathy with the injured priest and, while apologizing for his soldiers' behaviour (who however might be excused for mistaking him for one of the enemy), promised that a search should be made for the missing mule and carriage. He directed a Staff Officer to see to this at once, and informed the Frenchman that the offender, if discovered, should be flogged before all the troops.

This dreadful threat made my blood run cold and decided me to take immediate action. So, with apologies for intruding, I presented myself before the G.O.C., informing him that one of our Indian Officers had a remarkable talent for tracking criminals, and I would guarantee that if they would allow me to put the matter in his hands they would obtain news of the missing carriage before nightfall.

This plan was accepted and the complainant was invited to make himself comfortable in the G.O.C.'s Mess while a thorough search was being made in the precincts of the camp. I then hastily sought my Pathan Officer and put the facts clearly before him.

In an hour's time he returned to me with the information that he was ready to carry on. I took him to Camp Head-Quarters and informed the anxious priest that this intelligent officer had succeeded in tracing a mule and cart that seemed to resemble his. On this we all set out in the dark with lanterns, headed by the Pathan Officer.

He led us out of camp for about half a mile and then by various winding paths to a small deserted Chinese hut, behind which we discovered, to our joy and surprise, a very fine mule tethered beside a very handsome Pekin cart. The Frenchman was delighted, and after harnessing the mule with the aid of some of his Chinese attendants, set off in the direction of home, begging that his expressions of gratitude might be translated to the clever officer who had succeeded in recovering his property for him.

The General also thanked the officer and turning to me said, 'I don't want to ask too much about his methods, but he's a clever fellow. You ought to make a note of him,' to which I replied, 'Yes, sir, I will do so.'

So the incident ended happily for all except the Mess President who, however, was able to get a cart next day from a Chinaman, who was a Chinaman.

CHAPTER XIII

RAILWAY WORK

In November we marched back to Tientsin, and soon
after our arrival I was sent off to Tongku to take over
the duties of Railway Staff Officer.

Before proceeding further I must explain the situation as regards this railway. It was a purely Chinese
concern but financed with British capital and controlled
by a British Staff. The line ran from Tongku as centre
northwards to Shan-hai-Kuan — where after passing
through the Great Wall it linked up at Newchang with
the Russian Manchurian Railway — and westward to
Pekin. Tongku is an important port for the Pekin-
Tientsin trade, at the mouth of the Peiho River, close
to the Taku forts.

In the summer of 1900 the railway fell into the
hands of the allies who made use of it for military
purposes, and as the Russians were the only contingent with trained railwaymen, they were invited to
work the line on behalf of the allies. This was convenient but unfortunate because international jealousies
came into play.

As I stated before, the line was an Anglo-Chinese
one, but was very much coveted by the Russians, forming as it did an extension of their Siberian and Manchurian railways and linking up Moscow direct with
Pekin. The natural result was that having once got
hold of the line they were very unwilling to give it up
again. At last after heated discussions and a good deal

G

of threatening we succeeded in getting them to hand it over to the Germans, who passed it on to us, we having in the meantime procured the necessary personnel to secure efficient working.

In December 1901 I took up my employment at Tongku under the British Railway Administration, making my home in one of the rooms of the railway station. I had no knowledge of railway work, but that was not required of me as I had a very able staff of English and Chinese subordinates who were mostly old servants of the line, and who performed their duties in a highly efficient manner.

My principal duties were to see that trains started punctually, to keep certain records, to meet allied and commercial demands for transport, and to keep order among the various nationalities making use of the railway. In the performance of this latter duty my knowledge of languages was of great assistance to me; in fact, I do not know how I could have got on without it. My only regret was that I did not speak Italian or Japanese; all the others I could manage.

Although the allies were supposed to be very fond of each other, the exact opposite was the case, and nearly every train that came in gave me practice in languages and tact in settling quarrels between French and Germans, English and Russians, Italians and Austrians and so on.

· The first difficulty I had to cope with was the punctual starting of trains and I was determined to set this matter right without delay. I succeeded in a short time in securing departures fairly up to time, but nothing less than perfection would please me, and I think we eventually reached this standard. There were, however, pitfalls by the way.

Until I took over, nobody minded very much when the train started, and the obliging Chinese station-master was always glad to keep the train waiting for an officer 'whose kit would be here in a minute'; and demands of this sort were my chief difficulty, especially when they came from my own friends. But I gradually gave people to understand that the convenience of individuals could not be considered, and that the 10.20 train would leave at 10.20 to the tick.

On one particular morning one of these unpunctual officers arrived on the platform about 10.15, and begged me to keep the train till his kit came, which would certainly not mean more than ten minutes. I was on the platform with my watch in my hand to insist on a punctual departure, and I told him that the train could not possibly be delayed. We were only running one or two passenger trains a day at that time as we were short of engines and rolling-stock, owing to the damage due to the war, and consequently to miss a train was a rather serious affair.

He argued with me till it was time for the train to start, but I was not to be dissuaded from the strict performance of my duty. Accordingly at exactly 10.20 I turned to Mr. Ho, my Chinese station-master who was by my side, and, to the dismay of my friend, said, 'Let the train go.'

A smile of triumph, however, spread over his features when Mr. Ho replied, 'Sir, there is no engine on the train.'

Although I felt I had made rather an idiot of myself, I could not fail to appreciate the humour of the situation, and I was obliged to share in the smile. A Chinaman's face is usually impassive, but I thought I could detect the beginnings of a smile even on Mr. Ho's stolid features.

I had by this time acquired an undeserved reputation as a linguist; I am sorry I cannot lay claim to that however, but I have a facility for picking up a superficial knowledge of any language in a very short time, and in this way have been able to make myself quite well understood in eight languages, besides my own. But that is not to be a linguist.

What interests me is to see how when a man starts with a slight reputation for anything good or bad his friends and the general public outvie one another in building up on that slight foundation a most exaggerated estimate of his abilities or failings.

My fame as a linguist was greatly enhanced by the following incident. Among the passengers frequently passing through Tongku was a Chinaman who had been brought up in the Russian service and could speak Russian perfectly. I found this out by accident and he and I struck up a great friendship. When he passed through he would alight and tell me all the latest news from his part of the world in Russian, and I always looked forward to a pleasant chat with him in that language. Somebody noticed us walking up and down the platform and talking freely, and naturally assumed that we were talking Chinese. A few days later in the Club at Tientsin, I overheard some one say, 'Wonderful fellow that Dunsterville is, talks any language. He's only been this short time in China and the other day I saw him talking Chinese with a Chinaman as freely as if it were his own language.'

I was employed on railway duties for about a year and a half, and I never had a dull moment. Each nation had a small detachment at Tongku, to watch their interests, that is to say, to try and claim any odd tracts of the valuable river frontage, not apparently claimed by any of the other Powers, and to prevent any of the other Powers from making similar claims. It was quite an amusing game played with pretty little flags. As British business firms had acquired legitimately before the war all the land they needed for wharfage, godowns, etc., we did not join in the game except to the extent of putting up our flag over ground on which we noticed other Powers casting covetous glances.

Tongku is a dirty little place, an insignificant town on a mud flat, and at that time the only flourishing local business appeared to be that of the drinking-shops, which constituted about half the business establishments. These havens of rest for tired soldiers and sailors sold the very best brandy and whisky (made in Japan), guaranteed to produce delirium tremens quicker than any other kind, at about a shilling a bottle. In such drab surroundings the flag-game formed quite a pleasant relief, the national emblems being so thickly scattered about the country that a new arrival stepping ashore at the landing-stage on any day must have thought that we were celebrating the Emperor of China's birthday.

It amused me to look out from the station in the early morning and note the changes that had taken place during the night, it being of course only possible to shift your adversary's flag, or put up a new flag of your own, in the dark.

As a rule the game was played with good temper, but now and then we got rather cross with each other, and it even sometimes looked as if any two of the Great Powers might render themselves ridiculous by going to war over these trifles. I myself was called upon to face a rather desperate situation when, one morning on making my usual inspection I discovered a whole nest of German flags on a triangular plot of ground quite close to the station and certainly forming part of the railway property which was in my care. I immediately called on the German Commandant to point out the hopelessness of his claim and to beg the removal of the flags. This he refused to do, saying something heroic to the effect that where once the German flag had flown no power on earth could effect its removal.

I did not imagine that we would care to go to war with Germany over this incident, and I really did not mind the flags being there as they helped to brighten up the landscape, so I contented myself with demonstrating our claim to the ground in a more efficacious way, by covering it with heavy iron bridging material and putting a guard of the Royal Welch Fusiliers over this property. It was quite a small area and I found that the ostensible reason for its annexation by the Germans was in order to build a German Post Office there. The matter got as far as being mentioned in Reuter's telegrams, and *The Morning Post* of Delhi referred to it under the heading

'STALKY HOLDS UP THE GERMANS.'

The incident led to a discussion between the two Head-quarters at Tientsin, which ended in the flags being withdrawn. Troubles of this sort frequently arose among the various Powers, and one of a more serious nature broke out in Tientsin where the Russians opposed our constructing a railway siding, on the ground that the proposed line would pass over land to which they laid claim. They posted two sentries at the end of the partially finished line with orders to prevent the further progress of the work. As it appeared likely that they might even go so far as to attempt removing the rails already laid, we placed two sentries of ours immediately facing them. Thus, in this ridiculous fashion, these two great nations stood face to face for some days, until at last the Russians agreed to submit the matter to arbitration, which was done; the award, given some time later, was in our favour.

But while the tension lasted the matter seemed serious enough, and both I and the Russian Commander at Tongku, Captain Gomziakoff, spent sleepless nights devising plans by which we could outwit each other, our military strength being about equal. We were great friends and heartily disliked the idea of having to kill each other to satisfy the pride of our respective nations, but we agreed that under the circumstances our efforts to exterminate each other should not prejudice our private friendship.

The situation was reminiscent of the great battle between Tweedledum and Tweedledee, though likely to have more serious results. Every morning Gomziakoff would come up to see me and talk matters over, leaving each time in a temper because I would not tell him exactly what my strength was and what arrangements I was making to defeat him.

The nearest Russian detachment from which he could expect help was in the Peitang forts, to which he had a telephone line that crossed my station, using our railway telegraph posts.

By a coincidence, on the evening when matters were at their most serious point, a sergeant of our Royal Engineers employed in supervising the railway telegraph system, while readjusting our lines at the station, accidentally cut the Russian telephone wire, and poor Gomziakoff spent a night of terror finding himself deprived of all means of communication with his nearest supports.

In the morning he came to see me in a great rage, having discovered where the breakage in his line was, and I had quite a lot of trouble to convince him that the damage had been caused by inadvertence. It really looked at one time as if we should have to fight a duel. But in the end he calmed down, and news coming soon after that the crisis was past and all extraordinary military precautions cancelled on both sides, we cemented our renewed friendship with a bottle of champagne.

We were great friends with the American detachment here and spent many happy evenings in their Mess. When they heard of the prospects of a row between ourselves and the Russians, the commandant came down to see me and to offer his services. It was a kindly thought, but what a fuss there would have been in Washington if trouble had really broken out and my good-natured but impetuous friend had involved the U.S.A. in a European War! Besides, I felt it wouldn't be fair on Gomziakoff, who had no friends at all. Gomziakoff was killed two years later, in the Russo-Japanese War.

The German commanders at Tongku, both naval and military, were very good fellows in spite of their irritating efforts to secure for their fatherland a 'place in the sun' by staking out claims on portions of the mud flats which belonged to other people.

The French and Russian commanders and also the Japanese were always civil and obliging, but there was occasional trouble between our men and the French soldiers, squabbles which were settled without bloodshed and in which we generally found one side as much to blame as the other.

The American army and navy were our best friends,

and never failed to give us all the assistance in their power, especially in the matter of water transport for which I had no facilities. For some time during the winter of 1900–1 we shared a mess with them, flying the Union Jack and the Stars and Stripes from one flagstaff with daily change of precedence.

During the time I served on the räilway I had most able assistants. The first was an officer of the Indian Cavalry and he was succeeded by an officer of the Royal Engineers. Both were men of fierce, determined character and helped to balance my suavity. When fair and gentle means had failed I had only to say 'Fetch Captain Doveton', or 'Ask Captain Hunter to arrange', and, amid a shower of sparks, the affair was satisfactorily settled.

As the Russians had held the railway some time before we took it over, a good many questions were bound to arise between us and them, but these were in every case settled amicably.

There is a great deal to be said for teetotalism, and a great deal more for temperance, but as regards these particular incidents, I think that if we had conducted our proceedings on refreshing draughts of lime-juice we should probably have had war between England and Russia, because the questions involved were on the lines of the 'irresistible projectile meeting the immovable post'. But by the judicious application of alcoholic beverages the projectile and the post simply met and shook hands and went home arm in arm. But it was a severe tax on one's constitution.

I remember one important committee meeting which was held at 8 a.m. and my adversary proposed a bottle of champagne and several liqueurs to start with — at that appalling hour of the morning. After some demur I yielded to his proposal, and in the twinkling of an eye all difficulties vanished and a declaration signed to the effect that the British claim was fair, just, and reasonable.

This question of alcohol is very much to the front on all occasions of international hospitality, and it is often a very embarrassing one, especially to officers who have not very strong heads. But the British army regards it from a point of view differing entirely from that of other nations.

If we have guests we offer them the best we have, and as much of it as they care to consume, but we are not in the least interested in the amount of their consumption. They, on the other hand, regard it as a mark of hospitality to insist on your taking very much more than you want. In fact, they want to make their guests drunk, and we would sooner ours left sober.

I had a rather quaint experience in this way at a small dinner I gave at which two foreign officers were present. After their first two glasses of champagne they both refused a third, and in consequence their liquid refreshment for the evening ceased at that point. They really wanted forty glasses, but they liked to be a little pressed. I had no idea at all of pressing people to take what they did not want, and accepted their refusal as positive and final. I heard afterwards that they confided to their friends that it was the most miserable evening they had ever spent. But perhaps it was a lesson to them.

In the spring of 1901 things had settled down in China and my wife came out from home to share a fairly comfortable little hut which I had built on the railway platform. Other ladies also began to arrive and to give trouble. Most of them wanted impossibilities and many were rather free in their criticism of railway facilities. Two very nice ladies, who formed an exception to the above, sent me later a Christmas cake from England as a token of their gratitude.

One lady, who arrived at Tongku after the last train for the day had left, wanted me to provide her with a 'special' free. I explained that this could not be done, but if she was really very anxious to get on I would put a deck-chair in the guard's van of a goods train and allow her as a special favour to travel in that. She examined the van and seemed to turn up her nose at it. So to encourage her I said, 'My wife has often travelled like that,' to which her laconic reply was, 'Thank God, I'm not your wife.'

One day on a through train from Tongshan to Pekin the guard reported on arrival that there was a lady in a first-class coupé who had no ticket. I went to inquire into the matter, and informed her that she would either have to take a ticket or get off the train. She flatly refused to do either and punctuated her remarks with some unkind criticisms of our poor little railway, and of myself.

What was I to do? I could not slap her as she deserved, and I could not bring myself to snatch her purse and extract the fare. I dealt with the problem in my usual masterly way by sending for Captain Doveton. When he arrived, I said, 'There's a lady in there who hasn't paid for her ticket. Make her pay or turn her out', and I turned on my heel just as he was about to ask 'How?' in order to escape witnessing the unpleasant altercation.

But for once my assistant failed. He never failed when it was a matter of a clenched fist, but you can't apply that to a woman. So as the best way out of the matter, I let the train go and wired to the Railway Staff Officer at the next station, Sinho, 'Lady on train no ticket. Take necessary action.'

But he was a coward, too. I heard afterwards that she got through triumphantly to Pekin without paying a penny, each R.S.O. wiring to the next to take the necessary action and no one providing an answer to the conundrum 'What was the necessary action?' I had many other adventures of the sort, but the above will suffice to give an idea of my troubles in this line.

After all, I was not quite so badly treated as another Railway Staff Officer farther up the line who I heard had been bitten by a foreign Countess who 'had drink taken'.

As station-master at the port of embarkation, I met at one time or another nearly every one of every nationality in the Expeditionary Force. Nobody left or entered China without passing through my hands.

On one occasion an old friend, Captain Roland of the Royal Engineers, arrived from Tientsin by the afternoon train and dropped in to have a cup of tea with me. He informed me that his leave had been granted and he was embarking in two hours' time, unless a wire arrived recalling him to H.Q.

He had been employed in the task of levelling the Peitang forts, and as the work was not quite completed he was afraid that they might stop his leave at the last moment. This was deliberately asking for it. As station-master I also owned a telegraph office, and nothing was simpler than to step across to the office and give a few instructions to the corporal in charge, which resulted in an urgent wire being handed a few minutes later to Roland. The wire was from A.H.Q. and read 'Leave cancelled. Return at once'.

I have never heard anyone express their opinion of A.H.Q. in more fluent or reprehensible language than my friend did on this occasion. I enjoyed the situation for a few minutes and then got under cover before I informed him that the cancellation was cancelled.

Early in 1902 my regiment left for India where they joined the garrison at Mian Mir, while I remained on in the railway service in China. In September of that year, my eldest son was born in Tientsin, and, before he was a month old, I was ordered back to India. In October peace had been declared and order restored; affairs returned to normal, and the railway was handed back to the Chinese.

About this time I had a trifling accident on the

railway which resulted in my putting my knee out. I had to go down a long siding on a trolly to visit the Russian gunboat in the direction of the Taku forts. Some clever Chinaman, seeing me go down late in the day and realizing that I must return in the dark, amused himself by putting a big stone across the line with the result that as we hurried home at top speed in the dark the trolly was suddenly jerked off the line and we were all shot into space, I landing rather uncomfortably on my right knee which rendered me lame for several months, but not unfit for duty.

I left for India soon afterwards, but was taken off my ship at Hong-Kong, where I was kept for three weeks to hold an examination in Punjabi. Soon after leaving Hong-Kong my knee became worse and the doctor on board ship decided to put it in plaster of Paris. He carried out this operation one afternoon in the smoking-room on the upper deck and, after neatly finishing the bandages, warned me that I must remain perfectly still for some time until the plaster had set. He had no sooner left me than there was an alarm of 'man over-board', which was much too exciting an event to miss, so I hopped out of the saloon and watched an exciting rescue in a shark-infested sea off Singapore. This proved altogether too much for my knee, which continued to give me trouble for a year and a half but finally decided to behave itself when threatened with an operation.

CHAPTER XIV

MANŒUVRES AND MALARIA

THE voyage from China provided a rest-cure of which both of us were somewhat in need, and by the time we reached Calcutta I was freed from my plaster of Paris and was able to hop about with reasonable agility.

We reached Mian Mir just after the regiment had left to take part in the grand manœuvres that preceded the Delhi Durbar. I hurried after it and caught it up on the eve of a desperate conflict near Karnal. Here I was introduced, much to my annoyance, to several alterations in drill based on the lessons of the late war in South Africa. There were certainly no lessons in the art of War to be learnt from our operations in China, though much to be added to our private store of experiences in the matter of dealing with peculiar and difficult situations.

The principal lesson from the Boer War that was being rubbed into us at that time was the necessity for officers to carry rifles. As I had just been promoted Major it seemed to me a harmless order enough for officers up to the rank of Captain, but when I found there was no escape even for a Major I felt annoyed, and with good reason.

I had bought a rather wild animal at a moment's notice for a charger, and as I had not been trained as a Mounted Infantryman I guessed that the horse and I were going to have trouble over the rifle, and we did — the horse especially.

A long rifle loosely slung over the shoulder is not an easy thing to mount with, especially if your mount is a fidgetty country-bred that refuses to stand steady. At my first effort I grasped the reins, put my foot in the stirrup, and swung gracefully into the saddle, but the butt of the rifle got there first and hurt me a good deal. I repeated this performance several times in the next few days and then became fairly expert.

Dismounted at a halt I bent down to examine my horse's near fore foot, and in doing so jabbed him in the eye with the muzzle of my rifle. Similar unintentional prods with the rifle roused his resentment and made him still more difficult to mount, as whenever he saw me approaching he naturally suspected me of evil intent. I was consequently glad when the order for carrying rifles was cancelled. During the remainder of my service each new war produced similar futile lessons which had to be learnt, and then a little later happily unlearnt.

The manœuvres were on a grand scale, fairly realistic, and very interesting — especially so to the native ranks, as Indians have more imagination than we have and can consequently put greater zeal into mimic warfare than we do.

It is hard to get them to realize that umpires' decisions should never be questioned, as any discussion in the absence of bullets merely leads to interminable argument.

For myself, I have seldom felt indignant at being put out of action even when I was convinced that the umpire was in the wrong; in fact, I generally welcomed it as giving me the opportunity for a quiet pipe, and, if the Mess mule were handy, a welcome sandwich and a bottle of beer. But the Indian Officers were seldom resigned to their fate, and could with difficulty be restrained from giving their point of view to the umpire.

In one case I helped to explain to one of them why he was put out of action. I showed him that all the time that he had been firing at the enemy in his front, a small body of the enemy had been firing into his men from the right rear. But to that he objected that he had previously fought and conquered that detachment and they were all dead men an hour ago.

He gained some comfort, however, when I put before him the point of view that umpires were just 'catastrophes'. You cannot use bullets in peace-time operations, so umpires are sent about to create imaginary havoc; otherwise the battle would never come to an end. When an umpire puts you out of action, don't bother about the rights and wrongs, but just imagine that a shell has burst in the middle of your company.

Personally I have always found manœuvres, in decent weather, both instructive and amusing. You may or may not learn much at the 'pow-wow', but you can be learning all the time if you make your own mental notes, and your own deductions. As regards pow-wows they can be, and often are, most instructive, but there are occasions when there is practically nothing to be said, and at such times it is sad to note that a senior officer will often forget the golden rule, 'If there is nothing to say, say it.'

We fought many fierce battles with varying success, convincing ourselves when the umpire's decision was against us that if it had been real business and bullets had replaced umpires the victory would have been ours. Troops defeated at manœuvres can always cheer themselves with this reflection, which does them good and does no one else any harm. Besides, we all know that troops have to be fed, and food must be collected for them beforehand in certain places; therefore umpires' decisions must in the end be given so as to bring the troops at nightfall into the vicinity of their supplies. It is better to be defeated and fed than to be victorious and starving — I mean at manœuvres.

About lunch-time one day we captured all the Mess equipment of one of the enemy units. It was a capital joke, but of course we did not intend to be too realistic, especially as in this case the enemy were our best friends. We should not have eaten their lunch and left them to go hungry. We meant to keep the mules just long enough to annoy our friends, and then release them. But before we could do this a General on the other side came over to protest and to order their release. At this moment an umpire came up and explained to the General that, as he was in the midst of the enemy, he must consider himself a prisoner.

This naturally annoyed him very much, and as the umpire only held the rank of Lieut.-Colonel, the General constituted himself a bigger umpire and reversed his decision on the plea that he had not come over to us in a tactical way but merely to adjust a matter connected with the feeding of the troops. To this the umpire was about to yield when another umpire came up, a General this time and a bigger one than the first one, and he confirmed our capture.

We were not allowed to lead the captured General about with us for the rest of the day as we should have liked to have done, but he was put out of action and released.

That really was a day of triumph. Towards the evening we happened to be the nearest troops to the supply depot for that night and the result was that nothing could dislodge us. The enemy hurled his best troops at us in masses, and we were out-numbered ten to one, but the decision had always to be given in our favour, and we won a glorious victory. That, coupled with the capture of a General, and the Mess mules, constituted a day of really splendid memory.

Operations came to an end at Delhi, where we went into camp and polished ourselves up to take part in the great Durbar organized by Lord Curzon to celebrate the Coronation of King Edward VII.

After the Durbar we returned to Mian Mir, where we spent the whole summer without leave, in the midst of a very bad cholera epidemic.

Having no leave we had to extract what fun we could out of life by open-air concerts and theatricals. Soldiers are fond of melodrama, and I remember, on one of the hottest nights of the year when the thermometer was over 100 degrees at midnight, a play in which the heroine was dying in a snowstorm. The snow was represented by falling pieces of newspaper which looked most unconvincing, but the freezing heroine looked still more unreal with streams of perspiration pouring down her face.

To get some little change I decided to bicycle to Ferozepore with my wife on a nice sunny day in June. I never want to do it again. The distance is only fifty miles, but with the thermometer at 122 degrees in the shade on a blinding white shadeless road, I wonder now that either of us ever reached our destination.

At the end of this year, 1903, I left for a year's leave in England which I felt I badly needed. My malaria continued to trouble me till we were on board ship, but I comforted my wife by telling her that the sea air would soon put me right. But it did not. On the contrary, I grew worse and worse, and just when we were off Gibraltar the disease suddenly took the form of bleeding, and in a few minutes I lost nearly all the blood in my body. Then I laid down and died. I was not in any great pain and the sensation of dying was soothing and pleasant. The doctor informed me that he had no hope of saving my life, and warned me to bid farewell to my wife, which I did, handing her my keys and giving her a few parting words of advice. Then I grew cold and stiff and turned up my toes and slipped into oblivion.

A few minutes later (which I believe was in fact twenty-four hours) I came to life again, much to every one's astonishment, and have continued so ever since. As usual in such tragic moments, farce was always at my elbow. I remember being amused, just before the crisis occurred, at the bewilderment of the young doctor who was in charge of the ship's hospital.

I fancy he had only just emerged from the chrysalis stage and was in fact not much more than a fairly competent but unpractised medical student. He had probably looked forward to the voyage as a sort of yachting holiday and had never dreamt of being landed with a case of complicated malaria; a disease of which I am sure he knew nothing. But at least he knew the rules of correct medical procedure and firmly refused to cut me open, as I begged him to do, to see what was going on inside me; and he was a good nurse too, sitting by my bedside throughout the five days until we reached Liverpool.

I remember his last words to me just before I left for the evergreen shore were to the effect that if I could keep still for twenty-four hours I might pull through. Considering that I am the most restless of individuals, never lying quiet even in my sleep, I smiled at the hopelessness of his advice. But I did for the first and only time in my life succeed in remaining motionless · for the necessary length of time.

Before leaving the ship he wrote out a detailed account of my malady, which I presented to the great malaria specialist Sir Patrick Manson when I was conveyed to his residence in London the day after landing. On reading the account he said that there must be some mistake in it because if I had had the symptoms described I must be dead. I replied that I thought the doctor's account was probably correct and his surmise equally so because, as far as I knew, I had been dead.

He gave me a very drastic treatment which involved daily injections into various muscles of my body for a long period, at the end of which I was quite restored to health and I have never had malaria since. I suppose that in losing all the blood out of my body the poor little microbes had to go along with it, and as I have had to lead a more careful life from that time with a wife to prevent me from doing stupid things, they have never had another chance of getting hold of me.

Two bouts of rheumatic fever and all this malaria ought to have left me a wreck, but as a matter of fact I soon found myself as fit as I had ever been.

Having suffered myself from very acute malaria it has interested me to note how the British Public is hypnotized by the mention of this common disease.

I frequently notice in the accounts of proceedings in a magistrate's court, cases where a prisoner is being tried for some such offence as the theft of a gold watch, or the embezzlement of a large sum of money. The evidence is all against the prisoner who pleads guilty, but just as the judge is about to pronounce sentence a comrade of the accused rushes into court and gives evidence that the prisoner once suffered from an attack of malaria. On receipt of this information the judge bursts into tears and in a voice trembling with emotion orders the prisoner to be discharged. I do not see why similar rules should not apply with regard to chicken-pox, but for some obscure reason malaria appears to hold a monopoly.

Nearly every one who has been in India has suffered at one time or another from malaria — at least I may say that in my time all the best people had it — and as I have suffered more severely than most, I want some one to explain to me the connection between malaria and freedom of responsibility for crime.

After spending a sufficient time at home to enable me to visit my relations, I decided to set off on a prolonged tour in Europe with my wife. Endeavours were made to dissuade us on the grounds that I was not yet well enough and also that we could not afford so expensive a trip.

The first objection was trifling, but the second was more serious. I had no money, but I seldom have had, and there are ways of getting round that difficulty, and I reflected that one only lives one's life once and that it is one's duty to get as much out of it in a reasonable way as one can. Knowing that the Angel of Death is very close to us all our lives, we may as well fill up the little time we may have on this earth as usefully as possible. There is nothing gloomy in dwelling on this fact. More than anything it has helped me to be in life the pronounced optimist that I am known to be. A reflection of this nature taken in the proper way tends to make one all the more lively, both spiritually and materially. Do what you can as quickly as you can while in this world without forgetting that there certainly is another life beyond. We know this without having to call upon the Spirits for corroboration.

With the kind assistance of people who do that sort of thing, I procured a large bag of money and set forth to revisit my favourite haunts in Europe. In this way we were able to see Paris, Moscow, Petersburg, Helsingfors and Stockholm, and I have never regretted the undertaking.

We left for Paris in June, and passing through Dover old friends who were living there kindly came down to the steamer to see us off by the morning boat. The party consisted of a lady, her daughter, a schoolgirl of about fourteen years of age, and a schoolgirl friend of hers.

They came on board and we had a pleasant chat, but when I observed signs of activity on the part of the ship's crew I gathered that the ship might be about to leave, and knowing that cross-Channel steamers dart off like lightning and give little warning, I suggested that our friends might like to go on shore. But I was told that there was no hurry; they lived in Dover and were accustomed to these boats and would know quite well when it was time to go. Feeling snubbed I subsided, and a few minutes later we were bounding over the sea *en route* for France. My friend then suggested that I should ask them to stop the ship as they did not want to go to France. I knew that we might as well try to stop the stars in their courses, but as a matter of politeness I could not do less than ask. So I addressed a man with some gold braid on his cap and begged him to stop the ship and go back to Dover. I cannot remember his reply, but I know that it was expressed in words that I could not allow myself to repeat and it was to the effect that the ship would not stop. So, while anxious friends in Dover awaited in vain their return to lunch, they were having a pleasant and unexpected trip to France. It was very amusing, but rather a costly joke for them.

Upon arrival at Calais they kindly offered to come and see us off by the Paris train, but this I firmly forbade. I had visions of the same thing happening again and the whole party doing a tour in France, while anxious relatives in Dover were organizing search parties and informing the police of their strange disappearance.

In Paris we renewed our acquaintance with friends in the French army whom we had known in China, but saw little of a military nature. From Paris we went to Friederichshafen on Lake Constance to inspect the airships being constructed by Count Zeppelin, whose name was given to this new engine of war which was destined to play a large part ten years later in the Great War. The inventor did not live, happily for him, to see the complete failure of his dirigibles in the early years of the war.

From there we went to Berlin, where we had many acquaintances in the German army and navy who received us most hospitably. Here I was able to see a good deal of the troops, being permitted to ride on the Tempelhof parade-ground and watch the infantry at their training. Their equipment was better than ours in several respects and especially in the matter of range-finders. But in efficiency it appeared to me that we had nothing to learn from them.

From Berlin we went to Moscow and saw the Russian troops there and at Petersburg, but I was not able to see anything in the way of manœuvres. We crossed to Helsingfors by steamer from Petersburg and thence to Stockholm, whence we travelled across Sweden by canal and took steamer back to England from Göteborg.

The financial result of this pleasant trip was disastrous, and as my prospects in the army looked very gloomy – I was quite blocked for promotion – I decided once more to leave the service and accept an offer of civil employment in North China. But the Russo-Japanese War upset all arrangements in that part of the world and I stayed on. It was fortunate that I did so, as the promotion block was just about to melt away.

CHAPTER XV

FAKIRS AND FINANCE

On my return to London I found that I had been appointed officiating second-in-command of the 26th Punjabis and I left.in November to join that regiment on the frontier at Dera Ismail Khan, arriving there soon after Christmas 1904. I had no sooner reported my arrival than I was ordered to Rawal Pindi for railway work in connection with a large concentration of troops assembled for manœuvres on the occasion of the visit to India of H.R.H. the Prince of Wales – now King George V. On completion of this duty I returned to my new regiment which was then commanded by Colonel Dillon, one of the most able officers of the Indian Army.

I had the prospect of succeeding to the command of this regiment in three years' time when Colonel Dillon's tenure would end, and though I regretted leaving my old regiment I felt that I was fortunate to have joined a particularly smart battalion and one famous for its good shooting.

Early in 1905 there was fresh trouble in Waziristan and we mobilized with great rapidity, reaching Tank by forced marches in record time, only to find that we were not needed as the tribes had submitted. After a short delay in Tank we returned to cantonments and settled down to our usual training with nothing to enliven us except the disastrous earthquake that destroyed Dharmsala; we felt it severely, though no damage was done.

By a peculiar coincidence my old regiment, the 20th Punjabis, was now ordered to Dera Ismail Khan, and I was soon fated to rejoin it, owing to the sudden death of Colonel Dillon, which left the command of the 26th Punjabis vacant while I was still too junior to hope for the appointment. I accordingly returned to the 20th as second-in-command under Colonel P. Walker.

During the following eight years, up to the outbreak of the Great War, we led the usual uneventful life of soldiers in peace-time. In 1906 we marched through the Sherani country, where there had recently been some trouble with the tribesmen. It was an interesting march through new country, but as a military affair it was not exciting as we met with no opposition. The Sheranis must have thoroughly enjoyed a visit from troops who paid high prices for all supplies and were able to help them in various ways.

The country was roadless, and we often found it impossible to get even pack-mules over some of the hill tracks. On such occasions the Sappers came to the front and soon cleared a road by means of explosives. The sight of solid rocks being blown to smithereens delighted the tribesmen, who besieged us with requests for private performances of the same nature.

All their cultivation is dependent on a rough-and-ready irrigation system, and in a country mostly composed of rocks and stones it is often difficult to make a water-channel run just where you want it to. It is all right up to a certain point and then a big boulder blocks the way and the channel can go no farther. It was in such cases that they found the Sirkar's troops a heaven-sent blessing, as we were able to blast a rock for them in a few hours that would have taken them years to move by ordinary methods. If we had granted all their requests, we should have soon had no explosives left.

In January 1908 I succeeded to the command of the 20th Punjabis and found that the fad for that year was semaphore signalling by Officers and N.C.O.'s. The semaphore alphabet is very easy to learn and with a little practice fair efficiency is attained, but as a method of conveying information it has very weak points.

The first is that with a megaphone the voice will reach, especially in the hills, as far as the sight. If you are near enough to read the small flag signals you are also near enough to hear a megaphone. To this the advocate of the semaphore will reply: 'Yes, perhaps. But in action the sound of firing will render the voice useless.' That is quite true, but it cuts both ways. If the noise of firing prevents me from using my voice the enemy's bullets will prevent me from using my flags.

At manœuvres, however, they are splendid, and no amount of blank ammunition will prevent an officer standing up in the open within 800 yards of the enemy's position and signalling 'Where is the Mess mule?'

Although I did not believe that we were likely to

derive much benefit from this system of signalling, I had to carry out the orders I had received and I eventually succeeded, as I thought, in getting the officers fairly proficient.

A little later we marched out into the hilly country round Pezu to carry out our annual test and I think we acquitted ourselves pretty well. As a matter of fact, we gained a very good report. But the semaphore let me down badly.

I knew the G.O.C. was very keen on it, and while he happened to be standing by my side I saw a splendid opportunity of displaying our skill. The General and myself were standing on the edge of a cliff overlooking a deep nullah on the other side of which my transport officer was guiding a string of camels to their destination.

From my higher position I could see the lie of the land better than he could, and I saw that if he wheeled to the left he would get on to a better track. So I pulled out my flags and called him up. He produced his flags and prepared to take my message which was 'Left wheel better path.' As he ticked off each word with his flag and sent R.D. in the correct manner, I turned to the General with a sycophantic smile to receive his approbation, when, to my horror, this miserable officer (who did not know the General was by my side) put his megaphone to his lips, awakening the echoes among the rocks as he bellowed, 'I can't understand a word of your message.'

Well, well. Just another of life's little tragedies.

Soon after this inspection the regiment marched to Jhelum, where it remained until the outbreak of the Great War. Jhelum as a training centre for infantry is ideal. The cantonments lie on the right bank of the river and are surrounded at a distance of a few miles by low hills and broken ground which afford splendid sites for battalion or company training camps. By dividing the circle into four segments we could secure fresh ground every year for four years.

There was good mahseer-fishing in the neighbourhood, but not much in the way of shooting. There were always plenty of quail, however, in the autumn and, as I am not a particularly good game shot, I looked forward to the quail season.

Shooting in England, I have been able to hold my own, but have sometimes not done very well. A gamekeeper on one occasion had the temerity to say within my hearing that he did not think much of my shooting. I wish I could have sent him to the Punjab to learn politeness. In that happy land when one misses the birds the shikari is always ready to attribute it to anything but your own lack of skill. The well-known story of the Colonel and shikari is a fine example of this. The Colonel fired off quantities of cartridges, but did little execution among the birds. Some one said to the shikari: 'The Colonel is a very bad shot, isn't he?' To which the shikari replied: 'Not at all. He is a wonderful shot. But God is merciful to the birds.'

While in Jhelum we had quite a glut of night marches, some instructive, but all amusing. Led by a

Staff Officer with a compass, on one occasion, the leading battalion of the Brigade, winding along the bed of a dry torrent in the dark, became suddenly aware of troops in front of them, but before any disastrous action could take place it was luckily discovered that the enemy troops were the tail of their own column, which had tied itself up in a knot and formed a complete circle.

On another occasion we attempted a very risky form of night march, and the result showed very clearly the danger of it. It helped to impress on my mind the sound rule, 'Do not do anything at night except the very simplest and most straightforward of movements. Do not attempt anything the success of which depends on any combination of movements.'

In this case the enemy held a position in a low range of hills facing south.

We crept up by night in two columns, by different routes, timed to meet at a certain point at dawn and combine in rushing the position.

Our column carried out its march apparently quite successfully, but just as dawn was beginning to break, and before we could get in touch with the other column, we suddenly found ourselves face to face with the enemy at a distance of 600 yards.

This was clearly no case for hesitation, so we let him have it with a volley and then charged with a ringing cheer, only to find that the supposed enemy was none other than our missing column. How the two columns got so far astray I do not know — I am

H

glad I was not leading – but the fact is that instead of facing north, as we should have been, we were facing east and west, and while we were endeavouring to slaughter one another, the enemy quietly took us in flank and we were decimated.

We hoped to be able to extricate ourselves before the Divisional General could be roused from his camp to see the fun, but unluckily he was a particularly wakeful man and was on the spot in good time to witness our discomfiture. He was very liverish in the early morning and had none of that 'Kruschen feeling' about him. What he said will not really bear repeating.

Generals have an unfortunate knack of turning up where they are not wanted and of hearing or seeing what they are not meant to hear and see. Even a deaf General can hear at a time when he should not.

I knew one General, a man of great keenness and ability, who was really quite deaf, in fact, it was this disability that prevented him going farther than he did in the army. Yet even his deafness would yield as by a miracle when something was said that he should under no circumstances be allowed to hear. Remarks from one Staff Officer to another (very bad form) in an ordinary voice could be made with impunity within a few yards of him. Such remarks, for instance, as 'the old man is very stuffy this morning' never caused the tympanum of his ear to vibrate, but I remember one occasion when he suddenly heard what was certainly not meant for his ears.

It was in cantonments during part of the annual

inspection of a battalion. The General had been minutely examining the equipment and accoutrements of the men, and after spending some four hours of the forenoon in this way appeared quite untired. The Staff were hungry and looked anxiously at their watches. At last one said to another, 'Can't you get him off it for a bit? We shan't get any lunch this way. Tell him you've got some urgent papers for him to sign.' The suggestion was acted on and the General was begged to hasten home to sign important papers, to which he replied: 'All right. I can do that very well in the office with the Head Clerk, and I'll take the opportunity of a bit of lunch while I'm away. You can keep busy till I come back. I don't like the way these accoutrements are marked. Let three of the companies go and have their food while you check the numbers on the belts, frogs and clings of the fourth company, then carry on with the others. I'll be back soon.'

He returned with a grim smile at 4.30.

In Jhelum many of our old pensioners turned up to visit the regiment. One old friend came to see me about his son who had got into trouble. Arsla Khan had retired as a Subadar, and his son was now a Jemadar on probation in the regiment. The latter had, after several warnings, committed a serious breach of discipline, and his general behaviour had been such that I had reluctantly to tell him that I could not keep him in the regiment and that he had better return to his home. On receiving this intimation, he showed his

intelligence by dispatching at once an S.O.S. telegram to his father, who had now arrived to plead his
cause.

I pointed out to the old man the heinousness of his
son's offences, but he continued to beg that I would
forgive him for the sake of our old friendship. I
remained obdurate, however, until he deprived me
of all further power of argument by saying: 'Well,
Sahib, after all, what does it amount to? Just the usual
high spirits of a young man. You yourself, I well
remember, were young once, and I can call to mind
many wild pranks in which you were concerned.'
Terrified at what he might be going to recount of my
youthful misdemeanours before my Adjutant, who was
in the room with me, I beat a hurried retreat and
agreed to pardon his son. I am glad I did. He lived
to create a splendid record in the Great War, and was
killed in action in Mesopotamia.

Another old friend whom I had known for many
years, 'Dumbari', the eccentric fakir, paid me frequent
visits. He was a quaint fellow with a saucy humour,
and very picturesque in his coat of many colours,
carrying his wooden rifle and pistol decorated with
regimental badges. I hope he is alive still, but I have
not heard from him for some years.

He and I first met several years before the China
War, and I remember receiving from him while I was
in China a memo of dues claimed. He said: 'I shall
require from you at least a hundred rupees on your
return to India. Your absence at the war has pre-

vented you from bestowing alms on me for the last two years, and as you have also had a son born to you, you will be glad to grant additional charity, in God's name, to this humble fakir.'

I had no objection to his visiting the men's barracks on pay-day to pick up what he could, but I had to draw the line when he wanted me to issue an order that every man should be compelled to give him a fixed sum out of his salary.

He was very outspoken and his witticisms often got him into trouble. Meeting the regiment on the march one day, he presented arms to me with his wooden rifle and then fell in behind my horse at the head of the regiment. The leading company was commanded by a very old Subadar whom Dumbari greeted with a salaam. Then in course of conversation I heard him say: 'You are getting very old, Subadar-Sahib, yet you keep well, and may God grant you continued health and long life, but you are blocking promotion. Why don't you get out of the way and let one of the younger men have your place?' The Subadar was very angry, all the more so because there was so much sense in Dumbari's remarks.

At the time of the Delhi Durbar he came to me and induced me to pay his railway fare to Delhi, where he expected to reap a rich harvest, but he came back to me the next day very forlorn, having been deported from Delhi by the police as a dangerous character and forbidden to return on pain of imprisonment. He certainly looked startling enough in his gaudy rags, but he was quite harmless and not half as mad as he pretended to be. He received large sums in charity, but he spent most of his gains in feeding other less fortunate fakirs.

The Christian idea of charity is that one should conceal one's virtues in this respect and give in secret. But this was not possible with Dumbari, who, in gratitude to me for my offering, used to advertise largely and with great exaggeration the amount of my gift. Thus, when I gave him five rupees he would run through the bazar, leaping in the air, brandishing his wooden rifle, and crying: 'May God grant health and long life to the Colonel Sahib Bahadur, who has just given me five hundred rupees!'

If I had only known it, I could better have afforded to have given him five hundred rupees than to have undertaken the small financial operation into which some kind friends led me about that time.

A man had invented some wonderful boots with changeable heels and soles. The uppers did for all purposes and you slid on suitable heels and soles as required. You could carry several changes in your pocket, and after coming in from shooting, if you wanted to play tennis, you just slid off your heavy soles and put on rubbers. After tennis you might wish to dance, in which case you exchanged the rubbers for dancing-soles in the twinkling of an eye. The fact that you might be needing a bath in the intervals does not affect the matter. The idea was a clever one and I put £100 into the venture, which I never saw again.

I had not got £100, and I did not want to invest in anything. But my friends insisted on my securing a share in this golden enterprise, so I got the £100 from somewhere else, and had to pay it back again after it had disappeared.

During the whole time we were in Jhelum, plague was rampant in the city, and it shows the wonderful result of proper sanitation that we never had a single case in cantonments. The only white people living and working in the city were the missionaries, and these wonderful people carried on, as they always do, as if circumstances were quite normal.

Before leaving Jhelum I paid a visit to the Pir Sahib at Makhad, which I shall remember all my life. The Pir Sahib is a Mahomedan hereditary saint, guardian of a holy shrine. To reach it you have to wander along the frontier railway line in slow trains, and after many changes you arrive at a small station called Makhad Road. From there you ride about seven miles till you arrive at the shrine on the left bank of the Indus.

I was due at the station at about 8 p.m., and knowing that there were no facilities for food there, I had a big dinner in the refreshment-room at Daud Khel Junction. I ate heartily because I was hungry and I saw no prospect of any more food for a long time. About an hour later I reached Makhad Road station and was met by a large party of old regimental pensioners and attendants of the Pir Sahib, who conducted me in state to a large room in the station where I was

horrified to find an enormous dinner prepared for
me!

Such is Oriental hospitality. This good man had
sent some hundreds of miles for the complete rig-out
– cooks, table-servants and wines included. I said I
was very sorry but I could not eat. An influential
native officer of my regiment drew me aside and said:
'Sahib, you've got to eat it, and to eat it all. It is for
the honour of the regiment. The Pir Sahib will be
mortally offended, and we shall all be covered with
shame if you don't eat it.' So I let out my belt and
sat solemnly down to eat my second dinner.

As usual on these occasions, there were numerous
onlookers, and they were careful to see that I omitted
nothing – I was told that if I did, some of the Pir
Sahib's attendants would let him know and the honour
of the regiment would be trailed in the mud. There
wasn't even a dog handy to accept surreptitious
morsels under the table!

It may not be a proud record to boast of, but I think
it probably is a world's record – two complete dinners
in a space of three hours.

I took the opportunity while I was up in this part
of the world of visiting a very distinguished old
retired Indian Officer of the regiment. He had been
twice to England and had been Orderly Officer to
His Majesty the King. After all this grandeur and
the fine achievements of his lifetime in the army, it
was quaint to find him in his little village, far from
civilization, in a rough country that was mostly rocks

and where the only occupations were the tending of a few goats or the tilling of very unlikely-looking patches of barren soil. 'It certainly is a poor country,' he said, 'but it's my home, and it's all I want.'

In the course of his travels he had collected a good many *souvenirs*. One of the towels he gave me to wash with bore the monogram of a well-known English railway, another proclaimed the ownership of the s.s. *Mongolia*. Tumblers also indicated a similar origin, the P. & O. being the principal sufferers.

I called his attention to these, and he said: 'Yes, I generally take all I need in that way. These big companies have lots of things like that, and they would hardly mind my keeping one or two for myself.' He had no idea that he was 'robbing' the companies, but regarded these articles as gifts from them to him.

I never saw him again till he came to visit me in Peshawar in 1915. It was a long way for him to travel and, although we were always good friends, I wondered if it was pure friendship that had brought him. It looked like that because he had no petition of any sort to urge, which is unusual in the case of such visits.

Afterwards I found he was engaged in a plot which culminated in a lawsuit, and his visit to me had been craftily arranged to provide an 'alibi'. But it did not work and the whole family came to sad grief over the failure of the plot, which involved the murder of several people. There was, of course, a woman in the case, and what we call murder was just retribution under Pathan law; but, unfortunately, the Pathans on the left bank of the Indus come under our tamer laws and have to suffer for it.

It seems hard to apply our laws to people of another civilization who have laws of their own differing drastically from ours. This is especially the case where women are concerned. Our whole outlook on the position of women is diametrically opposed to theirs.

The freedom of our women with their uncovered faces is always a shock to them, their women living always in strict seclusion and never showing their faces to any man but their husband. Imagine the feelings of the young Indian soldier who joins the band and takes part for the first time in playing at a regimental dance. He sees, to his horror, the Colonel's wife, not only with face uncovered, but many other odd bits here and there, dressed in a fantastic costume and smiling or chatting with all the men. Then, more dreadful still, he sees a Captain of another regiment place his arm round her waist, clasp her firmly to his bosom, and whirl her round in the giddy maze of the dance. It is all very shocking to a man who will not even mention the name of his wife outside the family circle.

Once a year we have to write up the men's kindred rolls, and the name of the wife is important, as without it she will be unable to draw her widow's pension in the case of his death on service. Even when this is explained to the man, one may have to argue and persuade for half an hour before he gives you the required information in a whisper. So one sees that East is East and West is West, and the gulf must for ever remain unbridgeable, if for no other reason than for the entire divergence of our points of view regarding womenfolk.

In the summer of 1911 I was delighted at the birth of a daughter. As is usual on such occasions, the Indian Officers came in a body to offer their congratulations. The spokesman ended up by saying: 'We do this because we know that with your people the birth of a female is considered a matter of congratulation. For ourselves we regard it as a misfortune.' Female infanticide would save India from a preponderance of women, but a tyrannical Government will not permit it. Perhaps, after all, India is not so bad as China, where a notice-board may be seen beside the village pond bearing the inscription, 'Girls may not be drowned here.'

During the last year of my command I obtained long leave to pay a farewell visit to our favourite haunts in Kashmir. We badly needed a change – the baby was very ill, my wife was not very well, and I was certainly out of sorts.

As usual, we started our trip by wandering about the river and lakes in house-boats with matting roofs. It rained heavily and the roofs leaked, but no other boats were procurable and we had to make the best of what we could get.

Boat-life in rainy weather is a dull affair, but the only medical assistance procurable was in Srinagar, so I dared not venture moving off into camp in the higher mountains. The only break in the monotony was

afforded by my small son, aged seven, who fell into the
river. I luckily heard the splash and ran out in time to
see one small foot above water being carried down
stream. Being lightly clad, it was not a difficult task to
jump in and rescue him.

At last, as the doctors seemed unable to cure our ail-
ments, I decided on a desperate measure — to take the
responsibility of the baby, who appeared to be dying,
and to move the whole family up into camp at a higher
elevation, away from any prospect of assistance.

So we discharged our boatmen and started up the
Sind Valley, doing the three marches to Sonamarg without any catastrophe. Here I selected a beautiful site
for a camp, on the edge of the meadows at the foot of a
big forest, and looking out over the glaciers of the
Tejwaz Valley. We arrived on June 1, in the last snowstorm of the year, and remained until snow was ready to
fall again on October 1. The change of climate did
wonders for us all from the very first day of our arrival.
The river at Srinagar is about 5,000 feet above sea-
level and our camp was at 9,000 feet.

It takes a long time to settle a large party comfortably into camp. For the first month there was constant
work to be done, making paths, digging a garden, and
constructing an irrigation channel to water the garden.
After that we spent our time climbing the mountains
and exploring the glaciers. Many friends joined us and
we soon had a very large camp. Its fame spread so far
that one lady wrote asking my wife what her terms
were!

I had chosen Sonamarg for our camp, because it is the least crowded of all Kashmir camping-sites. It has no attractions beyond those of natural beauty. Most visitors go to Gulmarg, where there are hotels and clubs, and golf, tennis and bridge. Sonamarg was therefore left almost entirely to us and some missionary friends of the C.M.S., and also some American Presbyterians — not at all dull companions, although so many people have a stupid idea that missionaries cannot be cheerful.

A strange man came to the Marg one day and decided to pitch his tent a few yards from my camp. I thought it rather bad manners, but said nothing about it. The nearest tent of my camp to his abode was the one outside which I used to invite the missionaries to hold a Sunday service.

These services in the open air were very inspiring and we sang our hymns with great vigour. Perhaps the idea of the old tunes of the Ancient and Modern ringing through these primeval forests may sound a little incongruous to those inclined to cavil, but there is another side to that question.

In any case, the singing had an unexpectedly happy result, as it drove the stranger away from my camp. I really had no cause at all to dislike the poor man, but he had pitched exactly on the source of my water-supply and that annoyed me very much. So I was not at all sorry to find one morning that he had packed up and gone. I was wandering round my camp when I suddenly noticed that his tent had disappeared. On walking up to inspect the site he had recently occupied, I found a poetic effusion pinned on the trunk of a tree. It was quite wittily written in the style of Omar Khayyam, and was to the effect that he had travelled all the way from Lahore to find rest and quiet amid the charms of nature, only to find that his life was made intolerable by the bawling of hymns during his late morning slumbers.

Poor fellow! He may read these lines and know that I am sorry. But my obvious reply, which he may also read, is that, if he desired rest and solitude, he should not have tucked himself up as it were under my wing when he had at least 4,000 acres of suitable ground to pitch his tent on.

During our Sonamarg period we had no adventures, but the majority of our friends or guests were ladies and they kept things fairly lively among themselves. The meadows are a favourite grazing-ground for large herds of cattle, and buffaloes, inspired by curiosity, have a way of poking their heads into your tent at night.

The snorting of a buffalo is very terrifying, and when one is roused from one's slumbers by this blood-curdling sound, one assumes a tiger, or at least a bear, as the author of the snorts.

One lady, awakened in this way, bravely bashed a kettle in the face of the intruder. The kettle-handle got round his horn and he danced away through the camp in a panic, and neither he nor the kettle were ever seen again.

Unfortunately, this was a very patent sort of kettle borrowed from another lady, and the incident led to a certain coolness. There is no need to give more of such incidents, which were frequent enough.

In October we returned to Jhelum with renewed health. About Christmas-time the head Yogi from Yogi-Tillah, whose acquaintance I had made long ago, came to see me, bringing with him his 'chela' or disciple. We had long talks together on spiritual subjects, and my vanity was much flattered by his turning every now and then to his chela and saying: 'Note what he says.'

But the real object of his visit was to borrow a rifle with which to shoot a leopard that was causing much trouble in his neighbourhood. Students of the occult will be as surprised as I was at this request. I should have thought he ought to have been able to down that leopard with a glance of his eye.

In January 1914 my tenure of command, with one year's extension, making six years in all, came to an end, and I severed my connection with my old battalion twenty-five years after the date of my joining. I think there is possibly nothing so sad in life as this parting from a regiment in which one has spent all the best years of manhood. There is nothing quite comparable to it in civil life. Soldiers of all ranks are thrown so closely together in peace and war that they become knit by ties which are stronger than any other human ties, the breaking of which is a sad episode in one's life.

It is a pleasure to me to feel that those ties have been

in a measure restored by my having been appointed, in 1924, Colonel of my old regiment, which helps me to keep in touch with it, and not to feel entirely cast out of the fold.

CHAPTER XVI

THE GREAT WAR – FRANCE

AFTER handing over my command I left for England, where I had leisure to enjoy life while awaiting further employment in the higher grades, which I had been told I might hope for. I expected to return to India in the autumn.

Meantime I did what I could to prevent myself from getting rusty, and had the very good fortune to be invited by General Maxse to attend the manœuvres of the 1st Guards' Brigade near Aldershot in July. Here I had the opportunity of seeing to what a high standard efficiency can be brought, and on the whole I learnt a great deal. I was treated with great hospitality and was shown everything there was to see. A good many harmless witticisms were indulged in at my expense, and I was referred to as 'the Indian Colonel'. Surprise was expressed at my not having a red face and white whiskers, which were supposed to be the outward sign of Indian Colonels. When iced claret-cup was on the table, I was asked if I would prefer brandy-pawnee. When I accepted a slice of chicken, apologies were made for the absence of curry, which was assumed to be my normal diet. And at three o'clock in the afternoon came the daily joke: 'Hullo, Dunsterville. You still here? I thought you Indian gentlemen always had a siesta about this time!'

During the manœuvres I also had the opportunity of my first flight in an aeroplane, being taken up by my

gallant nephew, Bay Harvey-Kelly, who was among
the best of our airmen at the beginning of the war, and
continued to harass the Germans until his plane was
shot down and he joined the vast host of brave men who
gave their lives for their country.

Thus, when war broke out in the beginning of
August, I felt that I was as ready as any man could be,
and immediately applied to the War Office for employment in any capacity. There was at this time no hint of
the Indian Army being called on to take part in the
European phase of the struggle, and, as many people
thought the war would be over by Christmas, I felt I
could not afford to waste any time.

I was more or less informed by the War Office that
Indian Colonels weren't particularly wanted, but at last
I succeeded in being appointed a train-conducting
officer in France, on the grounds of my knowledge of
the French language. So I scrambled together some
uniform and kit in twenty-four hours and reported myself at Le Havre on August 23.

Family finance at this period was in a tragic state,
and but for the courtesy of my bankers things would
have been very difficult. I wrote explaining the situation, and asking for an overdraft for the family, and
received an immediate reply to the effect that at a crisis
like the present they considered it their duty to do what
they could to help, and so would be glad to allow what
I asked for. I may freely say that, throughout my
career, my bank has been to me — as the Indians say — a
father and mother.

In order to explain the duties of a train-conducting officer, it will be necessary to give some idea of the difficulties of the railway-supply system.

Owing to the natural confusion of the early stages of a war, intensified by the rapid retirement from Mons, the French railways were not working very smoothly. I do not reproach them for it; it is wonderful that they were able to do as much as they did when most of their best men had been called away to join the colours.

Of course, the nearer you were to the railhead the greater the confusion became, and it was found that trains conveying British rations failed to reach their destinations. So one of us was allotted to each train, and it was our business to see that the train reached its proper destination, if that had not already fallen into the hands of the enemy, and to bring back the empty trains to the Base to be refilled. It was extremely interesting work, though not of a heroic nature. Still, it was better than doing nothing at home, and I hoped I might be able to secure something more lively later on.

It was pretty rough work at first. We spent several days away on each trip from the Base, and during that time had to get what comfort we could in an ordinary covered railway truck. The train was naturally full, but one could generally find a half-filled truck in which one could sleep fairly comfortably among cheeses and sides of bacon. But I never knew before what goods-train shunting is like. I wonder if any railway-man knows what it is like from the inside of a truck: to get the best effect, it must be a half-filled truck, and it must be on a

French railway and in war-time – the two latter points for the reason that all shunting was 'fly' shunting, which is unusual, or forbidden, in England, and the shortage of Staff meant generally that some fellow who should have been at hand to put on a brake was generally among the missing numbers. In 'fly' shunting the line of trucks is pushed over an elevation of some ten feet or so, sufficient to give a tremendous impetus to your un-coupled truck when you break away from the line of trucks being manœuvred. Then you fizz down one of the forming-up lines until you hit something. Then you stop. But the things in the half-empty truck do not stop. They contain the momentum of the original speed and employ this by hurtling through the air from one end of the truck to the other. I dreaded that night-time rearrangement of trains at junctions. It was just a series of violent collisions, and not always successful attempts to defend oneself from cheeses and sides of bacon that hurled themselves at one. All very funny and amusing, perhaps, to read about, but you can be killed by a flying cheese as well as by a shell – and what an ignominious epitaph that would furnish!

Fancy our widows sharing condolences. 'My hus-band was killed in an aeroplane after having downed six enemy planes in one morning. And yours, dear?' 'Mine was killed in a railway truck by a Double Glou-cester.'

As a matter of fact, my orderly was nearly killed on one occasion by the crashing of boxes of stores, but they just missed his head and he escaped with cuts and bruises the whole length of his legs. Later on, when things got into order, one passenger carriage was attached to each train for our use and that of officers proceeding to and from the front.

The French people were full of enthusiasm for the British troops who had come over to help in the war, and whenever we stopped at a station we were offered fruit and other eatables and bottles of wine. In vain I pointed out that we were not among the heroes, that we had not fought and probably never would. I begged them to keep all these good things for the fighting men, but they would not listen to me and continued to shower gifts on us while robbing us of all our buttons and badges as 'souvenirs'. They were extremely nice and kind to us then, but twelve years is a long time and memories are short.

Many amusing incidents occurred to relieve the dullness of our duties. One day my train was in the goods yard on the far side of the passenger station at Boulogne. To leave on its journey it had to pass through the main station. While waiting for the start, another train-conducting officer came into my carriage to talk to me. Presently the train began to move off, and I warned him to jump out. But he said: 'Oh no, it's quite all right. They always pull up at the main station.' So he remained till we came to the main station, but there were no signs of a stop; on the contrary, we continued to gather speed, until it became obvious that we had made a definite start on our journey.

On this the officer flew to the window and, thrusting

his head and arms outside with fierce gesticulations, screamed, 'Arrêtez le train. Arrêtez le train.' The French officials on duty, and the private individuals on the platform, seeing a British officer gesticulating in this fashion, said to themselves: 'Here at last is an Englishman who has some life in him. He waves to us kind messages of *l'entente cordiale.*' So they responded with 'Bravo, les anglais. Hurrah, hurrah!'

To this my visitor responded with oaths and expressions of hatred, accentuated by clenched fists. But the more he shouted 'Arrêtez le train', the more they responded 'Bravo, les anglais', until the train passed out of the station, bearing the indignant officer away to the back of beyond. When he sank back exhausted on his seat, I informed him that according to my time-schedule I was a non-stop train for 100 miles. I exaggerated a little, but I wanted to enjoy myself. Fortune, however, favoured him in the end. We were stopped by signal some few miles down the line, and a train proceeding in the opposite direction being also stopped at the same point for a moment, he leaped from one to the other and got back to his train. This joke was in *Punch* later on, but there may have been two occurrences of the same nature.

On another occasion I had an amusing example of bounce. I was doing the duty of a junior officer, but I held the unusual rank of full Colonel, denoted by one crown and two stars on the shoulder-strap. One crown and two stars by moonlight look very much like three stars.

I brought back some German prisoners from the front, arriving somewhere in the middle of the night. A tall Major, the Railway Staff Officer, came to meet the train. I told him that I had 100 German prisoners to hand over. He asked me what escort I had. I replied that I had one N.C.O. and six men of the London Scottish. He suggested that that was ridiculously insufficient. I, who knew much more about it than he did, retorted that it was excessive. I said that if he dismissed the escort I would lead them all home on a string by myself. They were tired and glad to be prisoners, and wanted food and rest and no more war. Without concluding the argument, he turned on his heel and left me. I, knowing what a job it is to wake sleeping soldiers, thought to save time by rousing my Germans and forming them up on the platform, which I did, congratulating myself on having them all ready to march off in fours as soon as the Railway Staff Officer reappeared with instructions.

On his return, instead of the applause I had expected, this tall officer towered over me in wrath and asked what the devil I meant by getting the prisoners out when he had said that the escort was insufficient, and so on and so on.

I meekly retorted that I was doing my little best, whereupon he stormed at me: 'Now, look here, my lad, orders are orders. I am a Major and you are a Captain.' Here I cut him short with: 'Oh no. I'm sorry, I'm a Colonel.' I don't know who he was and I have never met him again so far as I know, but I would like to do

so and talk it over. He left me standing on the platform and disappeared into the darkness of the night,
while I made my own arrangements for the removal
of the prisoners. It was hard luck on him that by the
feeble illumination of the railway lamp one crown and
two stars should look so much like three stars.

I extracted a great deal of amusement also out of my
frequent conversations with the French soldiers. My
exalted rank was always an excellent joke for them,
because, when I was forced to mention it, they never
for a minute believed what I said — it was taken to be
an example of English dry humour. I suppose this
misunderstanding was due to their inability to believe
that a Colonel could be the best of pals with a private
soldier without risking the slackening of discipline.
Perhaps it is only in our army that there is this spirit
of genuine camaraderie pervading all ranks, which, so
far from loosening the ties of discipline, is a great
strengthening of those bonds.

I was sitting on a bench in the railway station of
Creil during the retirement. Our troops were withdrawing and my train was probably the last to leave
that station before the Germans marched in. Two
French soldiers came up and flung themselves down
on the bench, one on each side of me, and when they
found I could talk a little French they started an
animated conversation, in the course of which we
exchanged many friendly jokes.

The rank of full Colonel is indicated on the sleeves
of the khaki tunic by a great many lines of light-

coloured braid. One of my companions, observing this, asked me: '*Quel grade avez vous?*' to which I replied quite simply: '*Moi? moi je suis Colonel.*' This produced roars of delighted laughter from my two friends, one of whom slapped me on the back and said: '*Et moi – serai bientôt Général.*'

Of all armies, I think we are the most modest. We carry our modesty to such lengths that we deliberately conceal our rank by covering ourselves up in Burberrys or trench-coats, which are of the same pattern for all and show nothing to indicate rank. This is rather stupid and leads to trouble and misunderstanding. In some cases rank may be denoted by the head-dress, but in war-time even that distinction is usually missing.

I was with my train one morning in France at a station where a British sentry had been posted to stop any of our troops leaving the precincts. I walked out of the station, wearing my Burberry, without noticing him, he having at the moment carelessly turned his back on the exit to speak to some one. I had gone a few yards when I heard a voice say: ''Ere. Come back 'ere. Where are you goin' to?' It didn't interest me at all, but as it was somewhat angrily repeated, I turned round and became aware that it was I who was being addressed.

I obeyed his orders and moved in his direction, but not quick enough to satisfy him, for he shouted: 'Get a move on, you blighter. Come 'ere, and look slippy abaht it.' So I 'looked slippy' and hurriedly convinced him, to his confusion, that I had the necessary permission to leave the station. I also took the trouble to explain to him that he had taken quite the right action. A man in a Burberry may be a Field Marshal, or he may be a recruit.

The type of officer who wishes to catch his men out by coming upon them unawares is fortunately rare in our army. But, owing to this lack of distinguishing marks and to other circumstances, it has often happened to me to be an unwilling detective in such cases. Travelling with these ration-trains and living in a truck brought many such opportunities. You would hardly expect a recumbent figure wrapped in a Burberry, curled up with his head on a cheese in a railway truck, to prove to be a Colonel.

On one occasion I was awakened at night by two Frenchmen with a lantern who wanted to know if I would sell my warm underclothing! They fled in a hurry when they heard my reply.

As I mentioned before, we were soon shorn of our buttons and badges, which charming French ladies took away as 'souvenirs'. And our soldiers quickly learnt the use of this word, to which they gave a rather extended meaning. Thus on one occasion a soldier was seen to take up a large codfish from a fishmonger's stall and walk away with it. When the indignant fishmonger ran after him for payment, he waved the cod at him, smiling and repeating the magic word 'souvenir'.

On the Aisne I saw an old French peasant digging out his potatoes. A private soldier approached with a large bucket, which he calmly proceeded to fill. When he had done so he waved his arm in grateful thanks to the farmer, exclaiming 'Souvenir. Savvy? Souvenir', as he trotted off to camp with his spoil.

I might have stayed the rest of the war on the French railways, if I had wanted to, but by March 1915 it had really become nothing but a 'cushy' routine job. I resolved, therefore, to make a bid for something more lively. I accordingly wrote in and begged that I might be given some active employment in the field.

Our work on the French railways had really been physically hard at the commencement. Among other things, when your train is the seventh of a mass of fifteen goods trains lying in the goods yard parallel to each other, it is quite good exercise to have to dive under, or climb over, six trains to reach it, and you need to be particularly 'nippy' over the job when it is quite likely that the train you are crawling under will start moving when you're in front of the wheels. But by now things were working so smoothly that we were not even called on to undertake these minor risks, and life became very dull. I was very pleased, therefore, when my application met with success and I was appointed to the Command of the Jhelum Brigade in India.

CHAPTER XVII

THE GREAT WAR – THE INDIAN FRONTIER

I SAILED from England with my wife and daughter in April 1915, and reported myself in Jhelum a month later. Within another month I was transferred to Peshawar to take over the command of the 1st Infantry Brigade, which had recently been in action with the Mohmands on the frontier near Shabkadr. In the autumn of the same year we marched out again against the Mohmands, going into camp at Subhan Khwar, to the west of Shabkadr fort.

Operations against these tribes continued on and off till the end of 1917, and we had one or two serious encounters, in one of which the 21st Lancers suffered severely, the Colonel being killed while charging the enemy on my left flank.

It was one of those rare occasions on the frontier when the enemy come down on to flat ground and give the cavalry a chance of which they cannot omit to take advantage, but unfortunately the cavalry in this case had to charge with their left on an almost impassable irrigation channel, on the other side of which were high sugar-cane crops concealing a body of the enemy who fired at short range into their left flank. It seemed to me to have been one of those unavoidable pieces of bad luck of which one has to take one's share in war-time.

The opportunity for a charge is a fleeting one – a matter of seconds. There is no time to consider risks,

or examine your ground. You have just got to go in
and take your chance.

On the frontier it is often hard to tell friend from foe,
and, when fighting against the very tribes from which
we enlist our men, the situation becomes quite Gilbertian, the same man being often both friend in one
sense and foe in another. He may be loyally fighting on
your side when his sympathies are really with his
brothers across the border, or he may be fighting for
the tribes when his sympathies are with the Sirkar —
who is quite likely paying him a pension.

My personal sympathies have frequently been with
the tribesmen. But a handful of wild highlanders living
without laws in their mountain fastnesses cannot be
permitted to hold up the progress of civilized nations
acting with laws and impelled by the irresistible force
of their particular brand of civilization — however that
word may be defined.

The case of the Mohmands is a very hard one. If
their tribal lands ended at the foothills, the demarcation
of the frontier could have been carried out without hard-
ship to them, but unfortunately they have overflowed
on to the plain, and the frontier line has to run through
the tribal area, leaving the majority across the border in
independent territory, and the minority on our side of
the border, subjects of King George V. So that while
we were fighting the trans-border Mohmands, we were
living amongst their brothers and cousins on this side
of the border. This made things more difficult for us
than for them, as we could not possibly tell friend from

foe. The man who sold you milk in the morning from the village alongside the camp could easily take part in night operations on the enemy's side and come round again cheerfully with the milk in the morning.

Among the cis-border men I had one old friend who came to see me frequently in camp. He was a quaint old thing and I liked a chat with him. But my Staff did not like him at all, and asked me to cut his acquaintance. I always do what a sensible Staff tell me to, so I warned him off.

I dare say the Staff were right. It is certain that it was generally after one of his visits that I got a volley into camp at night, pretty close to Brigade Head-quarters. I have never been wounded in action, but my camp kit suffered severely. My mosquito curtain, my tent, and my pillow each in turn received a mortal wound.

Inside the Mess-tent late one night Major H. Duncan, my Brigade-Major, was reading out orders for the next day while an orderly officer held up a hurricane lantern for him to read by. A volley! Crash! and the fizz of bullets. Well directed but no one hit. Trying to look as if I did not mind, I directed the Brigade-Major to continue reading. He looked at me with an expression in his eye that seemed to suggest 'I don't think', but I was adamant, until a second volley startled the midnight air, on which I said that the further reading might be indefinitely postponed.

My old friend came to see me one day to ask me for a blanket, as he said he felt the cold so much at night. Major Duncan suggested that he would feel the cold less if he tucked himself up in bed instead of sitting on the cold rocks potting at the camp.

According to regulations, the G.O.C. has a small red lamp burning at head-quarters during the night. The man who invented this regulation forgot that though the red lamp would help messengers to find their way, it would also enable the enemy to know the position of Brigade Head-quarters. We got a good many shots at our red lamp, but I stuck to it because I did not want the troops to say that the General wasn't taking his fair risks. Funnily enough the demand for its removal – with which I was delighted to comply – came from the troops themselves.

It is interesting to note that in gentlemanly warfare, as it is still on the N.W. Frontier where all enemy shots are aimed at individuals, it is seldom the man aimed at that gets hit, but those on his left and right. To convince yourself of this you have only to examine the target after firing on the range. The minority of hits are on the bull's-eye – that's me. The majority are centres to the left or right of the bull – that's my Staff.

In this case I got a message from the regiment holding one of the flanks that the line of fire from the enemy to my red lamp passed just over their parapet, so would I please put it out.

A tribesman with a rifle in his hand is very like a sportsman in the jungle. He wants to kill something if he can, and if possible an animal with record horns. The sportsman is not actuated by any hatred of the animal he aims at — he merely wants the trophy with which to decorate his ancestral halls — or furnished lodgings — in England. So the Mohmands, in directing their fire on me, were not actuated by any particular dislike, but merely wanted to bag a General. One can sympathize with that feeling.

On one occasion they nearly got me, and I had to send a message by my old enemy-friend to point out that in killing me they would be killing the goose that laid the golden egg, as no one on our side had in the slightest degree the sympathy that I had for them.

I was visiting the picquets with my Staff by daylight. After leaving one of the picquets we trotted off to the next, when suddenly a group of Mohmands opened fire on us at short range. It was quite uncomfortable. I was glad that I had started at a trot (though it was a slow one) and not at a walk. With all the picquets looking on I did not dare to alter my pace, though I felt more like doing a gallop! If we had been at a walk it would have been most unpleasant.

That afternoon I told my old Mohmand to tell his brothers not to be so silly. If they shot me they shot their last chance. But I did not really mean this message to have any effect on them — you cannot eradicate that sportsman's desire to secure a trophy. And one has to remember that even in peace-time the irresponsible tribesman will often take a shot at a passer-by, not actuated by any unkind motive, but just to try his rifle at a moving object or to keep his eye in. He won't shoot at one of his own lot, not because he loves him too much, but simply because that sort of thing is 'not done', and it sets up an unending blood-feud.

During the intervals of frontier-fighting one had much to interest one in cantonments.

To begin with, there were General Inspections, and, having been inspected by various Generals for thirty-one years, I rather looked forward to my first inspection. I set out with no other idea in my mind than that of doing my best to test the general efficiency of battalions. I had no fads, and no desire to find out hidden secrets, but a malign fate seems to guide people like that to sore places. Very often I only asked a question to fill up time, and with no interest in the probable reply, but in nearly every case the reply, or the hesitation, put me on the trail of something really good.

What has always astonished me is the absurd reluctance of men in all branches of life, in the army or out of it, to make use of the simple phrase 'I do not know'.

When I was studying the Russian army in 1897 I found that they had one very good point in the instruction of the private soldier. Russian soldiers being nearly all illiterate had to be taught everything by very simple stages. One of the first lessons was to learn the three replies that should always be made to an officer. They were:

(1) Exactly so.
(2) Certainly not.
(3) I do not know.

I came to the conclusion that inspections would go off much more smoothly if Commanding Officers could

I

only be trained to reply on the same lines. They answer most questions and avoid trouble.

For instance, at a pow-wow the G.O.C. may say something you totally disagree with. Do not yield to your impulse and endeavour to put your point of view before him. Just give him No. 1 reply and nobody will be any the worse. To put forward your point of view in the most brilliant and convincing manner will not please the General at all, and it will make your brother officers hate you because they are fed up with the whole show and want to hear the bugler sound the 'dismiss'.

But at inspections C.O.'s nearly always seem to think that they must make some sort of a shot at a reply, even if it leads them slightly astray from the narrow path of strict veracity.

So the General says to Colonel X., 'How many men have you had laid up with pneumonia this winter?' It is obvious that the C.O. doesn't know and he ought to say so. But instead, a lot of whispering goes on while the tactful G.O.C. turns his head slightly away. The Medical Officer whispers to the Adjutant 'seven', the Adjutant whispers to the Colonel 'seven', and the flustered Colonel says to the General 'eleven'. The General turns to his Staff and says, 'Just inquire into that. Anything over ten cases is serious.' All this would have been avoided if the C.O. had said 'I do not know'.

At one inspection I was filling up time by wandering round the lines. Suddenly I came across a pair of light

khaki wheels lying rather untidily in a corner. I took
no interest in them at all, but their untidiness was
obvious, and so, for the sake of saying something, I
asked, 'What are those old wheels over there?'

The C.O., looking rather startled, echoed, 'Those
wheels?' And I re-echoed, 'Yes, those wheels,' to
which he murmured, 'Oh, those wheels' as he stroked
his chin – an obvious sign of embarrassment, so I
tactfully turned my head away. Loud whispers succeeded, from the Adjutant to the Quartermaster, and
from the Quartermaster to the Subadar-Major and
then back again, by which time the C.O. was able to
inform me that they were the wheels of a *tum-tum* that
had belonged to one of the Indian Officers.

The questions of the wheels had never interested
me for a moment, so I was glad to receive this quite
unconvincing reply which enabled me to drop the subject. A little later I was visiting another battalion,
and thought for a change I would have a look at the
Quarter Guard. Here in a corner were some odds and
ends covered by a tarpaulin, which again only attracted
me by their untidiness. So I asked, 'What's under
that tarpaulin?' An orderly deftly removing this covering, I was astonished to find again, two light khaki
wheels. I really was getting interested in them by this
time, so I asked the C.O., 'What on earth are those two
wheels?' Whereupon succeeded the same scene of
guilty embarrassment and stifled whispers culminating
in the C.O.'s reply, 'Those wheels, sir, are part of an
obsolete equipment for a machine gun.'

I had no immediate intention of running this reply to earth and exposing a base falsehood, so I passed on after suggesting that units should not allow themselves to be burdened with obsolete equipment and that the wheels should be returned at once to the Arsenal.

On my return to the Brigade Office, feeling deeply intrigued by these ridiculous wheels, I set the Staff to work and by the following morning they were able to report to me that they formed part of an experimental wheeled ambulance for use in the field, which had been issued to all infantry units two years ago with instructions that they were to be carefully looked after, given a fair trial at company training, and returned within a month accompanied by a detailed report as to their utility.

And twenty-four months later, I had accidentally stumbled on them on their way to the rubbish-heap while the units in whose charge they were had not the faintest idea what they were for! Here was another case where the proper answer was 'I do not know', but no one said it.

I will give one more example of the way in which impish Fate always leads a General to find out weak spots. I was inspecting a British Infantry Battalion, and, as usual, had to pretend to take an interest in the Quartermaster's stores, which I really find intensely boring.

I was shown samples of cloth, buttons, badges, etc., and was struck with admiration at the neatness of the display. But it is dull looking at things they show you, it is much more amusing to look at the things they don't show you. So I wandered round behind a pile of bales and boxes, asking various questions, to which intelligent replies were promptly given.

While engaged in appreciating the extreme neatness of the stores I noticed thirty pair of rope slings for loading pack-mules. They only caught my eye because of their very neatness — the store-man had arranged them in a sort of pattern. I had no question to ask about them, but for some reason or another I just happened to remember that there were thirty of them.

By an extraordinary coincidence I found the next day among the correspondence on my office table a complaint from the Transport Officer that units were in the habit of keeping pack-mule slings instead of returning them with the mules, and that thirty pair were missing. With great detective ability and an unrivalled power of putting two and two together, I was able to state exactly where those slings would be found.

We suffer very much in peace-time from the lack of distinction between the various ranks. When I became a General it was immediately borne in on me, that the whole army, including all ranks, is divided into two categories. Those who wish to see the General, and those who do not wish to see the General. The first comprises, I suppose, about one per cent. and the latter ninety-nine per cent.

Therefore a General Officer should at all times wear something so remarkable that he can be spotted a mile away. Then the one per cent. can make a rush for him, and the ninety-nine per cent. can make a bolt for their burrows. Instead of which, when not wearing a forage cap, all he has to mark him out is his red tabs with a small strip of gold. The strip of gold cannot be seen until you are within a few feet and the red tabs are worn by all the Staff.

So in peace-time when the guard has to turn out to salute the General as he passes by, the unfortunate sentry is run in for not turning out the guard because he thought the G.O.C. was only the Staff Captain, or he gets the rough side of the sergeant's tongue for turning out the guard to the Staff Captain under the impression that it was the G.O.C.

I have always felt sorry for sentries. The above is one example of their difficulties, but in peace-time the whole position of a sentry is ridiculous. For example, he is given a rifle, bayonet and ammunition, and he is put on to guard some important post. But civil law gives him no rights towards civilians. His weapons therefore become useless encumbrances. If a civilian approaches his post and throws a lump of mud at him, he can only say 'please don't'. If the civilian approaches nearer and refuses to halt, the sentry will ultimately have to raise his rifle and fire, possibly killing the civilian. In such a case I suppose he is tried for murder and hanged,, or let off with penal servitude for life. And if he makes no resistance and something happens he is tried for neglect of duty and goes to prison for a long term.

When military law clashes with civil law, as it unavoidably must on many occasions, the soldier catches it both ways. In the troubles over the Reform Bill early in the nineteenth century, a Colonel in the Army was tried and sentenced for not firing on the rioters at Bristol. In recent years we have seen a General punished because he did fire on the rioters. Now that this sort of thing has been a standing joke for centuries, is it not time that it was put right?

Either give a sentry the right to use his arms in peace-time, or take away his clumsy rifle and give him a good catapult with some swan shot. That would make inquisitive intruders skip!

As an example of the unfairness in making Generals so inconspicuous I give the following instance. A very good Territorial Battalion was attached to my Brigade. They had only recently arrived from home and were for the most part quite young and only partially trained soldiers. I was asked to report as to whether they were fit for active service in the field or not. I knew that they were not, but in order to convince the authorities I put this battalion through a sort of modified 'Test'. In the old infantry test I think a battalion had to march fifteen miles in heavy field-service kit, to attack a position at the end of the march, cook their meals after the attack, and then go straight off into night operations.

In this case, I cut the march down to nine miles, and I

arranged an easy attack, but before night work could begin I saw that the men were not up to it, so I closed the operations and reported them as being not fit for active service. After the march and attack the battalion got into bivouac camp just before sunset. I dismounted at the entrance to the camp and sat down by myself on the edge of a dry ditch to light a pipe. Behind me a company commander had decided to assemble his men, and as they came up by twos and threes he allowed them to sit about and light up their cigarettes until he had got them all together.

As I have said before, Generals have little to distinguish them from other people, and, with their backs turned, practically nothing, so one by one the men sat down behind me, in front of me, and on both sides, and I gradually found myself the centre of a little group of private soldiers. There was still a blank space immediately in front of me and into this a cross and tired soldier flung himself, and before I could give him a chance of realizing that he was within a few inches of the General, he started giving a brief description of affairs from his point of view, interspersed with crimson and purple adjectives and ending up with 'It's a bloody shame. That's what I call it.' 'What's a bloody shame?' I asked, whereupon he turned round and gazed at me with horror-stricken eyes.

Soldiers really ought not to use such distressing language, and they really ought not to criticize military operations, but then again Generals ought not to be so difficult to spot, and they ought not to appear unawares in the middle of a group of tired soldiers. So I thought we had better call it quits.

Later, by a few words to the battalion as a whole, I had the opportunity of convincing my 'grouser' that Generals do not undertake operations of this sort just for fun, and the object of the day's performance was to save them from being sent to do under war conditions what I could now report they were unable to do even under peace conditions. In the British Army we do not regard our men as 'cannon-fodder', and I saved this battalion from that fate.

In the intervals of troubles with the Mohmands we had lots to keep us busy in cantonments between work and recreation.

I dislike office work intensely, but unfortunately one cannot escape from it. My Brigade office was very well run by an efficient staff who did most of my pen work for me, but occasionally I had to draft a letter to Army Head-quarters, which I did, I thought, with some skill.

My efforts, however, did not always meet with the approval of my Brigade-Major, who frequently turned down my effusions with the remark: 'I'm afraid, General, you can't say things like that. Please let me re-draft it for you in more official language.' This tactful behaviour on his part probably saved me a lot of trouble.

So many witticisms are hurled by regimental officers at the unfortunate Staff that I cannot do less than pay my personal tribute to the efficiency and hard work of

all the Staff Officers, without exception, with whom I
came into contact during the various phases of the war.
One of the wittiest calumnies was conveyed in the
following conundrum: 'If bread is the "staff of life",
what is the life of the staff?'

Answer: 'One long loaf.'

I mention this in order to give the lie to it. An eight-
hour day would have been a half-holiday to any of my
Staff.

Apart from his military duties, a G.O.C. Brigade in
India has to deal with a lot of cantonment matters of a
purely civil nature. In this way I was called on to evict
an officer's widow (and an old friend) from her bungalow which was one of several required by the military
authorities for the accommodation of officers.

It was a painful task and involved a protracted correspondence. I kept on saying to the widow – or rather
my Staff kept on making me say – 'You must get out
of your bungalow in 48 hours', and she kept on asking,
'Where am I to go?'

In the end we should have triumphed, but unfortunately she caught me alone one day when I was not
protected by my Staff – which is a most unfair way of
treating a General – and I spoilt all our chances by
telling her, as a friend, that if she kept on quietly living
in her bungalow and ignoring my fierce threats in my
official capacity, no power on earth could move her. I
wonder this thought had not struck her before. You
cannot apply force to a lady, and if we burnt the bungalow down with her in it we should have defeated our

own purpose; so she continued to stay on in spite of the
fact that I continued – in my official capacity – to
demand her evacuation in threatening language. She
is still there, I believe. This is a good example of a dual
personality, but it is also a good example of the worry
that is caused by women in war-time. I am no use at
all with women. If one of them looks as if she were
going to cry, I'm done for, and I have suffered much
at their hands owing to this deplorable weakness.

I have given one or two instances during the war in
China. Several instances occurred in France when I
was working on the railway. Even in Persia I was
worried by them. We had the misfortune to capture
an enemy officer in North Persia who had his wife
with him, so she had also to be treated as a prisoner and
conveyed to Baghdad. She was not a Russian but spoke
that language and so I had to take personal charge of
her, which was most unpleasant and embarrassing. In
order to convey her from Kasvin to Hamadan I gave
her a seat in my Ford touring car, there being no
other accommodation but Ford vans, which would have
been rather rough for a lady. As we started off on our
140-mile drive on a not very good road, she was as
delighted as a child with the motor-car, never having
been in one before.

For the first ten miles she kept on saying, 'Oh, this
is nice!' 'I do enjoy travelling like this', but her
expressions of approval grew fainter and fainter until
at about the twentieth mile she said, 'Please, stop the
car.' I did so and she got out and was sick by the

roadside. After this the operation was repeated about once an hour. It was a very depressing affair for me, but it had no effect at all on her spirits — she seemed to like being sick, and after each bout, on her return to the car, she repeated that she was enjoying herself very much.

There were a good many odd women knocking about Persia like that and we passed them on as fast as we could to Baghdad. Can you wonder that Baghdad Head-quarters took a great dislike to me?

My old friend Dumbari came to see me in Peshawar. The first news I got of his visit was a message from the police to the effect that they had taken into custody a wild-looking and disreputable man who, when asked for references as to character, had stated that the General Officer Commanding the Brigade was a life-long friend of his and would go bail for his good behaviour — in fact, he went further and said that he had come to Peshawar to stay as my guest. I had to corroborate all this, rather to the surprise of the police, and an hour later Dumbari drove up in a *tum-tum* to my bungalow, where I heard him tell my head servant that he had come to spend a day or two, and would he please prepare a room for him.

I had also a very dear friend, an old Sikh poet, who used to celebrate in song my fancied achievements on the field of battle, and any prominent event in canton-ments. I remember he composed one very striking ode on a 'march-past'. I wish I had it now, but when he had read it out to me and I asked him to give me the

Gurmukhi manuscript, he said he could not for the following reasons:

He was a shopkeeper, and being also, in the most literal sense, a genuinely inspired poet, when the Muse descended on him he had to record his frenzy on any piece of paper he could grasp. In this case the poem had been scribbled off on the backs of his customers' bills and, if I kept the poem, he would have no record of what they owed him.

CHAPTER XVIII

THE GREAT WAR – PERSIA – DUNSTERFORCE

Towards the end of 1917 the Mohmands began to think that they had had enough of it, and there seemed in consequence very little prospect of further operations on that part of the frontier. I was delighted, therefore, to receive orders that would convey me to a quite different scene in the theatre of war.

On Christmas Eve I received secret orders to hand over the command of the Brigade and to proceed to Delhi for further instructions with a view to my being employed 'overseas'.

It eventually appeared that my new destination was to be North-west Persia and the Caucasus, but before I briefly touch on my share in events in that part of the world it will be well to explain the general nature of the allied interest in Persia at that time.

First and foremost, the reader must realize the peculiar state of affairs under which Persia – while remaining officially neutral throughout the war – was the scene of military operations from first to last.

The educated and refined Persian of the governing classes, whose interests in life are almost entirely confined to things of beauty and pleasure – wine, women, rose-gardens, nightingales and poetry – was the last person in the world to interest himself in the murderous quarrel of the European nations. Through his country, however, lies the most favourable route for an invasion of India by a force advancing from the west, and India was the most vulnerable spot in the British Empire.

It was obvious, therefore, that from the outset of the war Germany would endeavour to threaten India from this direction, using the Turkish Army as her instrument. Once a small Turkish force had established itself in Afghanistan, the latent animosity of that country would have led to open hostilities against India, and with the backing of Kabul the fanatical tribes of the north-west frontier of India would not have hesitated to throw in their lot against us.

This was the moment for which the seditious propagandists of India were waiting, and it is practically certain that, in the event of any enemy success on these lines, the whole country would have risen, and our situation would have been extremely perilous, to say the least of it.

On the outbreak of war, our allies, the Russians, wielded considerable influence in North Persia, controlling the principal military force – the Persian Cossacks. But this gain to the allies was more than counterbalanced by the fact that the Persian Gendarmerie was under the control of Swedish officers, who favoured the German cause.

The proximity of the Turkish Army to the western frontier of Persia was another factor that told against us, as any move made by them had the advantage of very short lines of communications.

Shortly after the outbreak of war, the Russians and

Turks came to blows in the extreme north-west corner of Persia, with the result that the latter were driven back on Van.

During 1915 the enemy succeeded in despatching several missions into Central Persia. These missions were not of sufficient strength to undertake military operations, but they furnished centres of propaganda and served as bases to other missions. With the aid of forces raised locally they were able to attack the isolated and unprotected British and Russian colonies in this part of Persia, and by the end of the year the British had been driven out and forced to seek refuge at the coast.

Only the Russians now remained in the north and on the Kasvin-Kermanshah road in the west.

Against these the Turks despatched a force from Baghdad early in 1916, and serious fighting took place in the neighbourhood of Hamadan, resulting in the Turks being driven back to Mesopotamia. When Kut fell, a little later, large Turkish forces were released and a strong column was again sent up the Hamadan road, which successfully engaged the Russians, who retired northwards in the direction of Kasvin. The Russians at this juncture received further reinforcements and, taking up a position astride the road, succeeded in checking the further advance of the Turks, whose ultimate withdrawal was occasioned by the fall of Baghdad in the spring of 1917.

On the retirement of the Turkish Army from this area, the Russians held an unbroken line from the

Caspian Sea to Khanikin on the Mesopotamia frontier, where they were in touch with the right of the British line. Had they been able to maintain this position there would perhaps have been no further trouble in Persia; but unfortunately the revolution which took place in Russia early in 1917 resulted in the complete disintegration of this force, the soldiers refusing any longer to obey orders and having eventually to be withdrawn to the Caucasus.

By the end of 1917 few of the Russian troops were left in Persia, and it was to fill this gap of 500 miles on the right of our line from Khanikin to the Caspian Sea that my force was called into being. We were far from being the first in the field, and it will be interesting to record what other steps were being taken during this trying period to safeguard our interests in Persia and thwart the Turco-German schemes.

Besides the force that I commanded, there were operating in Persia (1) The South Persian Rifles, with about 2,000 Indian troops, under Brigadier-General Sir Percy Sykes, (2) a small force of Indian troops under Brigadier-General R. H. Dyer in Seistan, forming the Eastern Persia Cordon, and (3) a Mission under Major-General Sir Wilfrid Malleson in North-east Persia and Turkestan.

It was impossible for me to get into touch with any of these forces, the nearest being that of Sir Percy Sykes at Shiraz, 400 miles in a straight line from my head-quarters at Hamadan. This force had firmly established itself in Southern Persia and had succeeded in driving out the German missions, which up to June 1916 had had everything their own way.

Sir Percy Sykes' intimate knowledge of Persia and the Persians, gained during many years' residence in that country, gave him an advantage that none of us other commanders possessed, enabling him to make such a remarkable success with his local troops, the South Persia Rifles, and to extricate himself from his difficult position at Shiraz in March 1918.

My task differed entirely from that of the other commanders; the scheme was as follows:

I was to be given a nucleus of some 200 officers and N.C.O.'s, and with these I was to proceed from Baghdad through Persia to Tiflis, the capital of Georgia. From this centre it was hoped that I might be able to reorganize the revolutionary units, and by this means restore the line confronting the Turks. Thus it will be seen I had no troops at all, but merely a body of selected Officers and N.C.O.'s to act as instructors and organizers. I was presumably chosen for this task because I was known to like the Russians, and I spoke their language. The idea was as good a one as could be evolved under circumstances which precluded the employment of troops – there being none available for this new sphere of operations.

And I think that if we had reached Tiflis we should have had some chance of success, but the whole scheme broke down owing to Bolshevik opposition, which prevented me from crossing the Caspian Sea until the Turks had captured the railway line leading from Baku to Tiflis.

In accordance with my instructions, I proceeded to report myself at Army Head-quarters in Delhi, when the details of the scheme were explained to me. Two days later I left for Karachi, where I arrived just in time to catch a transport for the Persian Gulf, and I reached Baghdad on January 6, 1918.

In the course of a few days I was equipped with the necessary maps and intelligence reports, and found myself ready to start out on the Great Adventure, but my army had not yet put in an appearance. They began eventually to turn up in twos and threes, but as they were to be selected from all the forces on all the many fronts of the theatre of war, it was obviously quite hopeless to wait for a general assembly.

By January 29, 1918, I had collected twelve officers and with this small nucleus set forth on that date, travelling in Ford vans with an escort of one armoured car under Lieut. Singer. After fighting our way through snowstorms, and digging through twelve-foot snow-drifts on the mountain passes in Persia, we reached Enzeli, the southern port of the Caspian Sea, on February 17.

Here we found ourselves confronted by the hostile Bolsheviks who controlled the town and the shipping, while the Persians of the Gilan province, in which we were, threatened to massacre the party – and to this day no one knows why they did not. Possibly they were frightened by the armoured car, though one armoured car seems a trivial force with which to overawe 2,000 Bolshevik soldiers and 5,000 well-armed Gilanis under the dashing leadership of the renowned Kuchik Khan.

However, the fact remains that, while everybody kept on 'threatening', nobody did anything.

At last, when I saw that the situation was quite hopeless and that at any moment the threats might be put into action, I seized a favourable opportunity of running away – 'withdrawing' is the more correct military term – getting on the move before daybreak and slipping through the Gilan country without encountering opposition. We reached Kasvin, 140 miles from Enzeli, without mishap and, suffering no harm from renewed threats of massacre from the hostile inhabitants of this town, continued our retreat as far as Hamadan, which we reached on the fifth day after leaving Enzeli, having been considerably impeded by heavy falls of snow on the passes.

Hamadan provided us with a good water-supply, ample provisions, and a position suitable for defence, and, being almost exactly half-way between Baghdad and the Caspian Sea, seemed a convenient point at which to fix our permanent head-quarters.

Here we remained till summer, receiving gradual reinforcements from Baghdad and succeeding by various devices in creating a sort of line of resistance against the Turks. I say 'sort of' because the line of resistance was quite unreal and, at least till April, when the first reinforcements arrived, was entirely composed of bluff.

In March 1918 things were going very badly for

the allies. The Germans appeared to be driving everything before them in France, and the Persians naturally came to regard them as the ultimate winners of the war.

I was not in touch with Sykes' force, but heard through Baghdad of his being invested by the Kashgais in Shiraz. The outlook was very gloomy, and was made more so by the fact of our inability to do anything to help him. I had only 'bluff' to offer, and he had all he needed of that, and Shiraz was more than 400 miles distant from us. The clouds, however, soon began to show their silver lining. Spring came on, the snows melted, a fresh batch of officers arrived from Baghdad, and we received the welcome news of Sykes' defeat of the Kashgais.

My army was still a very small one, and would have been in a rather precarious situation had it not been for the presence in this part of Persia of the last disciplined remnant of the Russian Army – the Kuban Cossacks under Colonel Bicherakov.

The Russian troops still in Persia were nominally under the command of General Baratov, who was bitterly disappointed at the smallness of my army. 'Dunsterforce!' he snorted, 'I know Dunster all right, but where is the *Force*?'

I must agree that he had some excuse for his exasperation, as our growth was very gradual, and at the highest point our strength was never as much as a Brigade.

Up till April 3 we remained at our original strength

of 12 officers and 1 armoured car; on that date our first reinforcement arrived in the shape of Brigadier-General Byron with 20 officers and 20 N.C.O.'s.

This does not sound a great deal, but it was sufficient to enable us to expand into at least the semblance of an army. With the new arrivals we set to work raising local troops, and in a very short time we had some very fine-looking soldiers. I say 'fine-looking' because their chief merit lay in their looks – they were wonderfully fierce fellows to look at, and as in Persia everything goes by 'looks', that was all we needed.

So later on, when Colonel Toby Rawlinson joined us, he was able to improvise a very fine armoured car out of a Ford van and some tissue-paper. It was a terrific thing to *look* at and, as no one was allowed near enough to poke their fingers through the 'armour', it terrorized the whole countryside.

About the same time we also received some real troops in the shape of 30 rifles of the 1/4 Hants Regiment, and a few days later our first aeroplane arrived.

In this way by the middle of April our army consisted of 32 officers, 22 N.C.O.'s, 50 car-drivers, 1 armoured car and 1 aeroplane, to which must be added our local Persian levies of about 600 men. The arrival of the aeroplane caused great excitement as none had previously been seen in this part of Asia, and it consequently added much to our prestige.

Throughout the period covered by the expedition the Air Force rendered splendid service; among other fine performances, Lieutenant Pennington's flight to Urumiah deserves recording.

Urumiah was held by the Assyrian Christians, who were entirely surrounded by the Turks. We wanted to get in touch with them to enable them to continue their resistance. To do this I despatched Pennington with a message for the leader of the Assyrians, General Aga Petros; he flew over the investing Turkish troops and alighted on a very doubtful landing-ground, delivered the message and brought back the reply successfully, suffering from nothing worse than having been kissed by the entire population of the town.

Early in May our third party arrived, and on May 25 Colonel R. Keyworth brought up the fourth party of 50 officers and 150 N.C.O.'s.

With this last addition to our strength we felt we might begin to do something, and we renewed our efforts to get in touch with Baku, hoping eventually to cross the Caspian Sea and save that town from falling into the hands of the Turks, who were advancing against it from the west.

A squadron of the 14th Hussars, under Captain Pope, and 8 armoured cars had now joined us, and a mobile force of 1,000 rifles of the 1/4 Hants Regiment and the 1/2 Gurkhas with 2 mountain guns were on their way from Baghdad.

Bicherakov's Cossacks, reinforced by our armoured cars and the squadron of the 14th Hussars, fought and defeated Kuchik Khan at Menjil Bridge on June 11, and opened the road to the Caspian. The Russians continued to withdraw to the north and, as they withdrew, the road from Kasvin to the port of Enzeli was taken over by the mobile column under Colonel Matthews. This force established itself in Resht, the capital of the Gilan province, where it was attacked by Kuchik Khan's army of Jangalis on July 20. This action resulted in the final defeat of the Jangalis and put an end to all risk of trouble on the Kasvin–Enzeli road.

I ought not to omit to mention here the very fine services rendered by the Anzac Wireless troop, who kept us in touch with Baghdad throughout these operations.

By June, my 'army' having received the above-mentioned reinforcements, I decided to transfer my head-quarters to Kasvin, an ancient capital of Persia, about 90 miles from the present capital, Teheran, and 140 from the Caspian Sea. At Kasvin we had many amusing incidents to keep us cheerful. There were many Persian officials in the town plotting against us, but the vigilance of my Intelligence Staff always enabled us to forestall them.

I was not really exaggerating very much when I told a Persian gentleman who was calling upon me that I knew all about every one in the town, and the exact degree to which each was implicated in various plots. The news soon spread abroad and I was credited with supernatural powers of detecting crime.

One immediate result was that a very bad old man, whose wickedness had so far escaped the vigilance of my Staff, came to see me and made a full confession of the most dreadful iniquities, under the impression that I already knew all about them. He begged for forgiveness and promised better behaviour. So I forgave him and added his name to the Black List!

With the exception of Bicherakov's Cossacks, the Russian troops were a demoralized mob and were making for home in parties which looted and burned as they passed through the country. They had got a good grip of that wicked and misleading slogan, 'Liberty, equality, fraternity,' taking 'Liberty' to mean 'I shall do what I like without regard to my neighbour', 'Equality' to mean 'I am as good as you are, but you are not as good as I am', and demonstrating 'Fraternity' as Cain demonstrated it to Abel.

Bicherakov's Cossacks were now in Kasvin and we tried to work as far as possible together, but their methods were so very different to our own that we found it rather difficult. Bicherakov's right-hand man was a Lieutenant Sovlaiev – a very fine specimen of a wild and untamed Cossack. There was no 'finesse' about Sovlaiev. His methods were those of the mailed fist.

He spent all his time arresting people on the slightest grounds of suspicion, and generally handing them over to me for disposal. When I asked for a statement of the man's crime, he would say, 'I'm not sure. But he's a bad lot. Just look at him.'

I objected to punishing men without any evidence just because they were dreadful people to look at, so Sovlaiev hit on a very happy expedient. He said, 'All right; if you make so much fuss about innocence and guilt, don't punish them. Put them all in a lorry and send them down to Baghdad, and then let them walk home.' Quite a good idea — the distance was over 400 miles, and the long walk would take them over a month and give them time to reflect over their misdemeanours — if any.

He brought me one man whom I definitely refused to accept on any condition. His innocence was manifest and admitted. Sovlaiev had gone to an inn to arrest the proprietor, who was certainly a bad man. But the wily man got news of his coming and ran away. So Sovlaiev arrested the cook. 'I had to have somebody,' he explained.

I had on one occasion to have two Bolshevik leaders from Enzeli to lunch. We were, of course, implacable foes from the political point of view, but otherwise they were decent and harmless fellows enough, and I felt rather sorry for them having, with their very limited intelligence and education, to hold important Government posts for which they were (and knew they were) totally unfitted. Although we were antagonistic we were not at war, and business matters brought us together. They had lots of petrol and no cars, and I had lots of cars and no petrol. We were able to make a very satisfactory arrangement.

I mention this incident only to show how easily these fiery demagogues eat (or drink) their own principles. One of the principal planks in the Bolshevik platform was 'prohibition'. Alcohol of all kinds was strictly forbidden. So as they sat at lunch, one on either side of me, I broached this subject and asked them if they were really sincere. In reply they gave me a lot of platform oratory to the effect that drink was the downfall of man, etc. I did not want to put their principles to the test and I had not the least idea of persuading them to drink, but in the ordinary routine of politeness I asked, 'What would you like to drink? There is red wine or white wine or beer.' I might have added 'water', but before I could do so they both said in chorus, 'Red wine, please,' and after copious draughts of this during the meal they each had two liqueurs with their coffee.

I have recorded the principal events of this interesting expedition in my book *The Adventures of Dunsterforce*, so I need not dwell at length on these operations. In that book, however, I am afraid I failed to make clear what a lot we owed to the Imperial Bank of Persia and their most capable officials. I also had little to say about the important part played by the Royal Navy. But the action of the latter did not really begin to make itself felt till after I had withdrawn from the Caspian.

The naval forces were under the command of Commodore Norris, R.N., who joined us in Kasvin in the summer with sufficient naval ratings to enable him to develop a small fleet on the Caspian Sea by equipping suitable merchant vessels. The naval and military forces worked in perfect harmony, the only point of difference between Commodore Norris and myself being on the question of rank. The rank of Commo-

dore is not known in the Russian navy and was con-
fused by them with the lower rank of Commander.
I proposed to get over this difficulty by promoting
Norris to the rank of Admiral by a mere stroke of
the pen. He protested vigorously, however, against
my taking this action, threatening that if I persisted
he would issue naval orders gazetting me a Bishop.
So I decided to leave the matter alone.

During June and July all our thoughts were concentrated on Baku, towards which town the Turks were
pressing with all haste with a view of capturing the
valuable oil wells. Our friends in Baku were those of
the Social-revolutionary party – a party with a 'con-
structive' policy opposed to the purely 'destructive'
policy of the Bolsheviks.

We agreed with them that, if they could succeed in
ousting the Bolsheviks and establishing a reasonable
government in their place, we would come over to help
in the defence of the town. I promised to bring what
troops I could, but gave them fair warning that the
numbers could not be large. It is necessary to lay
stress on this, because we found later, when we got over
to Baku, that the Baku people were bitterly disappointed
at the smallness of our numbers. They apparently
expected me to bring enough troops to undertake the
whole defence, while they looked on and applauded.

On July 26 the long-expected *coup d'état* took place
at Baku; the Bolsheviks were driven out and their
place taken by a new government calling itself the
Central-Caspian Dictatorship, who invited our aid.

In response to their appeal, I at once despatched Colonel Stokes with a small party of the 1/4 Hants Regiment, followed by Colonel R. Keyworth with further reinforcements.

Baghdad sent up the 39th Midland Brigade in motor-lorries – the whole summer having been spent in making the roads passable for these – and No. 8 Field Battery. The first troops arrived in Baku on August 4, and the remainder, with my head-quarters, on August 10.

From the first day of our arrival we had friction with the local authorities, chiefly due to the fact of their disappointment at the smallness of our numbers. We found it difficult, also, to work with revolutionary troops. Every one was free and fraternal, and a private soldier was as good as the Commander-in-Chief. Troops ordered to march to a certain point held a committee meeting and decided unanimously to march in the opposite direction. It all sounds very amusing, but as the troops of the 39th Midland Brigade were now holding the line against the Turks, who made frequent attacks, this failure of the local troops to occupy their proper positions in the line of defence meant needless loss of life among our troops.

After endeavouring to hold a line of nearly twenty miles with 900 rifles, feebly supported by about 5,000 town troops, for about six weeks, it became obvious that further sacrifice of life would be in vain. We held on, however, till September 14, when the Turks made a determined assault at daybreak and broke through the line at a critical point. After fighting till sunset, the

British troops withdrew in order to the wharf, where I had three ships in readiness to receive them, and the whole force was embarked by 10 p.m. With some difficulty we succeeded in getting clear of the harbour and setting our course for Enzeli, the port from which we had set out, where we arrived on the following day.

Here the force was reorganized as the Northern Persian Force, with a new rôle, and I returned to India.

CHAPTER XIX

ANTI-CLIMAX

Soon after my return to India the Armistice was declared, and a few weeks later I was appointed to the command of the Agra Brigade. After the moving events of the past four years peace-time soldiering seemed unusually dull, but I enjoyed the period of my Agra Command, though I would have preferred to have been back among my old friends in the Punjab. However, as it was, I made many new friends in this new part of India, among others a fine old philosopher – a Hindu cloth-seller who was a rampant Home-Ruler. He said to me, 'Sahib, I am all for Swaraj. It has brought a lot of profit to me in my business. At a time when I had a lot of English white cotton drill on my hands, the politicians suddenly started a boycott on all European goods, proclaiming that only "Swadeshi" goods should be purchased. So there was I with all that cloth on my hands and ruin staring me in the face. But I soon thought of a way out. I bought an india-rubber stamp with my name on it and the words "Swadeshi. Made in Bombay." And with this I stamped each yard of cloth. The stamp only cost me five rupees and I charged two annas extra per yard for the cloth, so I did pretty well out of it.'

I enjoyed my talks with this old humorist and at his instigation interested myself generally in the great question of 'Home Rule for India'.

I cannot say I studied the question, but I learned a

good deal more about it from disinterested Indian
friends than many who profess to have done so – from
books and agitators. I found, what one always finds
with regard to these political terms, that Home Rule
means different things to different people.

To the sincere patriot – perhaps a quarter per cent
of the whole number – it means a return of the Golden
Age, with all the beautiful illusions that form the will-
o'-the-wisp of romantic revolutionaries in all ages.

To the not-so-sincere patriot it means getting rid
of the supercilious Englishman, and, most important
point of all, succeeding, with his highly-educated companions, to the inheritance of the large salaries now
drawn by English officials.

As the Hindu population is by far the most advanced
in education, and outnumber the less educated Mahomedans by four to one, the term means to them Hindu
Home Rule, with a promise (like pie-crust) of a kindly
toleration for Mahomedans. To the Mahomedans –
with the exception of a few fanatics – it signifies 'a jolly
old bust up', with a chance of some one securing some
of the prizes. To none of these people does the idea
suggest itself that men of the lowest castes should
compete on equal terms with the higher castes. If
they talk of 'equality', they use the term only to attract
the sympathy of Europeans, they do not use it for
home consumption.

To the frontier tribesmen it means truly the dawn of
the Golden Age, when our troops shall be withdrawn
from their duties of keeping the peace on the frontier,

and the Pathan tribes will be free to ravage, loot and destroy without let or hindrance.

To the average peasant, I do not know exactly what it means — no more does he. But from conversations with many of them, I find that most of them have been told the usual stories of that Golden Age we are all waiting for. When the British go, there will be no more taxes and every one who has land can enjoy the usual protection of a benign Government free, while those who have no land will be given as much as they want.

When the great change takes place and the deluded peasant finds that it means no more than the replacement of a white official by a brown one, he will wish himself back under the old régime, beyond a doubt.

With the fierce undying antagonism between Mahomedan and Hindu, no system of government for India that does not provide officials, and especially Magistrates, from a race that stands aloof from both can ever give peace and security to the people.

That wonderful Mogul, Akbar the Great, had a fine idea of impartiality. But what do Hindus think of the time they had under the rule of another Mogul, Aurungzeb?

And what sort of a time will Mahomedans have under a rule where they will find themselves outvoted on all occasions by four to one, if indeed they are allowed to have a say in the matter at all?

Then again, does Home Rule mean a rule by various monarchies, based on the present rule of the Native

K

States? Or does it mean rule of the lower castes by the higher? Or does it mean democratic rule on the lines of 'equality'?

I can hardly imagine under the latter system a highly-educated man of the Sweeper caste occupying a position of authority, with friendly Brahmins to hold his stirrup when he mounts his horse.

What does it mean when the question is put up before our legislators or before the sympathetic British public? Will some one please tell us?

In the meantime, to see how things work in a Native State under a semi-Royal rule, I visited one of them. The rule in these States differs considerably. Some have more or less adopted our system; others prefer the old-fashioned autocratic rule, which is all India will ever get if we allow her to break away from us in pursuit of a vain ideal.

The State I visited was run most efficiently on the latter lines and the people were smiling, contented, and apparently prosperous – it's their way and they like it.

Speaking to the Indian proprietor of a hotel I was staying at, I asked him if I need take any special precautions against theft. He replied, 'No, sir. There are no thieves in this city. If a man is only suspected of theft, he goes at once to prison.'

Political orators speaking on socialistic lines, with all the twaddle of liberty, equality and fraternity, share a like fate, so the subjects of this Raja enjoy a happy immunity from the speeches of Marble Arch politicians.

This was 'Rule' with a vengeance; whether it was 'Home' or not, I do not know.

The first point for students of this question to bear in mind is that the 350 million people of India, living in an area as large as the whole of Europe, have no point of union among themselves, but constitute a heterogeneous collection of varying religions, races and languages. There is far greater diversity in religion, race and language between a Punjab Mahomedan, a Poonah Brahmin, and a Dravidian from Madras than between any of the most contrasting groups in the whole of Europe. It is this which makes the Indian problem stand on quite a separate footing.

In 1919, the year of my command in Agra, the agitation fostered by the Indian political extremists was at its height. India was at this time in a very dangerous state, and had our system of intelligence been as imperfect, and our officials as slack as they were in 1857, we should have had the terrible events of the Mutiny repeated on a larger scale.

That we were spared this calamity is solely due to the action of two men in the Punjab – Sir Michael O'Dwyer, the Lieutenant-Governor, and General Dyer, commanding the troops at Amritsar. But in Agra, while the pot seethed a good deal, it never actually boiled over.

I had a good deal to do in the way of instructing new units and young officers, which interested me very much, but I was ordered to run a Staff Ride, which interested me not at all.

I would not mind a Staff Ride if the whole thing was done verbally, but there is so much paper work in connection with it that all the life is taken out of it. Among other things, you have to prepare a quantity of typed questions, and at intervals you get off your horse and hand these round to officers taking part in the entertainment. All this takes time and trouble, and one's normal work gets three days in arrears.

The Officer Commanding a Territorial battalion in the Brigade came to talk over the Staff Ride with me and the gist of his conversation (cutting out polite phrases) was:

'I have been at Aldershot more recently than you, and so I know more about Staff Rides than you do. Now this is the way they ought to be run,' etc., etc.

He was certainly right in saying he knew more about Staff Rides than I did. There was nothing he didn't know about them.

So I got a brain-wave and said, 'I'll tell you what, Colonel X, you're the very man for the job. You shall run the Staff Ride while I get on with my work.'

I don't think he really wanted all that work pushed off on to him, but he was distinctly 'asking for it', and I was delighted to be relieved of the burden.

He ran the Staff Ride very well indeed and I made a note to entrust him with the next one as a mark of recognition, but unfortunately the Brigade broke up before another was due.

Agra was distinctly a peaceful period in my life, but there were occasionally amusing or exciting incidents.

We had for the last year of my service two of the best *feu-de-joie* parades that I have ever taken part in. The mounted officers simply excelled themselves on January 1, 1919, and January 1, 1920.

On the first occasion the glory of command was taken away from me owing to a visit of the General Officer Commanding the Northern Army, who took his place with his Staff opposite the flagstaff while I remained with my Staff at the head of the Brigade.

I looked forward to the proceedings with complete equanimity. I was mounted on a young and spirited animal, but, while he was full of disconcerting tricks at odd moments, he had a complete contempt for sounds of firing. Twice he had nearly got me off by shying at a butterfly that flitted out of a bush just under his nose, but he never even cocked an ear at the most deafening of explosions. So I could watch the others in ease and comfort.

G.O.C. Northern Army was some fifty paces in front of me, with his Brigadier-General on his right and his A.D.C. on his left.

At the flagstaff, not on parade, was my Station Staff Officer, whose duty it was to see to the flag, and the proper placing of onlookers and odd jobs of that sort. For this duty he should have been on foot, but I noticed that he had taken it on himself to ride. I suppose he wanted to show the ladies that he could ride. His conceit brought disaster on his head.

The parade begins with the artillery firing on the flank, and horses seldom mind that much, especially as the guns are a fairly long distance from them. But this particular animal that my S.S.O. had selected was a world's record in his dislike of guns.

With the discharge of the very first gun, I saw the unfortunate young man rise high into the air as if the gun had been a bomb that had exploded beside him and blown him up into the sky.

He fell with a resounding thud and I saw his inanimate form carried off on a stretcher. His share in the proceedings was over for the day as he had broken a rib or two, and he was borne from the ground while his horse happily cantered home to his stables, delighted to have been dismissed from parade.

During the remainder of the artillery firing the horses only got a little fidgety, but when the infantry fire began it was altogether too much for them. At the first round the Brigadier-General's horse got rid of his burden, and at the second round the A.D.C.'s horse followed his example, and the G.O.C. Northern Army was left in solitude.

It is quite inexplicable to me why people should think the sight of a man tumbling off his horse irresistibly comic, but it is a fact that we all do so. There is nothing really funny about it at all and the rider is probably going to break a leg, or possibly his neck – yet every one roars with laughter.

At the next parade, January 1, 1920, it was I who afforded the most amusement. Various mounted officers got into trouble, but I was so occupied with myself I had no time to enjoy their misfortunes.

My Brigade was one of those 'axed' in the post-war
reduction of units, and as I was giving up my command
in a few days, I had sold my charger, having arranged
to go on leave just after Christmas, and a horse being
unnecessary for those few remaining days. But for
some reason or another. – I can't remember now what
it was except that it was a good one – my Brigade-
Major begged me to stay and take the parade. I accordingly did so, and that was my last appearance in this
world as a mounted officer on parade – and it was
nearly a case of a 'dismounted' officer.

Having no charger, I borrowed a horse of some sort
from somebody who guaranteed him to be quite quiet
and to stand fire. He came up to this guarantee most
thoroughly – I never saw such a miserably tame animal,
and he took no notice whatever of the firing.

But to my surprise, I found it was my voice that he
took exception to. Among the many horses I have
ridden in my life, I have never before or since met with
that form of timidity. I possess powerful lungs, and
on such a parade a General has to use his voice to the
full in order that he may be heard clearly at a considerable distance.

In the earlier stages of the parade I noticed that the
sound of my loud voice produced a corresponding
tremble in the muscles of my charger, but in the final
stage the poor animal was terrified out of its
senses.

This final stage is reached when the General, holding
his sword in his right hand and his reins in his left,

removes his helmet with his third hand and addresses his gallant troops as follows:

'The Brigade will give three cheers for His Most Gracious Majesty the King-Emperor, taking the time from me.'

He then says 'Hip' and the troops prick up their ears. Then another tremendous 'Hip' and they prepare to open their mouths. Then, with a wave of the helmet and all the power of his stentorian voice, he shouts 'Hooray!' This is repeated, of course, three times, making in all nine yells.

In this case, when I turned my back on the ladies and spectators, with their cameras a few yards away near the flagstaff, and faced the troops with the opening remarks quoted above, I felt a sort of ripple run through the limbs of my astonished steed — who was apparently under the impression that I was directing these fierce remarks to him in anger.

But when I came to the 'hips' he began to sink into the ground. Although he remained quite still, he began to disappear beneath me. When I came to the 'hooray' he was half-way down on his haunches.

Before I began the second lot of 'hips' I hoped that he would come back to normal, and then, starting from that point, the second 'hooray' would just bring him down again to the half-way point, which I could do with. But the poor beast remained rigid in the half-crouching attitude and an application of the spur did nothing to improve matters. So I embarked on the second series, which brought him down with his quarters two feet from the ground.

I made a lightning calculation that another twenty-four inches and he would be sitting up like a puppy for a biscuit while I slid ignominiously out of the saddle, so allowing eight inches for each of the three yells, I decided to cut out the two 'hips' and merely bellowed 'hooray'. This left us sixteen inches to spare and the situation was saved. But the cameras were busy behind me, and unkind people sent me proofs of their snapshots afterwards.

After the parade a Commanding Officer said to me, 'I may be wrong, General, but the reason we rather messed up that last cheer was that we did not hear your preliminary "hips" to give us warning for the "hooray".' I said 'Most extraordinary'.

In this ignominious way I bid farewell to the army after a very happy career of over thirty-six years. My final pleasure was to disappoint the troops I loved so well. I could see that all the front-rank men, British and Native, instead of being inspired with a desire to give vocal expression of their feelings of loyalty, were merely wondering 'Is the old man going to come off or not?'

I hope my troops loved me as much as I loved them. But you cannot be human and not want to see the General tumble off on parade.

Eight years have passed by since the curtain fell on my active career. My life is still extremely active in

my new incarnation, but I find leisure for philosophic
contemplation and I reflect on the words of that great
Persian poet, Sheik Saadi:

'The world, oh my brother, is passing away. Let it
suffice you, then, to fix your heart on Him who created
it and you. Put not your trust in land, wealth, or
raiment; for the World has pampered many such as
you – only to annihilate them in the end.

'When the pure soul wings its last flight from earth,
at that hour what matters it if one is seated on a throne,
or lying in the dust?'

A LIST OF THE
VOLUMES NOW PUBLISHED
IN THE
TRAVELLERS' LIBRARY

3s. 6d. net
each

JONATHAN CAPE
AND WILLIAM HEINEMANN
LONDON

THE
TRAVELLERS' LIBRARY

A series of books in all branches of literature designed for the pocket, or for the small house where shelf space is scarce. Though the volumes measure only 7 inches by 4¾ inches, the page is arranged so that the margins are not unreasonably curtailed nor legibility sacrificed. The books are of a uniform thickness irrespective of the number of pages, and the paper, specially manufactured for the series, is remarkably opaque, even when it is thinnest.

A semi-flexible form of binding has been adopted, as a safeguard against the damage inevitably associated with hasty packing. The cloth is an attractive shade of blue and has the title and author's name stamped in gold on the back.

A NOTE

ON THE ARRANGEMENT OF

THIS CATALOGUE

The main body or text of this list is arranged alphabetically under the names of AUTHORS. But, in addition, and for the convenience of readers, there will be found at the end two indexes. The first (page 31) is arranged numerically under the series numbers given to the volumes. The second (page 35) is arranged alphabetically under the titles of the books.

ANDERSON, Sherwood

HORSES AND MEN. Stories   *No.* 54

'*Horses and Men* confirms our indebtedness to the publishers who are introducing his work here. It has a unity beyond that of its constant Middle West setting. A man of poetic vision, with an intimate knowledge of particular conditions of life, here looks out upon a world that seems singularly material only because he unflinchingly accepts its actualities.' *Morning Post*

ARMSTRONG, Martin

THE BAZAAR. Stories   *No.* 77

'These stories have considerable range of subject, but in general they are stay-at-home tales, depicting cloistered lives and delicate, finely fibred minds. . . . Mr. Armstrong writes beautifully.' *Nation and Athenæum*

ATKINS, J. B.

SIDE SHOWS. Essays. With an introduction by JAMES BONE   *No.* 78

Mr. J. B. Atkins was war correspondent in four wars, the London editor of a great English paper, then Paris correspondent of another, and latterly the editor of the *Spectator*. His subjects in *Side Shows* are briefly London and the sea.

BELLOC, Hilaire

SHORT TALKS WITH THE DEAD   *No.* 79

In these essays Mr. Belloc attains his usual high level of pungent and witty writing. The subjects vary widely and include an imaginary talk with the spirits of Charles I, the barber of Louis XIV, and Napoleon, Venice, fakes, eclipses, Byron, and the famous dissertation on the Nordic Man.

BERCOVICI, Konrad

BETWEEN EARTH AND SKY. Stories of Gipsies.
With an Introduction by A. E. COPPARD   *No.* 117

Konrad Bercovici, through his own association with gipsies, together with a magical intuition of their lives, is able to give us some unforgettable pictures of those wanderers who, having no home anywhere, are at home everywhere.

BIERCE, Ambrose

CAN SUCH THINGS BE ? Stories   *No.* 1

'Bierce never wastes a word, never coins a too startling phrase ;
he secures his final effect, a cold thrill of fear, by a simple, yet
subtle, realism. No anthology of short stories, limited to a score
or so, would be complete without an example of his unique artistry.'
Morning Post

THE EYES OF THE PANTHER. Stories   *No.* 49

It is said that these tales were originally rejected by virtually every
publisher in the country. Bierce was a strange man ; in 1914, at
the age of seventy-one, he set out for Mexico and has never been
heard of since. His stories are as strange as his life, but this volume
shows him as a master of his art.

THE MONK AND THE HANGMAN'S DAUGHTER.

Written by Ambrose Bierce in collaboration with Adolphe
    Danziger de Castro   *No.* 34

'They are stories which the discerning are certain to welcome.
They are evidence of very unusual powers, and when once they
have been read the reader will feel himself impelled to dig out more
from the same pen.' *Westminster Gazette*

BIRRELL, Augustine

MORE OBITER DICTA   *No.* 140

'A volume delightful to read, packed with urbane and shrewd
criticism, and distinguished by a pleasant vein of kindly humour.'
Daily Mail

'Age has not wearied Mr. Birrell's humour ; nor have the years
condemned his whimsicality. He remains as delightful a companion
as ever.' *Nation and Athenæum*

BOURNE, George

A FARMER'S LIFE   *No.* 32

The life-story of a tenant-farmer of fifty years ago in which the
author of *The Bettesworth Book* and *The Memoirs of a Surrey
Labourer* draws on his memory for a picture of the everyday life
of his immediate forbears, the Smiths, farmers and handicraft men,
who lived and died on the border of Surrey and Hampshire.

4

BRAMAH, Ernest

THE WALLET OF KAI LUNG   *No.* 18

'Something worth doing and done. . . . It was a thing intended, wrought out, completed and established. Therefore it was destined to endure, and, what is more important, it was a success.' *Hilaire Belloc*

KAI LUNG'S GOLDEN HOURS   *No.* 16

'It is worthy of its forerunner. There is the same plan, exactitude, working-out and achievement ; and therefore complete satisfaction in the reading.' *From the Preface by* HILAIRE BELLOC

BRONTË, Emily

WUTHERING HEIGHTS   *No.* 30

'It is a very great book. You may read this grim story of lost and thwarted human creatures on a moor at any age and come under its sway.' *From the Introduction by* ROSE MACAULAY

BROWNE, Louis

THE STORY OF THE JEWS   *No.* 146

Here is a history which is more absorbing than any work of fiction. The author traces the beginnings of the Jewish race from the wandering Semitic races of Arabia, through interminable strife and conflict, slavery, oppression, expatriation, up to modern times.

BUTLER, Samuel

EREWHON. A Satire   *No.* 11

'To lash the age, to ridicule vain pretension, to expose hypocrisy, to deride humbug in education, politics and religion, are tasks beyond most men's powers ; but occasionally, very occasionally, a bit of genuine satire secures for itself more than a passing nod of recognition. *Erewhon* is such a satire. . . . The best of its kind since *Gulliver's Travels*.' *Augustine Birrell*

EREWHON REVISITED. A Satire   *No.* 12

'He waged a sleepless war with the mental torpor of the prosperous, complacent England around him ; a Swift with the soul of music in him, and completely sane ; a liberator of humanity operating with the wit and malice and coolness of Mephistopheles.' *Manchester Guardian*

BUTLER, Samuel

THE NOTE BOOKS   *No.* 75

'To us Butler stands not chiefly as a satirist or an amateur in fiction
or in the fine arts, but as the freest, most original and most varied
thinker of his generation. . . . Neither *Erewhon* nor *The Way of
All Flesh*, but the posthumous work entitled *Note Books* will stand,
in our judgment, as the decisive contribution of Samuel Butler to
the thought of his age.' *Nation*

SELECTED ESSAYS. This   volume   contains   the
following essays :   *No* 55

THE HUMOUR OF HOMER	HOW TO MAKE THE BEST OF LIFE
QUIS DESIDERIO . . . ?	THE SANCTUARY OF MONTRIGONE
RAMBLINGS IN CHEAPSIDE	A MEDIEVAL GIRLS' SCHOOL
THE AUNT, THE NIECES, AND	ART IN THE VALLEY OF SAAS
THE DOG	THOUGHT AND LANGUAGE

THE WAY OF ALL FLESH. A Novel   *No.* 10

'It drives one almost to despair of English Literature when one
sees so extraordinary a study of English life as Butler's posthumous
Way of All Flesh making so little impression. Really, the English
do not deserve to have great men.' *George Bernard Shaw*

CANOT, Theodore

MEMOIRS OF A SLAVE TRADER. Set down by
BRANTZ MAYER and now edited by A. W. LAWRENCE   *No.* 126

In 1854 a cosmopolitan adventurer, who knew Africa at the worst
period of its history, dictated this sardonic account of piracy and
mutiny, of battles with warships or rival traders, and of the
fantastic lives of European and half-caste slavers on the West Coast.

CARDUS, Neville

DAYS IN THE SUN : A Cricketer's Book   *No.* 121

The author says 'the intention of this book is modest – it should be
taken as a rather freely compiled journal of happy experiences
which have come my way on our cricket fields.'

ARLETON, Captain George

MILITARY MEMOIRS (1672–1713). Edited by
A. W. LAWRENCE   *No.* 134

> A cheerful sidelight on the war of the Spanish Succession, with a remarkable literary history. Johnson praised the book, Scott edited it, and then the critics declared it to be fiction and suggested Defoe or Swift as the author ; now it has come into its own again as one of the most vivid records of a soldier's actual experiences.

CLEMENTS, Rex

A GIPSY OF THE HORN. Life in a deep-sea sailing ship *No.* 136

> A true and spirited account of a phase of sea-life now passing, if not passed, fascinating from the very vividness and sincerity of its telling. Mr. Clements loves the sea, and he makes his readers love it.

COPPARD, A. E.

ADAM AND EVE AND PINCH ME. Stories   *No.* 13

> Mr. Coppard's implicit theme is the closeness of the spiritual world to the material ; the strange, communicative sympathy which strikes through two temperaments and suddenly makes them one. He deals with those sudden impulses under which secrecy is broken down for a moment, and personality revealed as under a flash of spiritual lightning.

CLORINDA WALKS IN HEAVEN. Stories   *No.* 22

> 'Genius is a hard-ridden word, and has been put by critics at many puny ditches, but Mr. Coppard sets up a fence worthy of its mettle. He shows that in hands like his the English language is as alive as ever, and that there are still infinite possibilities in the short story.' *Outlook*

FISHMONGER'S FIDDLE. Stories   *No.* 130

> 'In definite colour and solid strength his work suggests that of the old Dutch Masters. Mr. Coppard is a born story-teller.' *Times Literary Supplement*

THE BLACK DOG. Stories   *No.* 2

> 'Mr. Coppard is a born story-teller. The book is filled with a variety of delightful stuff : no one who is interested in good writing in general, and good short stories in particular, should miss it.' *Spectator*

7

COYLE, Kathleen

LIV. A Novel. With an Introduction by REBECCA WEST
No. 87

'*Liv* is a short novel, but more subtly suggesting beauty an
movement than many a longer book. Liv is a young Norwegia
girl whose father is recently dead. She is engaged, half against he
will, to a young man, a neighbour ; but she desires above all thing
to go to Paris to "see life." . . . There is something cool and rar
about this story ; the reader finds himself turning back to re-rea
pages that must not be forgotten.' *Times Literary Supplement*

DAVIES, W. H.

THE AUTOBIOGRAPHY OF A SUPER-TRAMP.
With a Preface by G. BERNARD SHAW
No. 3

Printed as it was written, it is worth reading for its literary styl
alone. The author tells us with inimitable quiet modesty of how
he begged and stole his way across America and through Englan
and Wales until his travelling days were cut short by losing hi
right foot while attempting to 'jump' a train.

LATER DAYS. A pendant to *The Autobiography of a Super-Tramp*
No. 48

'The self-portrait is given with disarming, mysterious, anc
baffling directness, and the writing has the same disarmingness anc
simpleness.' *Observer*

A POET'S PILGRIMAGE
No. 56

A Poet's Pilgrimage recounts the author's impressions of his nativ
Wales on his return after many years' absence. He tells of a walking
tour during which he stayed in cheap rooms and ate in the smal
wayside inns. The result is a vivid picture of the Welsh people, the
towns and countryside.

DELEDDA, GRAZIA

THE MOTHER. A Novel. With an Introduction by D. H. LAWRENCE. (Awarded the Nobel Prize 1928.)
No. 105

An unusual book, both in its story and its setting in a remote
Sardinian hill village, half civilised and superstitious. The action
of the story takes place so rapidly and the actual drama is so inter-
woven with the mental conflict, and all so forced by circumstances,
that it is almost Greek in its simple and inevitable tragedy.

DE MAUPASSANT

STORIES. Translated by ELIZABETH MARTINDALE   *No.* 37

'His "story" engrosses the non-critical, it holds the critical too at the first reading. . . . That is the real test of art, and it is because of the inobtrusiveness of this workmanship, that for once the critic and the reader may join hands without awaiting the verdict of posterity.' *From the Introduction by* FORD MADOX FORD

DE SELINCOURT, Hugh

THE CRICKET MATCH. A Story   *No.* 108

Through the medium of a cricket match the author endeavours to give a glimpse of life in a Sussex village. First we have a bird's-eye view at dawn of the village nestling under the Downs ; then we see the players awaken in all the widely different circumstances of their various lives, pass the morning, assemble on the field, play their game, united for a few hours, as men should be, by a common purpose – and at night disperse.

DOS PASSOS, John

ORIENT EXPRESS. A book of travel   *No.* 80

This book will be read because, as well as being the temperature chart of an unfortunate sufferer from the travelling disease, it deals with places shaken by the heavy footsteps of History, manifesting itself as usual by plague, famine, murder, sudden death and depreciated currency. Underneath, the book is an ode to railroad travel.

DOUGLAS, George

THE HOUSE WITH THE GREEN SHUTTERS.

A novel. With an Introduction by J. B. PRIESTLEY   *No.* 118

This powerful and moving story of life in a small Scots burgh is one of the grimmest studies of realism in all modern fiction. The author flashes a cold and remorseless searchlight upon the back-bitings, jealousies, and intrigues of the townsfolk, and his story stands as a classic antidote to the sentimentalism of the kailyard school.

DUNSTERVILLE, Major-General L. G.

STALKY'S REMINISCENCES

'The real Stalky, General Dunsterville, who is so delightful
character that the fictitious Stalky must at times feel jealous of hi
as a rival. . . . In war he proved his genius in the Dunster For
adventure ; and in this book he shows that he possesses anoth
kind of genius – the genius of comic self-revelation and burbli
anecdote. And the whole story is told in a vein of comedy th
would have done credit to Charles Lever.' *The Observer*

FARSON, Negley

SAILING ACROSS EUROPE. With an Introduction
by FRANK MORLEY

A voyage of six months in a ship, its one and only cabin measurir
8 feet by 6 feet, up the Rhine, down the Danube, passing from on
to the other by the half-forgotten Ludwig's Canal. To think
and plan such a journey was a fine imaginative effort and to wri
about it interestingly is no mean accomplishment.

FAUSSET, Hugh I'Anson

TENNYSON. A critical study

Mr. Fausset's study of Tennyson's qualities as poet, man, an
moralist is by implication a study of some of the predomina
characteristics of the Victorian age. His book, however, is
pictorial as it is critical, being woven, to quote *The Times*, 'li
an arras of delicate colour and imagery.'

FLAUBERT, Gustave

MADAME BOVARY. Translated by ELEANOR MARX-
AVELING. With an Introduction by PERCY LUBBOCK.

'. . . It remains perpetually the novel of all novels which th
criticism of fiction cannot overlook ; as soon as ever we speak o
the principles of the art we must be prepared to engage wit
Flaubert. There is no such book as his *Bovary* ; for it is a nov
in which the subject stands firm and clear, without the least shad
of ambiguity to break the line which bounds it.' PERCY LUBBOC
in The Craft of Fiction

FORMAN, Henry James

GRECIAN ITALY. A book of Travel   *No.* 29

'It has been said that if you were shown Taormina in a vision you would not believe it. If the reader has been in Grecian Italy before he reads this book, the magic of its pages will revive old memories and induce a severe attack of nostalgia.' *From the Preface by* H. FESTING JONES

GARNETT, Edward

FRIDAY NIGHTS. Critical Essays   *No.* 119

'Mr. Garnett is "the critic as artist," sensitive alike to elemental nature and the subtlest human variations. His book sketches for us the possible outlines of a new humanism, a fresh valuation of both life and art.' *The Times*

GARNETT, Mrs. R. S.

THE INFAMOUS JOHN FRIEND. A Novel *No.* 53

This book, though in form an historical novel, claims to rank as a psychological study. It is an attempt to depict a character which, though destitute of the common virtues of everyday life, is gifted with qualities that compel love and admiration.

GAUGIN, Paul

THE INTIMATE JOURNALS. Translated by
VAN WYCK BROOKS   *No.* 101

The confessions of genius are usually startling ; and Gaugin's *Journals*, now made accessible to the wider world, are no exception. He exults in his power to give free rein to his savage spirit, tearing the shawl from convention's shoulders with a gesture as unscrupulous as it is Rabelaisian.

GIBBS, J. Arthur

A COTSWOLD VILLAGE   *No.* 138

'For pure observation of people, places and sports, occupations and wild life, the book is admirable. Everything is put down freshly from the notebook, and has not gone through any deadening process of being written up. There are stories, jokes, snatches of conversation, quotations from old diaries, odds and ends of a hundred kinds about squires, gamekeepers, labourers and their wives.' *Morning Post*

GOBINEAU, Comte de

THE CRIMSON HANDKERCHIEF, AND OTHER STORIES. Translated from the French by HENRY LONGAN STUART

> The three stories included in this volume mark the flood tide o
> Comte de Gobineau's unique and long-neglected genius. No
> even Nietzsche has surpassed him in a love of heroic characters and
> unfettered wills – or in his contempt for bourgeois virtues and
> vices.

GOSSE, Sir Edmund

SELECTED ESSAYS. First Series

> 'The prose of Sir Edmund Gosse is as rich in the colour of young
> imagination as in the mellow harmony of judgment. Sir Edmund
> Gosse's literary kit-kats will continue to be read with avidity long
> after the greater part of the academic criticism of the century is
> swept away upon the lumber-heap.' *Daily Telegraph*

SELECTED ESSAYS. Second Series

> A second volume of essays personally chosen by Sir Edmund
> Gosse from the wild field of his literary work. One is delighted
> with the width of his appreciation which enables him to write with
> equal charm on *Wycherley* and on *How to Read the Bible*.

GRAHAM, Stephen

A PRIVATE IN THE GUARDS

> In his own experiences as a soldier Stephen Graham has conserved
> the half-forgotten emotions of a nation in arms. Above all, he
> makes us feel the stark brutality and horror of actual war, the
> valour which is more than valour, and the disciplined endurance
> which is human and therefore the more terrifying.

HEARN, Lafcadio

GLEANINGS IN BUDDHA-FIELDS

> A book which is readable from the first page to the last, and is full
> of suggestive thought, the essays on Japanese religious belief calling
> for special praise for the earnest spirit in which the subject is
> approached.

HEARN, Lafcadio

GLIMPSES OF UNFAMILIAR JAPAN. First
Series   *No.* 57

Most books written about Japan have been superficial sketches of a passing traveller. Of the inner life of the Japanese we know practically nothing, their religion, superstitions, ways of thought. Lafcadio Hearn reveals something of the people and their customs as they are.

GLIMPSES OF UNFAMILIAR JAPAN. Second
Series   *No.* 58

Sketches by an acute observer and a master of English prose, of a Nation in transition – of the lingering remains of Old Japan, to-day only a memory, of its gardens, its beliefs, customs, gods and devils, of its wonderful kindliness and charm – and of the New Japan, struggling against odds towards new ideals.

KWAIDAN. Stories   *No.* 44

The marvellous tales which Mr. Hearn has told in this volume illustrate the wonder-living tendency of the Japanese. The stories are of goblins, fairies and sprites, with here and there an adventure into the field of unveiled supernaturalism.

OUT OF THE EAST   *No.* 43

Mr. Hearn has written many books about Japan ; he is saturated with the essence of its beauty, and in this book the light and colour and movement of that land drips from his pen in every delicately conceived and finely written sentence.

HEYWARD, Du Bose

PORGY. A Tale   *No.* 85

This fascinating book gives a vivid and intimate insight into the lives of a group of American negroes, from whom Porgy stands out, rich in humour and tragedy. The author's description of a hurricane is reminiscent in its power.

HILDEBRAND, Arthur Sturges

BLUE WATER. The story of an ocean voyage   *No.* 36

This book gives the real feeling of life on a small cruising yacht ; the nights on deck with the sails against the sky, long fights with head winds by mountainous coasts to safety in forlorn little island ports, and constant adventure free from care.

HOUSMAN, Laurence

ANGELS AND MINISTERS, AND OTHER
PLAYS.   *No.* 17

> Imaginary portraits of political characters done in dialogue
> Queen Victoria, Disraeli, Gladstone, Parnell, Joseph Chamberla
> and Woodrow Wilson.
> 'It is all so good that one is tempted to congratulate Mr. Housma
> on a true masterpiece.' *Times*

HUDDLESTON, Sisley

FRANCE AND THE FRENCH. A study   *No.* 86

> 'There has been nothing of its kind published since the war. H
> book is a repository of facts marshalled with judgment ; as suc
> it should assist in clearing away a whole maze of misconceptio
> and prejudices, and serve as a sort of pocket encyclopædia
> modern France.' *Times Literary Supplement*

HUDSON, W. H.

MEN, BOOKS AND BIRDS: Letters to a Friend. With
Notes, some Letters, and an Introduction by MORLEY
ROBERTS   *No.* 11

> An important collection of letters from the naturalist to his frien
> literary executor and fellow author, Morley Roberts, covering
> period of twenty-five years.

JEWETT, Sarah Orne

THE COUNTRY OF THE POINTED FIRS. Stories *No.* 28

> 'The young student of American literature in the far distant futu
> will take up this book and say "a masterpiece!" as proudly as
> he had made it. It will be a message in a universal language – t
> one message that even the scythe of Time spares.' *From the Prefa*
> *by* WILLA CATHER

JONES, Henry Festing

DIVERSIONS IN SICILY. Travel impressions   *No.* 12

> Shortly before his sudden and unexpected death, Mr. Festing Jon
> chose out *Diversions in Sicily* for reprinting in the Traveller
> Library from among his three books of mainly Sicilian sketch
> and studies. These chapters, as well as any that he wrote, reca
> ture the wisdom, charm and humour of their author.

14

JOYCE, James

DUBLINERS. A volume of Stories   *No.* 14

A collection of fifteen short stories by the author of *Ulysses*. They are all of them brave, relentless and sympathetic pictures of Dublin life ; realistic, perhaps, but not crude ; analytical, but not repugnant. No modern writer has greater significance than Mr. Joyce, whose conception and practice of the short story is certainly unique and certainly vital.

KALLAS, Aino

THE WHITE SHIP. Stories. With an Introduction by
JOHN GALSWORTHY   *No.* 24

'The writer has an extraordinary sense of atmosphere.' *Times Literary Supplement*
'Stories told convincingly and well, with a keen perception for natural beauty.' *Nation*

KOMROFF, Manuel

CONTEMPORARIES OF MARCO POLO   *No.* 123

This volume comprises the Travel Records in the Eastern parts of the world of William of Rubruck (1253–5), the Journey of John of Pian de Carpini (1245–7), the Journey of Friar Odoric (1318–30). They describe the marvels and wonders of Asia under the Khans.

THE TRAVELS OF MARCO POLO   *No.* 59

When Marco Polo arrived at the court of the Great Khan, Pekin had just been rebuilt. Kublai Khan was at the height of his glory. Polo rose rapidly in favour and became governor of an important district. In this way he gained first-hand knowledge of a great civilisation and described it with astounding accuracy and detail.

LAWRENCE, A. W., edited by

CAPTIVES OF TIPU. Survivors' Narratives   *No.* 125

Three records of heroic endurance, which were hitherto unobtainable at a reasonable price. In addition to the well-known stories of Bristow and Scurry, a soldier and a seaman, who were forcibly Mohammedanised and retained in the service of Mysore till their escape after ten years, extracts are given from an officer's diary of his close imprisonment at Seringapatam.

LAWRENCE, D. H.

TWILIGHT IN ITALY. Travel essays — No. 19

This volume of travel vignettes in North Italy was first published in 1916. Since then Mr. Lawrence has increased the number of h.. admirers year by year. In *Twilight in Italy* they will find all th.. freshness and vigour of outlook which they have come to expec.. from its author.

LAWSON, Henry

WHILE THE BILLY BOILS. First Series — No. 38

These stories are written by the O. Henry of Australia. They te.. of men and dogs, of cities and plains, of gullies and ridges, o.. sorrow and happiness, and of the fundamental goodness that i.. hidden in the most unpromising of human soil.

WHILE THE BILLY BOILS. Second Series — No. 39

Mr. Lawson has the uncanny knack of making the people he write.. about almost violently alive. Whether he tells of jackeroos, bush.. children or drovers' wives, each one lingers in the memory long.. after we have closed the book.

LESLIE, Shane

THE END OF A CHAPTER — No. 110

In this, his most famous book, Mr. Shane Leslie has preserved for.. future generations the essence of the pre-war epoch, its institutions.. and individuals. He writes of Eton, of the Empire, of Post-Victorianism, of the Politicians. . . . And whatever he touches.. upon, he brilliantly interprets.

LITHGOW, William

RARE ADVENTURES AND PAINEFULL PEREGRINATIONS (1582–1645). Edited and with Introduction by B. I. LAWRENCE — No. 109

This is the book of a seventeenth-century Scotchman who walked.. over the Levant, North Africa and most of Europe, including.. Spain, where he was tortured by the Inquisition. An unscrupulous.. man, full of curiosity, his comments are diverting aad penetrating,.. his adventures remarkable.

LUBBOCK, Percy

EARLHAM. A portrait   *No.* 6

'The book seems too intimate to be reviewed. We want to be
allowed to read it, and to dream over it, and keep silence about it.
His judgment is perfect, his humour is true and ready ; his touch
light and prim ; his prose is exact and clean and full of music.'
Times

ROMAN PICTURES. Studies   *No.* 21

Pictures of life as it is lived – or has been or might be lived – among
the pilgrims and colonists in Rome of more or less English speech.
'A book of whimsical originality and exquisite workmanship, and
worthy of one of the best prose writers of our time.' *Sunday Times*

THE CRAFT OF FICTION. Critical essays *No.* 5

'No more substantial or more charming volume of criticism has
been published in our time.' *Observer*
'To say that this is the best book on the subject is probably true ;
but it is more to the point to say that it is the only one.' *Times
Literary Supplement*

LYND, Robert

BOOKS AND AUTHORS. Critical essays *No.* 135

Critical essays on great writers of modern and other times. Among
the modern writers we have appreciations of Mr. Max Beerbohm,
Mr. Arnold Bennett and Mr. H. M. Tomlinson, while Herrick,
Keats, Charles Lamb and Hawthorne are a few of the classical
writers who are criticised in the book.

MACDONALD, The Rt. Hon. J. Ramsay

WANDERINGS AND EXCURSIONS. Essays *No.* 132

Mr. Ramsay MacDonald has been a wide traveller and reader, and
has an uncommon power of bringing an individual eye – the eye
of the artist – to bear upon whatever he sees.

MACHEN, Arthur

DOG AND DUCK. Essays

No. 15

'As a literary artist, Mr. Arthur Machen has few living equals, and that is very far indeed from being his only, or even his greatest claim on the suffrages of English readers.' *Sunday Times*

MASEFIELD, John

CAPTAIN MARGARET. A Novel

No. 35

'His style is crisp, curt and vigorous. He has the Stevensonian sea swagger, the Stevensonian sense of beauty and poetic spirit. Mr Masefield's descriptions ring true and his characters carry conviction.' *The Observer*

MASON, Arthur

THE FLYING BO'SUN. A Tale

No. 47

'What makes the book remarkable is the imaginative power which has re-created these events so vividly that even the supernatural ones come with the shock and the conviction with which actual supernatural events might come.' *From the Introduction by* EDWIN MUIR

WIDE SEAS AND MANY LANDS. Reminiscences.

With an Introduction by MAURICE BARING   *No.* 7

'This is an extremely entertaining, and at the same time moving book. We are in the presence of a born writer. We read with the same mixture of amazement and delight that fills us throughout a Conrad novel.' *New Statesman*

MAUGHAM, W. Somerset

LIZA OF LAMBETH. A Tale

No. 141

Liza of Lambeth is W. Somerset Maugham's first novel, and its publication decided the whole course of his life. For if it had not succeeded its author could not have turned from medicine to letters, and his subsequent triumphs might never have been achieved. Originally published in 1897, it has since passed through eight editions before its present inclusion in the Travellers' Library. The story reflects much of the experience which Mr. Maugham gathered when he worked in the slums of the East End as a doctor.

AUGHAM, W. Somerset

ON A CHINESE SCREEN. Sketches   No. 31
> A collection of sketches of life in China. Mr. Somerset Maugham writes with equal certainty and vigour whether his characters are Chinese or European. There is a tenderness and humour about the whole book which makes the reader turn eagerly to the next page for more.

THE CASUARINA TREE. Stories   No. 92
> Intensely dramatic stories in which the stain of the East falls deeply on the lives of English men and women. Mr. Maugham remains cruelly aloof from his characters. On passion and its culminating tragedy he looks with unmoved detachment, ringing the changes without comment and yet with little cynicism.

THE MOON AND SIXPENCE. A Novel   No. 9
> A remarkable picture of a genius.
> 'Mr. Maugham has given us a ruthless and penetrating study in personality with a savage truthfulness of delineation and an icy contempt for the heroic and the sentimental.' *The Times*

ENCKEN, H. L.

IN DEFENCE OF WOMEN   No. 50
> 'All I design by the book is to set down in more or less plain form certain ideas that practically every civilised man and woman hold *in petto*, but that have been concealed hitherto by the vast mass of sentimentalities swathing the whole woman question.' *From the Author's Introduction*

SELECTED PREJUDICES. First Series. A Book of
Essays   No. 8
> 'He is exactly the kind of man we are needing, an iconoclast, a scoffer at ideals, a critic with whips and scorpions who does not hesitate to deal with literary, social and political humbugs in the one slashing fashion.' *English Review*

SELECTED PREJUDICES. Second Series   No. 60
> 'What a master of the straight left in appreciation! Everybody who wishes to see how common sense about books and authors can be made exhilarating should acquire this delightful book.' *Morning Post*

MEYNELL, Alice

WAYFARING. Essays *No.* 13

'Her essays have the merit of saying just enough of the subject, a
they can be read repeatedly. The surprise coming from that con
bined grace of manner and sanity of thought is like one's dream
what the recognition of a new truth would be.' Some of the essa
so described by George Meredith are here collected in book-for
for the first time.

MITCHISON, Naomi

CLOUD CUCKOO LAND. A Novel of Sparta *No.* 88

'Rich and frank in passions, and rich, too, in the detail which hel;
to make feigned life seemed real.' *Times Literary Supplement*

THE CONQUERED. A story of the Gauls under Cæsar *No.* 45

'With *The Conquered* Mrs. Mitchison establishes herself as the bes
if not the only, English historical novelist now writing. It seem
to me in many respects the most attractive and poignant historic
novel I have ever read.' *New Statesman*

WHEN THE BOUGH BREAKS. Stories of the time
when Rome was crumbling to ruin *No.* 46

'Interesting, delightful and fresh as morning dew. The connoisseu
in short stories will turn to some pages in this volume again an
again with renewed relish.' *Times Literary Supplement*

MONTAGU, Lady Mary Wortley

THE TRAVEL LETTERS OF LADY MARY
WORTLEY MONTAGU. Edited by A. W. LAWRENCE *No.* 143

The famous account of Lady Mary's journey to the East in 1716,
describing her visits to the German Courts and her residence in
Constantinople. In the words of a review by Tobias Smollett :
'The publication of these *Letters* will be an immortal monument
to the memory of Lady Mary Wortley Montagu and will show,
as long as the English language endures, the sprightliness of her
wit, the solidity of her judgment, the elegance of her taste, and the
excellence of her real character. These letters are so bewitchingly
entertaining, that we defy the most phlegmatic man on earth to
read one without going through with them.'

MOORE, George

CONFESSIONS OF A YOUNG MAN No. 76

'Mr. Moore, true to his period and to his genius, stripped himself of everything that might stand between him and the achievement of his artistic object. He does not ask you to admire this George Moore. He merely asks you to observe him beyond good and evil as a constant plucked from the bewildering flow of eternity.' *Humbert Wolfe*

MORLEY, Christopher

SAFETY PINS. Essays. With an Introduction by H.M. TOMLINSON No. 98

Very many readers will be glad of the opportunity to meet Mr Morley in the rôle of the gentle essayist. He is an author who is content to move among his fellows, to note, to reflect, and to write genially and urbanely ; to love words for their sound as well as for their value in expression of thought.

THUNDER ON THE LEFT. A Novel No. 90

'It is personal to every reader, it will become for every one a reflection of himself. I fancy that here, as always where work is fine and true, the author has created something not as he would but as he must, and is here an interpreter of a world more wonderful than he himself knows.' *Hugh Walpole*

WHERE THE BLUE BEGINS. A Fantasy No. 74

A delicious satirical fantasy in which humanity wears a dog-collar. 'Mr. Morley is a master of consequent inconsequence. His humour and irony are excellent, and his satire is only the more salient for the delicate and ingenuous fantasy in which it is set.' *Manchester Guardian*

MURRAY, Max

THE WORLD'S BACK DOORS. Adventures. With an Introduction by HECTOR BOLITHO No. 61

This book is not an account so much of places as of people. The journey round the world was begun with about enough money to buy one meal, and continued for 66,000 miles. There are periods as a longshore man and as a sailor, and a Chinese guard and a night watchman, and as a hobo.

MURRY, J. Middleton

THE EVOLUTION OF AN INTELLECTUAL   No. 62

These essays were written during and immediately after the Great War. The author says that they record the painful stages by which he passed from the so-called intellectual state to the state of being what he now considers to be a reasonable man.

O'FLAHERTY, Liam

SPRING SOWING. Stories   No. 26

'Nothing seems to escape Mr. O'Flaherty's eye ; his brain turns all things to drama ; and his vocabulary is like a river in spate. *Spring Sowing* is a book to buy, or to borrow, or, yes, to steal.' *Bookman*

THE BLACK SOUL. A Novel   No. 99

'*The Black Soul* overwhelms one like a storm. . . . Nothing like it has been written by any Irish writer.' 'Æ' in *The Irish Statesman*

THE INFORMER. A Novel   No. 128

This realistic novel of the Dublin underworld is generally conceded to be Mr. O'Flaherty's most outstanding book. It is to be produced as a film by British International Pictures, who regard it as one of the most ambitious of their efforts.

O'NEILL, Eugene

THE MOON OF THE CARIBBEES, AND OTHER
PLAYS OF THE SEA. With an Introduction by
ST. JOHN ERVINE   No. 116

'Mr. O'Neill is immeasurably the most interesting man of letters that America has produced since the death of Walt Whitman.' *From the Introduction*

O'SHAUGHNESSY, Edith

VIENNESE MEDLEY. A Novel   No. 51

'It is told with infinite tenderness, with many touches of grave or poignant humour, in a very beautiful book, which no lover of fiction should allow to pass unread. A book which sets its writer definitely in the first rank of living English novelists.' *Sunday Times*

PATER, Walter
MARIUS THE EPICUREAN No. 23

Walter Pater was at the same time a scholar of wide sympathies and a master of the English language. In this, his best-known work, he describes with rare delicacy of feeling and insight the religious and philosophic tendencies of the Roman Empire at the time of Antoninus Pius as they affected the mind and life of the story's hero.

THE RENAISSANCE No. 63

This English classic contains studies of those 'supreme artists' Michelangelo and Da Vinci, and of Botticelli, Della Robia, Mirandola, and others, who 'have a distinct faculty of their own by which they convey to us a peculiar quality of pleasure which we cannot get elsewhere.' There is no romance or subtlety in the work of these masters too fine for Pater to distinguish in superb English.

PICKTHALL, Marmaduke
ORIENTAL ENCOUNTERS No. 103

In *Oriental Encounters*, Mr. Pickthall relives his earlier manhood's discovery of Arabia and sympathetic encounters with the Eastern mind. He is one of the few travellers who really bridges the racial gulf.

POWELL, Sydney Walter
THE ADVENTURES OF A WANDERER No. 64

Throwing up a position in the Civil Service in Natal because he preferred movement and freedom to monotony and security, the author started his wanderings by enlisting in an Indian Ambulance Corps in the South African War. Afterwards he wandered all over the world.

POWYS, Llewelyn
BLACK LAUGHTER No. 127

Black Laughter is a kind of *Robinson Crusoe* of the continent of Africa. Indeed, Llewelyn Powys resembles Daniel Defoe in the startlingly realistic manner in which he conveys the actual feelings of the wild places he describes. You actually share the sensations of a sensitive and artistic nature suddenly transplanted from a peaceful English village into the heart of Africa.

RANSOME, Arthur
'RACUNDRA'S' FIRST CRUISE *No.* 65

This is the story of the building of an ideal yacht which would be a cruising boat that one man could manage if need be, but on which three people could live comfortably. The adventures of the cruise are skilfully and vividly told.

READE, Winwood
THE MARTYRDOM OF MAN *No.* 66

'Few sketches of universal history by one single author have been written. One book that has influenced me very strongly is *The Martyrdom of Man*. This "dates," as people say nowadays, and it has a fine gloom of its own ; but it is still an extraordinarily inspiring presentation of human history as one consistent process.' H. G. WELLS *in An Outline of History*

REYNOLDS, Stephen
A POOR MAN'S HOUSE *No.* 93

Vivid and intimate pictures of a Devonshire fisherman's life. 'Compact, harmonious, without a single – I won't say false – but uncertain note, true in aim, sentiment and expression, precise and imaginative, never precious, but containing here and there an absolutely priceless phrase. . . .' *Joseph Conrad*

RIESENBERG, Felix
SHIPMATES. Sea-faring portraits *No.* 107

A collection of intimate character-portraits of men with whom the author has sailed on many voyages. The sequence of studies blends into a fascinating panorama of living characters.

ROBERTS, Captain George
THE FOUR YEARS VOYAGES *No.* 40

The Manner of his being taken by Three Pyrate Ships which, after having plundered him, and detained him 10 Days, put him aboard his own Sloop, without Provisions, Water, etc.

The Hardships he endur'd for above 20 Days, 'till he arriv'd at the Island of St. Nicholas, from whence he was blown off to Sea ; and after Four Days of Difficulty and Distress, was Shipwreck'd on the Unfrequented Island of St. John, where, after he had remained near two Years, he built a Vessel to bring himself off.

24

ROBINSON, James Harvey

THE MIND IN THE MAKING. An Essay   No. 9

'For me, I think James Harvey Robinson is going to be almost as important as was Huxley in my adolescence, and William James in later years. It is a cardinal book. I question whether in the long run people may not come to it, as making a new initiative into the world's thought and methods.' *From the Introduction by* H. G. WELLS

ROSEBERY, The Earl of

NAPOLEON: THE LAST PHASE   No. 96

Of books and memoirs about Napoleon there is indeed no end, but of the veracious books such as this there are remarkably few. It aims to penetrate the deliberate darkness which surrounds the last act of the Napoleonic drama.

RUTHERFORD, Mark

THE AUTOBIOGRAPHY OF MARK RUTHERFORD.
With an Introduction by H. W. MASSINGHAM   No. 67

Because of its honesty, delicacy and simplicity of portraiture, this book has always had a curious grip upon the affections of its readers. An English Amiel, inheriting to his comfort an English Old Crome landscape, he freed and strengthened his own spirit as he will his reader's.

THE DELIVERANCE   No. 68

Once read, Hale White [Mark Rutherford] is never forgotten. But he is not yet approached through the highways of English letters. To the lover of his work, nothing can be more attractive than the pure and serene atmosphere of thought in which his art moves.

THE REVOLUTION IN TANNER'S LANE   No. 69

'Since Bunyan, English Puritanism has produced one imaginative genius of the highest order. To my mind, our fiction contains no more perfectly drawn pictures of English life in its recurring emotional contrast of excitement and repose more valuable to the historian, or more stimulating to the imaginative reader.' *H. W. Massingham*

SHELVOCKE, Captain George

A PRIVATEER'S VOYAGE ROUND THE WORLD.
With aspersions upon him by WILLIAM BETAGH. Edited by
A. W. LAWRENCE   *No.* 142

> A book of 1726, well known as the source of the albatross incident
> and other passages in the 'Ancient Mariner'; it describes the ex-
> ploits of a private ship of war on the coasts of South America, its
> wreck on the Crusoe island off Juan Fernandez, and the subsequent
> adventures of its company in various parts of the Pacific.
>
> Few among the true stories of the sea can rival this in psychological
> interest, because of the diverse villainies of captain and crew.
> Shelvocke was arrested on his return to England, for a successful
> conspiracy to defraud his owners of their due percentage of the
> profits, and he then wrote his book to defend his conduct.

SITWELL, Constance

FLOWERS AND ELEPHANTS. With an Introduction
by E. M. FORSTER   *No.* 115

> Mrs. Sitwell has known India well, and has filled her pages with
> many vivid little pictures, and with sounds and scents. But it is
> the thread on which her impressions are strung that is so fascinating,
> a thread so delicate and rare that the slightest clumsiness in defini-
> tion would snap it.

SMITH, Pauline

THE BEADLE. A Novel of South Africa   *No.* 129

> 'A story of great beauty, and told with simplicity and tenderness
> that makes it linger in the memory. It is a notable contribution to
> the literature of the day.' *Morning Post*

THE LITTLE KAROO. Stories of South Africa. With
an Introduction by ARNOLD BENNETT   *No.* 104

> 'Nothing like this has been written about South African life since
> Olive Schreiner and her *Story of an African Farm* took the literary
> world by storm.' *The Daily Telegraph*

SQUIRE, J. C.
THE GRUB STREET NIGHTS ENTERTAINMENTS *No.* 102
Stories of literary life, told with a breath of fantasy and gaily ironic humour. Each character lives, and is the more lively for its touch of caricature. From *The Man Who Kept a Diary* to *The Man Who Wrote Free Verse*, these tales constitute Mr. Squire's most delightful ventures in fiction ; and the conception of the book itself is unique.

SULLIVAN, J. W. N.
ASPECTS OF SCIENCE. First Series   *No.* 70
Although they deal with different aspects of various scientific ideas, the papers which make up this volume do illustrate, more or less, one point of view. This book tries to show one or two of the many reasons why science may be interesting for people who are not specialists as well as for those who are.

SYMONS, Arthur
PLAYS, ACTING AND MUSIC   *No.* 113
This book deals mainly with music and with the various arts of the stage. Mr. Arthur Symons shows how each art has its own laws, its own limits ; these it is the business of the critic jealously to distinguish. Yet in the study of art as art it should be his endeavour to master the universal science of beauty.

WILLIAM BLAKE. A critical study   *No.* 94
When Blake spoke the first word of the nineteenth century there was none to hear it ; and now that his message has penetrated the world, and is slowly remaking it, few are conscious of the man who first voiced it. This lack of knowledge is remedied in Mr. Symons's work.

TCHEKOFF, Anton
TWO PLAYS : *The Cherry Orchard* and *The Sea Gull*.
Translated by GEORGE CALDERON   *No.* 33
Tchekoff had that fine comedic spirit which relishes the incongruity between the actual disorder of the world with the underlying order. He habitually mingled tragedy (which is life seen close at hand) with comedy (which is life seen at a distance). His plays are tragedies with the texture of comedy.

THOMAS, Edward

A LITERARY PILGRIM IN ENGLAND *No. 95*

A book about the homes and resorts of English writers, from John Aubrey, Cowper, Gilbert White, Cobbett, Wordsworth, Burns, Borrow and Lamb, to Swinburne, Stevenson, Meredith, W. H. Hudson and H. Belloc. Each chapter is a miniature biography and the same time a picture of the man and his work and environment.

THE POCKET BOOK OF POEMS AND SONGS FOR THE OPEN AIR *No. 97*

This anthology is meant to please those lovers of poetry and the country who like a book that can always lighten some of their burdens or give wings to their delight, whether in the open air by day, or under the roof at evening ; in it is gathered much of the finest English poetry.

TURGENEV, Ivan

FATHERS AND CHILDREN. Translated by
CONSTANCE GARNETT *No. 83*

'As a piece of art *Fathers and Children* is the most powerful of all Turgenev's works. The figure of Bazarov is not only the political centre of the book, but a figure in which the eternal tragedy of man's impotence and insignificance is realised in scenes of a most ironical human drama.' *Edward Garnett*

ON THE EVE. Translated by CONSTANCE GARNETT *No. 82*

In his characters is something of the width and depth which so astounds us in the creations of Shakespeare. *On the Eve* is a quiet work, yet over which the growing consciousness of coming events casts its heavy shadow. Turgenev, even as he sketched the ripening love of a young girl, has made us feel the dawning aspirations of a nation.

SMOKE. Translated by CONSTANCE GARNETT *No. 84*

In this novel Turgenev sees and reflects, even in the shifting phases of political life, that which is universal in human nature. His work is compassionate, beautiful, unique ; in the sight of his fellow-craftsmen always marvellous and often perfect.

ERGA, Giovanni

MASTRO-DON GESUALDO. A Novel. Translated
by D. H. LAWRENCE   No. 71

> Verga, who died in 1922, is recognised as one of the greatest of
> Italian writers of fiction. He can claim a place beside Hardy and
> the Russians. 'It is a fine full tale, a fine full picture of life, with a
> bold beauty of its own which Mr. Lawrence must have relished
> greatly as he translated it.' *Observer*

OIGT, F. A.

COMBED OUT   No. 122

> This account of life in the army in 1917-18, both at home and in
> France, is written with a telling incisiveness. The author does not
> indulge in an unnecessary word, but packs in just the right details
> with an intensity of feeling that is infectious.

VATERS, W. G.

TRAVELLER'S JOY. An Anthology   No. 106

> This anthology has been selected for publication in the Travellers'
> Library from among the many collections of verse because of its
> suitability for the traveller, particularly the summer and autumn
> traveller, who would like to carry with him some store of literary
> provender.

VELLS, H. G.

CHRISTINA ALBERTA'S FATHER. A Novel   No. 100

> 'At first reading the book is utterly beyond criticism ; all the
> characters are delightfully genuine.' *Spectator*
> 'Brimming over with Wellsian insight, humour and invention. No
> one but Mr. Wells could have written the whole book and given it
> such verve and sparkle.' *Westminster Gazette*

THE DREAM. A Novel   No. 20

> 'It is the richest, most generous and absorbing thing that Mr. Wells
> has given us for years and years.' *Daily News*
> 'I find this book as close to being magnificent as any book that I
> have ever read. It is full of inspiration and life.' *Daily Graphic*

WHARTON, Edith
IN MOROCCO

Morocco is a land of mists and mysteries, of trailing silver vei
through which minarets, mighty towers, hot palm groves and Atl
snows peer and disappear at the will of the Atlantic cloud-drifts.

ITALIAN BACKGROUNDS
No. 114

Mrs. Wharton's perception of beauty and her grace of writing a
matters of general acceptance. Her book gives us pictures
mountains and rivers, monks, nuns and saints.

WITHERS, Percy
FRIENDS IN SOLITUDE. With an Introduction by
LASCELLES ABERCROMBIE
No. 131

Percy Withers, who lived for many years in the Lake Country, ha
his own experiences to relate ; but in seeking to widen them and
give them more vivid expression, he selects certain of the dale foll
his friends and companions, to tell in their own fashion so much th
manner of men they are, so much of their life-story, of its pros
perities, endurances, pathos, its reactions and responses to th
outward circumstances as may make the picture more comple
and give to it a more human significance.

YOUNG, E. H.
THE MISSES MALLETT. A Novel
No. 72

The virtue of this quiet and accomplished piece of writing lies i
its quality and in its character-drawing ; to summarise it would b
to give no idea of its charm. Neither realism nor romance, it is
book by a writer of insight and sensibility.

WILLIAM. A Novel
No. 27

'An extraordinary good book, penetrating and beautiful.' *Alla
Monkhouse*
'All its characters are very real and alive, and William himself is
masterpiece.' *May Sinclair*

NUMERICAL INDEX TO TITLES

ALPHABETICAL INDEX TO TITLES

STALKY'S REMINISCENCES. Major-General L. G. Dunsterville
STORIES. De Maupassant
STORY OF THE JEWS, THE. Louis Browne
TENNYSON. Hugh I'Anson Fausset
THUNDER ON THE LEFT. Christopher Morley
TRAVELLER'S JOY. W. G. Waters
TRAVELS OF MARCO POLO, THE
TWILIGHT IN ITALY. D. H. Lawrence
TWO PLAYS : *The Cherry Orchard* and *The Sea Gull*. Anton Tchekoff
VIENNESE MEDLEY. Edith O'Shaughnessy
WALLET OF KAI LUNG, THE. Ernest Bramah
WANDERINGS AND EXCURSIONS. The Rt. Hon. J. Ramsay
  MacDonald
WAY OF ALL FLESH, THE. Samuel Butler
WAYFARING. Alice Meynell
WHEN THE BOUGH BREAKS. Naomi Mitchison
WHERE THE BLUE BEGINS. Christopher Morley
WHILE THE BILLY BOILS. First Series. Henry Lawson
WHILE THE BILLY BOILS. Second Series. Henry Lawson
WHITE SHIP, THE. Aino Kallas
WIDE SEAS AND MANY LANDS. Arthur Mason
WILLIAM. E. H. Young
WORLD'S BACK DOORS, THE. Max Murray
WUTHERING HEIGHTS. Emily Brontë

Note

The *Travellers' Library* is published as a joint enterprise by Jonath
Cape and William Heinemann. The series as a whole, or any title in t
series, can be ordered through booksellers from either Jonathan Cape
William Heinemann. Booksellers' only care must be not to duplicate th
orders.

MADE AND PRINTED IN GREAT BRITAIN BY
THE GARDEN CITY PRESS LTD., LETCHWORTH, HERTS.